George Santayana's Political Hermeneutics

Value Inquiry Book Series

Founding Editor

Robert Ginsberg

Editor-in-Chief

J.D. Mininger

VOLUME 373

Social Philosophy

Editor

Andrew Fitz-Gibbon
(*State University of New York, Cortland*)

The titles published in this series are listed at *brill.com/vibs* and *brill.com/socp*

George Santayana's Political Hermeneutics

By

Katarzyna Kremplewska

BRILL

LEIDEN | BOSTON

Cover illustration: St Martin's Bridge, Toledo, Spain. Photo taken and edited by Katarzyna Kremplewska in 2018.

The Library of Congress Cataloging-in-Publication Data is available online at https://catalog.loc.gov
LC record available at https://lccn.loc.gov/2021057945

Typeface for the Latin, Greek, and Cyrillic scripts: "Brill". See and download: brill.com/brill-typeface.

ISSN 0929-8436
ISBN 978-90-04-50632-9 (hardback)
ISBN 978-90-04-50634-3 (e-book)

Copyright 2022 by Katarzyna Kremplewska. Published by Koninklijke Brill NV, Leiden, The Netherlands.
Koninklijke Brill NV incorporates the imprints Brill, Brill Nijhoff, Brill Hotei, Brill Schöningh, Brill Fink, Brill mentis, Vandenhoeck & Ruprecht, Böhlau Verlag and V&R Unipress.
Koninklijke Brill NV reserves the right to protect this publication against unauthorized use. Requests for re-use and/or translations must be addressed to Koninklijke Brill NV via brill.com or copyright.com.

This book is printed on acid-free paper and produced in a sustainable manner.

Contents

Acknowledgments   VII
Abbreviations   VIII

Introduction   1

1   Foundations and Contours   23
    1.1   Dualities   23
    1.2   Realms and Orders   27
    1.3   Powers, Dominations, and Virtues   33
    1.4   Human Nature, Condition, and Negative Anthropology   37

2   Liberty   44
    2.1   From Cultural Critique to Political Thinking   44
    2.2   Vacant Freedom and Vital Liberty   55
    2.3   Anarchist and Revolutionary Delusions   70

3   Servitude   75

4   Militancy   87
    4.1   Sources and Forms of Militancy   87
    4.2   War and Wars of Imagination   98
    4.3   The Limits of Relativism and Moral Ambivalence   113

5   Arts as Powers and as Dominations   122
    5.1   Mass Society, Business, and Culture   131
    5.2   Liberal Arts and the Artist   138
    5.3   A Digression on Secularization   144

6   The Fragility of Liberalism   148
    6.1   Ideas   148
    6.2   The Fate of the Liberal Ideals under the Liberal Rule   157
    6.3   Culture   169

7   Reflections on Self-Government, Democracy, and Justice   178
    7.1   A Few Remarks on Government by Politicians   178
    7.2   Perfection versus Freedom   179
    7.3   The Ironies of Democracy   185

7.4 The Aristocratic Ideal and a Democratic Society   196
7.5 Justice as Harmonizing Diversity and Justice as Charity   202

8 **Santayana on Communism**   216

9 **Conclusions and Further Reflections on Why Culture Matters**   235

Bibliography   249
Index   256

Acknowledgments

This book is the final result of a research project no. *2016/23/D/HS1/02274*, financed by National Science Center in Poland (NCN). Majority of the book consists of original, previously unpublished material. There are the following exceptions:

1. The ideas of managing necessity and negative anthropology, introduced in Chapter One of this book, appeared for the first time in my essay "Managing Necessity: Santayana on Forms of Power and the Human Condition," in: Charles Padrón and Krzysztof P. Skowroński, eds, *The Life of Reason in an Age of Terrorism*, Leiden and Boston: Brill, 2018, 28–42.
2. Subchapter 7.5 "Justice as harmonizing diversity and justice as charity" is going to appear as an article under the title "Harmony and charity as foundations of justice in Santayana's thought" in: *Limbo: boletín internacional de estudios sobre Santayana*, 41 (2021).
3. Chapter Eight is an expanded and modified version of my text: "Santayana on Communism in the Light of his Correspondence," *Overheard in Seville: Bulletin of The George Santayana Society* 37 (2019): 30–41, reprinted as "A story of disillusionment: George Santayana's views on communism and the Russian Revolution," *The Interlocutor. Journal of the Warsaw School of the History of Ideas* 2 (2019): 161–147.
4. The concluding chapter of this book contains parts of my text "Further Reflections on Culture, Humanism, and Individualism in the Context of Santayana's Political Thought," *Overheard in Seville: Bulletin of The George Santayana Society*, 38 (2020): 66–73.

Throughout the years leading to the publication of this book I have been engaged in a cooperation with The George Santayana Society – including participation in an ongoing reading group devoted to Santayana's *The Life of Reason* – which has been a source of inspiration and support for me.

I would like to express my sincere gratitude to my colleague, professor Dorota Zygmuntowicz, for her immensely helpful insights concerning Plato's political philosophy and its contemporary interpretations.

Abbreviations

Works by George Santayana

BR	*The Birth of Reason And Other Essays*
DL	*Dialogues in Limbo*
DP	*Dominations and Powers*
GTACOUS	*The Genteel Tradition in American Philosophy and Character and Opinion in the United States*
LGS	*The Letters of George Santayana*
LR	*The Life of Reason: Or, The Phases of Human Progress*
LR1	*The Life of Reason. Bk 1, Reason in Common Sense* (Critical Edition)
RB	*Realms of Being*
SiELS	*Soliloquies in England and Later Soliloquies*

Works by Other Authors

LIB	John Gray, *Liberalism*
PLIB	John Gray, *Post-Liberalism. Studies in Social Thought*

Introduction

In the late modern world, shaped, among other things, by the processes of industrialization, the rise of mass society, rapid technological progress, the evolution of capitalism, globalization on the one and the strengthening of nation-states on the other hand, the position of the individual in the West, though now empowered and protected by rights and liberties, became harder to understand and, in some sense, more precarious. The two World Wars, besides their devastating material effects, increased the anxiety and triggered self-questioning in the modern man. These changes evoked countless intellectual responses. New philosophical ideas, trying to grasp and explain the multifaceted change, appeared in the form of conservative, socialist, and Marxist critiques, hermeneutic analyses, as well as positive, liberal and progressivist projects. These responses, trying to cope with the increasing complexity of the world, often trespassed the borders between different areas of humanities and social sciences. In the first half of the twentieth century a number of thinkers, including figures such as Bergson, Adorno, Cassirer, Husserl, Heidegger, Babbitt, Benjamin, Dewey, Arendt, y Gasset, Berdyaev, or Zdziechowski, were grappling with the meanings and perspectives made available to humans in the modern world. It is among these thinkers, rather than political philosophers *par excellence*, that I place George Santayana. The modern, Western perception and experience of life and death evolved in a direction which, as should be honestly admitted, Santayana did not sympathize with, but neither altogether dismissed. Given the critical-hermeneutic dimension of his political thinking, its incentive to raise doubt, reveal paradoxes, interrogate and deconstruct prevailing ideals, myths and opinions, I call it *political hermeneutics*. Intimately related to his cultural criticism, his vision of a human being and the world of human affairs at large, as well as his materialist ontology, devoid – with a few exceptions – of references to other political thinkers, it diverges considerably from the contemporary, highly specialized and formalized discourse of political philosophy and science. Rather, in its integral approach, it is heir to the ancient thought. If we add to this Santayana's poetic language, as well as his inclination to remain, as Krzysztof Skowroński remarked, "submerged in imagination," we are left with an inspiring yet idiosyncratic kind of political reflection.[1]

---

1 See: Krzysztof Piotr Skowroński, *Santayana and America. Values, Liberties, Responsibility* (New Castle (UK): Cambridge Scholars Publishing, 2007), 199.

If judged in terms of impact, the contribution of Santayana into the field of political thought has been modest. He neither proposed a groundbreaking perspective on socio-political reality nor attracted a crowd of enthusiasts, even though his position in the intellectual milieu of the era had long been established. The reception of his final book, *Dominations and Powers: Reflections on Liberty, Society and Government*, was mixed. But prior to discussing the book and its reception in more detail, for those unfamiliar with the biography of Santayana, let me sketch, in a few strokes, the contours of his adult life in the twentieth century, which formed the background for the evolution of his ideas about society, culture, and politics.

The final years of Santayana's life (born in 1863, in Madrid, died in 1952, in Rome), which he spent at the Blue Nuns Convent in Rome, were filled with work on the completion of what may be regarded as the most mature and complete synthesis of his political thinking – the already mentioned work, *Dominations and Powers*. The task, almost exceeding the abilities of a philosopher in his late eighties and of ailing health, consisted in gathering, organizing and rewriting of what he had written on politics and society within a span of more or less half a century.[2] The volume, rich in reflections on a multitude of topics, amounts to what one might describe as a synthetic, critical, and predominantly naturalistic (albeit not deprived of idealistic elements) *hermeneia* of society and government. Inspired by Plato as he was, Santayana, in some respects, situates himself in opposition to the line of idealists, which began with Plato and culminated with Hegel, of whose political thought he writes:

> [they] preached a conceptual idealism with a militant philosophic and political zeal. The ideal to which they wished to sacrifice natural freedom was not the many-sided ideal radiation of spontaneous life, but a particular type of society or a particular method of change which they chose to impose on mankind or to attribute mythically to the universe.[3]

In contrast to those thinkers, it is on behalf of the "many-sided ideal radiation of spontaneous life" rather than as an advocate of any specific socio-political arrangement that Santayana undertakes his inquiry into the promises and limitations of society and government.

---

2   According to Herman J. Saatkamp, it is doubtful whether Santayana added any new material to the book after he moved to the clinic run by the convent in 1941. He relied on his secretary, Daniel Cory, to prepare *Dominations and Powers* for publication.

3   George Santayana, *Dominations and Powers. Reflections on Liberty, Society and Government* (New York: Charles Scribner's Sons, 1951), 392. Subsequently I will refer to this source as DP.

INTRODUCTION 3

Looking back in time, in 1911, when the philosopher was in his late 40s and had lived nearly forty years in the United States – he was of Spanish origin and spent his early childhood in Avila – he decided to resign from the professor's position at the Department of Philosophy at Harvard University and return to Europe. The same year, he delivered his well-known address, a kind of farewell to America, "The Genteel Tradition in American Philosophy." The speech was to become the basis for his later book of essays, which "was widely read in circles where it counted, and properly has since been assessed as a document of first importance in recent American intellectual history."[4] Today scholars agree that the value of his critique of American culture, and of modernity in general, is not unrelated to the specific and complex personal circumstances, his condition of being torn between his Spanish, Catholic roots, his Protestant professional milieu, and a sort of enlightened agnosticism inspired by his father. This multitude of familiar perspectives, which may have given rise to what is described as Santayana's relativism, "made him so valuable an observer of American civilization, for these gave him the detachment necessary to see American life without first accepting its premises."[5] This opinion may well be extended beyond American context and one may say that the autonomy of his thinking made him a valuable critic of Western politics and culture.

Feeling tired, as he declared, with teaching and the American way of life, he left for Europe, where he remained until his death.[6] At the time of his departure he felt he had achieved maturity and a clear sense of what would be his vocation for the years to follow. A "stubbornly independent spirit,"[7] no longer interested in academic career, he wished to devote his experience and talents to the pursuit of truth and writing. Relative financial stability attained due to a family legacy after his mother's death, and the independence that he owed to the fact that he had avoided deep personal commitments, allowed him to travel freely in Europe, socialize as much or as little as he felt necessary or convenient and engage in writing. The author of his biography, John McCormick, notes that the philosopher

---

4 John McCormick, *George Santayana: a biography* (New York: Alfred A. Knopf, 1987), 208.
5 Wilfred M. McClay, "The Unclaimed Legacy of George Santayana," in *The Genteel Tradition in American Philosophy and Character and Opinion in the United Sates*, by George Santayana, ed. and introduction by James Seaton (New Haven and London: Yale University Press, 2009), 129. Subsequently I refer to this book as GTACOUS.
6 As evidenced, for example, by a letter to his sister, Susanna: Letter to Susan Sturgis de Sastre, 7 Dec. 1911, *The Letters of George Santayana, Book 2, 1910–1920* (Cambridge, MA: MIT Press, 2002), 62–63. Subsequently, I will use the abbreviation LGS in reference to the volumes of this edition of Santayana's letters.
7 McClay, "The Unclaimed Legacy," in GTACOUS, 128.

took with him to Europe a great deal of the United States. He had found that he could not use his weapons properly in the United States, whereas he could use them with a remarkable efficiency in Europe, where his American vigor and industry meshed beautifully with the slower pace of life.[8]

Upon leaving America, Santayana already had on his mind writing a system of philosophy. But it took him years to settle down. Until the outbreak of the First World War, he was travelling unceasingly in-between continental Europe and Britain. The War found him in Oxford, from where, moved by its atrocities, he wrote in a letter to a friend: "what every fresh person tells you returning from the front is so horrifying ... that one is not allowed to forget the troubles of others in one's own comfortable and stupid routine of life." One also learns about a disagreement with his sister over their political sympathies. " 'You imagine that my sympathetic way to tolerate absurdity and fiction in religion,'" he says in an imaginary dialogue with his pro-German sister, " 'will extend to perversity and fiction in politics: but not at all. ... Politics is a matter of fact, of history, of morals: perversity in that is intolerable.' "[9] According to his diagnosis of Spanish opinion on the Great War, while his siter sided with the camp of "clericals and conservatives," Santayana, by sympathizing with England, joined the ranks of moderate liberals among his compatriots in Spain, who saw in England "the mother of parliaments, the home of free trade and of religious toleration."[10]

During the War, and under its partial influence, Santayana wrote *Egotism in German Philosophy*, where he presented his ideas about the dangers posed by a combination of certain cultural and intellectual trends in German thought, such as subjectivism, egotism and philosophy of will. Originating in transcendental philosophy, Protestant theology and romanticism, they evolved into a militant tendency, a political manifestation of which was a sort of collective individualism, where units such as nations and nation-states were treated as integral, self-conscious subjects and agents, whose essential identity involved a sense of superiority and a historical mission to perform. Santayana's deep distrust of nationalism and a sort of patriotism that accompanies it resonates

---

8   McCormick, *George Santayana: a biography*, 212.
9   Letter to Mary Williams Winslow, 4 Nov. 1915, LGS2: 233–234.
10 George Santayana, "Spanish Opinion on the War," *The New Republic*, 10 April 1915. More specifically, Santayana divides Spanish opinion into three "camps": pro-German conservatives, pro-English moderate liberals, and pro-French advanced liberals and revolutionists. Twenty years later, in a private letter, he would confess that his "Anglomania" had faded away. See: letter to Robert Shaw Barlow, 19 Oct. 1935, LGS5: 248–249.

in his later works.[11] From a couple of his letters one also learns that as early as in 1918 Santayana was intending to write "a sort of *psychology of politics*," a book "on the war, or rather on the psychological question, how governments and religions manage to dominate mankind," and was considering "calling it 'Dominations and Powers'."[12]

After the war, Santayana, having resisted the temptation of returning to academia, moved to the continent but did not abandon his nomadic lifestyle. The list of the places of his temporary residence included: Paris, Florence, Rome, Cortina D'Ampezzo and his hometown Avila. Meanwhile, Santayana's popularity increased considerably. In 1922, a collection of essays *Soliloquies in England and Later Soliloquies* was published. The same year he completed *Scepticism and Animal Faith* – a major work, containing his theory of essences and intuition, which was to become an introduction to his later system of philosophy, and, "without question, the single most distinctive work of Santayana's productive postwar period."[13] The book was well received in the English-speaking world, even by thinkers of an altogether different mindset, to mention only John Dewey. At the same time, he was working on a couple of other books, including his only novel *The Last Puritan* and the future four-volume magnum opus *Realms of Being*.

Soon after Santayana moved to Italy (1924), his personal favorite – *Dialogues in Limbo* – was published, followed by, among other things, *The Realm of Essence*, the first part of *Realms of Being*, the remaining volumes of which were to appear within the following two decades. To escape the World War II, he tried to leave for Switzerland but was unable to cross the border due to the fact that he held Spanish passport while there had arisen a political tension between the two countries. Thus, in 1941 "the war concealed Santayana in Rome as behind a curtain."[14] In the meantime, he reached his final destination and the place of retirement – the already mentioned Blue Sisters Convent in Rome. Meanwhile, Santayana's philosophical novel, *The Last Puritan*, and

---

11   For a very interesting comparison with the ideas of another philosopher of the era concerned with a number of issues raised also by Santayana, such as the persistent presence of myths in political beliefs, German nationalism, the consequences of Machiavellism in modern politics, and the relation between anti-individualism and totalitarianism, see: Ernst Cassirer, *The Myth of the State* (New Haven and London: Yale University Press, 1946.)

12   Letters to: Benjamin Apthorp Gould Fuller, 10 Sep 1918, LGS2: 327, and Mary Williams Winslow, 6 Apr. 1918, LGS2: 314. My emphasis. Note that it was Plato who was the forerunner of the idea of an intimate connection between psychology and politics.

13   McCormick, *George Santayana: a biography,* 256.

14   McCormick, 425.

the first two (out of three) volumes of his autobiography, *Persons and Places* and *The Middle Span*, gained recognition and were selling very well – a success that the thinker, due to the circumstances of war, could not cherish fully, neither mentally nor materially. Their popularity may be explained, among other things, by the merits of Santayana's style. As described by one of the scholars, it was "a style of power and suppleness, exemplary in its elegance, lucidity, sparseness, and directness; filled with wry and understated humor; made wonderfully vivid by ingenious but unforced metaphors."[15]

When the synthesis of his political thought, *Dominations and Powers*, was finally published in 1951, Santayana, as evidenced by his correspondence, was anxious about its reception. And it came as a disappointment to him, although perhaps not a great surprise -before the book was published he had expressed concern about its lack of discipline – that some of the initial reviews, like the one by his colleague, the pragmatist, Sydney Hook, were critical. The author of the introduction to Santayana's book, John McCormick, describes it as "a fascinating demonstration of Santayana's strengths and weaknesses," thoroughly original and "beautifully written," but, at the same time, uneven, suffering from an untamed diffuseness and marked by a profound skepticism towards the socio-political reality at large, which overwhelmed Santayana during the Cold War.[16] Moreover, McCormick finds a problematic disparity between the parts of the book – the first and the second one being critical and analytical, and the final, third one, projective, a model of what an ideal state might be. An unprepared reader might be tempted to read the final part in a close correspondence with the actual reality, as a recipe for a political regime that should actually come into being – something remote from Santayana's intentions, being rather speculative.

There are some other features of the book potentially preventing its readers from appreciating it and gaining a full grasp of the depth and richness of its palette of meanings. The overwhelming multitude of themes, Santayana's tendency to an abrupt switching in-between different perspectives, meant to present diverse standpoints in a possibly impartial way, his use of irony, and his preference to assume a detached and aesthetic tone, all conspired to making the book a demanding read and creating an impression of indifference – if not coldness – of the author. Critics have noted a "strain of irresponsibility" in Santayana's naturalism and aestheticism applied to the political realm, while

---

15   McClay, "The Unclaimed Legacy," in GTACOUS, 127.
16   All quotations in this paragraph: John McCormick, introduction to *Dominations and Powers Reflections on Liberty, Society and Government*, by George Santayana (London and New York: Routledge, 2017), xiii-xiv.

some of his comments have been regarded as misplaced – a tendency confirmed by some of his private letters.[17] Without any intention to neutralize these facts, what may be said in Santayana's defense is that such problematic passages are rare and do not constitute a dominant characteristic of the body of his work. Besides, it is far from clear whether the detachment present in his style bespeaks indifference or, alternatively, expresses a kind of protective shield assumed by a solitary intellectual. Having said this, I share the view of James Seaton that, regardless of Santayana's intentions, his "approach has its own dangers."[18] I am convinced that while Santayana scholarship today is based on the recognition of the value of his legacy, its thoughtful defense cannot be but highly selective.[19]

Santayana himself had a sense of being misunderstood and gave voice to it in his letters, saying that some of his readers were too immersed "in the controversies of the day" and, one may add, in the pursuit of concrete solutions, to attune to his perspective, which was broad and anthropological rather than local.[20] Today, Santayana's "philosophical distance from too much topicality" – a characteristic of his political thinking, as noted by Till Kinzel – is reconsidered in a much more appreciative tone.[21] As for the early friendly reviewers of *Dominations and Powers*, Michael Oakeshott praised both the aesthetic and intellectual aspect of the book. It

> is not, in fact, an anthology of miscellaneous reflections strung together on the thin thread of an arbitrary attitude to the universe. It is an

---

17   McClay, "The Unclaimed Legacy," in GTACOUS, 139. See also John McCormick's discussion of a display of "harshness and heartlessness" on Santayana's part in his letter to Horace Kallen, being a response to a suggestion that Santayana might want to sponsor a volume of Nicola Sacco's and Bartolomeo Vanzetti's – the famous victims of the Red Scare – letters. See: McCormick, *George Santayana: a biography*, 356. For a discussion of Santayana's relation to the Jews see: Daniel Pinkas, "Santayana, Judaism, and the Jews," *Overheard in Seville* 36 (2018): 69–78. For a concise but telling comment on what Santayana – more or less deliberately but, in any case, unfortunately – overlooked in his reflections on history and politics, see: Skowroński, *Santayana and America*, 198.
18   James Seaton, "Santayana as a Cultural Critic," in: *Under any Sky: Contemporary Readings of George Santayana*, ed. Matthew Caleb Flamm, Krzysztof Piotr Skowroński (Newcastle (UK): Cambridge Scholars Publishing, 2007), 119.
19   James Seaton, introduction to GTACOUS, xxxiii. See also: James Seaton, "The Genteel Tradition and English Liberty," in GTACOUS: 171–173.
20   Letter to Rosamond Thomas (Sturgis) Little, 4 May 1952, LGS8: 444.
21   Till Kinzel, "Santayana, Self-Knowledge and the Limits of Politics," in *The Life of Reason in an Age of Terrorism*, ed. Charles Padrón and Krzysztof P. Skowroński (Leiden and Boston: Brill, 2018), 94.

intellectual structure, a vertebrate and well considered philosophy. It is true that articulation is inobtrusive ... but not to have detected the articulation is to have missed the proper quality of the book.[22]

Another scholar who recognized the value of Santayana's reflections on society and politics was Russell Kirk, who, in his book published shortly after Santayana's death, noted: "He wrote on, nobly sane in a generation of frenzy; and surely the civilization which possesses a Santayana retains some chance for regeneration."[23]

Nevertheless, John McCormick was not the only scholar to think that "the book [*Dominations and Powers*] has never had the readership it deserves."[24] This underestimation of Santayana's political thought may be viewed in a broader context of the neglect of Santayana's legacy, which, according to another scholar, stood "in such stark contrast to his achievement, not to mention his reputation at the height of his long and productive career, that one is led to wonder whether part of the explanation lies in the unwelcomeness of the messages he sought to convey."[25] Today, after a few decades of a modest but steady process of uncovering and reclaiming Santayana, scholars agree upon the enduring value of his work and note that the actuality of some of its parts has been increasing in our century. Despite the fact of a recent revival of interest in Santayana's political thought and cultural criticism – the most recent evidence of which is a collection of essays, edited by Charles Padrón and Krzysztof Piotr Skowroński, *The Life of Reason in an Age of Terrorism* (2018) – up to the point of writing this book, or, at least, over the past half a century, no single-authored monograph in English, devoted specifically to Santayana's political thought has appeared in print.[26] "The dearth

---

22   Michael Oakeshott, "Philosophical Imagination," review of *Dominations and Powers. Reflections on Liberty, Society and Government* by George Santayana, *The Spectator*, November 2, 1951.
23   Russell Kirk, *The Conservative Mind: From Burke to Santayana* (Chicago: Henry Regenery Co., 1953), 394.
24   McCormick, introduction to *Dominations and Powers*, xix.
25   McClay, "The Unclaimed Legacy," in GTACOUS, 127.
26   Two important secondary sources that engage in the topic of Santayana's political ideas are: Beth J. Singer's book *The Rational Society. A Critical Study of Santayana's Social Thought* (Cleveland/London: The Press of Case Western Reserve University, 1970) and Krzysztof P. Skowroński's *Santayana and America. Values, Liberties, Responsibility* (New Castle (UK): Cambridge Scholars Publishing, 2007). The former book, rather forgotten today, offers an overview of what the author considers to be the main constitutive elements of Santayana's conception of society and a more in-depth discussion of selected issues, such as the relation between his naturalism as reflected in his controversial views

of systematic studies on his political ideas is surprising," according to Daniel Moreno.[27]

The present book, by offering an attempt at reconstruction and interpretation of Santayana's political hermeneutics, aims to fill – or, rather, to begin filling – this gap. Except for *Dominations and Powers*, the most mature and synthetic exposition of Santayana's ideas, a number of other, relevant primary sources have been taken into account, to name only *The Life of Reason* (1905–6), *Dialogues in Limbo* (1925), essays in cultural and political criticism, gathered in a few collections, as exemplified by *Soliloquies in England and Later Soliloquies* (1922), as well as Santayana's correspondence, published in this century in an eight-volume collection (*The Letters of George Santayana*, 2001–2008), which offers illuminating insights into the thinker's sympathies and his uncensored comments on the current events. An acquaintance with Santayana's ontological premises and epistemological assumptions, contained in *Scepticism and Animal Faith: Introduction to a System of Philosophy* (1923) and his opus magnum *Realms of Being* (1927–1942) has been of help for the interpretation of his political ideas.

The image of Santayana that emerges from an inquiry into his socio-political thought and cultural critique is anything but unequivocal. An attempt to classify Santayana's views with reference to traditional categories, although instructive as a process, may in the end leave one perplexed. The reader may experience, alternately, illumination and frustration when trying to find the key to a (difficult) alliance between elements of orthodoxy and moderate fatalism on the one hand, and an individualistic nonconformity, on the other. This does not result from a lack of clarity or intellectual inconsistency. According to my reading experience, Santayana expresses his thoughts – and does so independently of the poetic quality of his writing – in a way that may be described as synthetic, dense, yet – with some exceptions – lucid enough. Save for the fact that Santayana avoided committing himself to any set of views associated with this or that political tradition, school, or party,[28] the confusing aspect of

---

on race (and/or ethnicity) and civilization. Santayana's political views are interpreted by the author in terms of an interplay of the natural, the moral and the rational. I'd suggest that from the perspective of a contemporary reader, Beth Singer's book may be considered a valuable prolegomena to Santayana's social thought. It also is a source of useful elucidations of some of the terms – such as "rationality" – that were central to Santayana's thinking yet used by him in an inconsistent way.

27 Daniel Moreno, *Santayana the Philosopher. Philosophy as a Form of Life*, trans. Charles Padron (Lewisburg: Bucknell University Press, 2015), 93. In Moreno's book there is a chapter devoted to Santayana's political thought, which is an important contribution to this area of research.

28 See: Letter to Rimsa Michel, 22 Sept. 1949, LGS8: 201.

his socio-political writings rests rather in their very density, enormous thematic scope, frequent and often unexpected use of irony and humor, and what I would describe as a *consistent and intended ambiguity*, which may be partly explained by the author's relativism and, partly, as an expression of an inner dialogue with an *alter ego*. As Morris Grossman remarked, "Santayana confesses his errant tendencies, but at the same time his pervasive irony extends (after the manner of Schlegel's irony of ironies) to his confessions. Consistency remains for him a relative virtue." Still, the author admits, Santayana remains consistent in "the refusal to relinquish any alternatives that are humanly important, even if they lead to the brink of contradiction."[29]

Attaining an integral insight into the meaning and spirit of his work, then, requires an attentive reading and rereading, a constant reevaluation by taking, alternately, the positions of proximity and distance, and by juxtaposing fragments with their broader contexts and the book in its entirety. It also requires distinguishing between the levels of description and norm, between mock, irony, sarcasm and seriousness, between arguments put forth in favour of the author's standpoint and figures (often analogies or parabolas) meant to illuminate an imaginary interlocutor's reasoning. Knowledge of the historical and personal context may be of help too. Juxtaposition of Santayana's views with those of other critics of politics and culture of his era, as well as the thinkers he read and might have been influenced by, is another aspect of the hermeneutic method employed by me when writing this book. It is easy to misunderstand Santayana and recognize in him, for example, a panegyrist of war.[30]

What we are presented with in Santayana's final work – in the form of a panoramic overview – may be described as, first, an examination of human powers and limitations, of possible gains and losses that human life, individually and collectively, may be subject to under different socio-political configurations and in different cultural landscapes. Second, and at a deeper level, we get a description of the dynamics of the political realm, viewed as interconnected with human nature and condition, or, in other words, the existential (human and non-human) constants and variables defining the precarious situation of humans. This apparently impartial description is enriched with an individualistic, moral perspective, where the possibility of recognizing

---

29 Morris Grossman, *Art and Morality. Essays in the Spirit of George Santayana*, ed. Martin Coleman (New York: Fordham University Press, 2014), 215.

30 See a text by Eduardo Mendieta, "Assassination Nation: the Drone as Thanatological Dispositif," in *The Life of Reason in an Age of Terrorism*, 61–87. In this overall interesting essay, the author too hastily, in my view, places Santayana among philosophers attuned to a kind of war mode.

one's true interests and attaining happiness (the early Santayana of *The Life of Reason*), or achieving vital liberty tantamount to completion (the Santayana of *Dominations and Powers*) are at stake. It is with this horizon in view that the pair powers-dominations becomes meaningful and turns into a triad powers-dominations-virtues. These moral criteria are not utterly divorced from aesthetic ones insofar as a spiritual perspective is taken into consideration. Hence, according to my interpretation, Santayana's criticism stems from, among other things, his preoccupation with the fate, authenticity, and liberality of liberal arts as essential for the vitality of culture and as venues for discharging individual potential and imagination, his respect for finite forms and living traditions as vehicles of continuity, and a belief that the preservation of (the idea of) virtues works to the benefit of common life. As for the political ideal, it is focused, on the one hand, on the pragmatic need to face the challenge of necessity in a competent way, and, on the other, on the idea of a harmonious organization of human diversity. The two, in my reading, represent a specific, *Santayanan formula of the separation of powers, competences, and virtues, namely – managing necessity and harmonizing diversity.*

What Santayana offers, then, is a sort of critical and interdisciplinary hermeneutics of politics and society as embedded in culture. Alternatively, one might want to describe it as an attempt at a "political anthropology," perhaps a sort of prelude to a political philosophy, which is not inconsistent with the way the thinker himself conceived of his endeavor, as evidenced by some of the earlier quoted passages from his private correspondence, where he speaks of a "psychology of politics." To understand the origins of Santayana's endeavor, one may also look into *The Life of Reason*. While some of his views changed significantly within the span of nearly half a century, when it comes to political ideas, one can see more of an evolution than discontinuity. Thus, I would suggest that one of the tasks that *Dominations and Powers* strives to fulfill has been outlined already in the earlier work, namely – "to unite a trustworthy conception of the conditions under which man lives with an adequate conception of his interests."[31] Here, as the philosopher admits, he feels most at home with the ancient thinkers, who have "drawn for us the outlines of an ideal culture at a time when life was simpler ... and individual intelligence more resolute and free."[32] Yet, he does not ignore later inspirations – from Catholicism to the French Revolution and industrialism, all of which embodied certain ideals worth consideration.

---

31 George Santayana, introduction to *The Life of Reason. Reason in Common Sense*, Critical Edition, by George Santayana, ed. Marrianne S. Wokeck, Martin A. Coleman (Cambridge, Ma: MIT, 2013), 17. Subsequently I will refer to this book as LR1.
32 Santayana, introduction to LR1, 19.

> There is no need to refute anything, for the will which is behind all ideals and behind most dogmas cannot itself be refuted; but it may be enlightened and led to reconsider its intent, when its satisfaction is seen to be either naturally impossible or inconsistent with better things.[33]

This generous, humanistic attitude of *humani nihil a me alienum puto*, is followed by a sort of post-modern manifesto, namely a contention that "[t]he age of controversy is past; that of interpretation has succeeded."[34] This declaration of the early Santayana, however, in his last work gives way to a more bitter tone of someone disillusioned with living in a "world false to its every promise,"[35] and prone to be suspicious, if not dismissive, of certain ideals and hopes which he enjoyed a few decades earlier. Regardless of this change, a continuous intellectual and moral articulation crystallizes itself throughout his *oeuvre* and consists in, to use John Gray's succinct phrase, "abandoning the romantic culture of limitless *hubris* for a classical ethos of limitation and constraint."[36]

Santayana's undertaking, meant to enhance our understanding of the political realm and provide criteria for judging it, cannot escape being dependent on the discernment of some lasting and universal elements and, hence, the assumption of an intelligible sort of continuity pertaining if not to the history of mankind then, at least, to the history of Western civilization. This is not to say that Santayana believed that history may be described in terms of any fixed and history-specific laws, for example as a repetition of cycles. Rather, the source of a relative unity is to be sought in the human condition, nature, and constitution, and, consequently, a certain organization of the world of human affairs. However, one needs to keep in mind that while Santayana was preoccupied with the fate of the human genius, he "entertained no illusions about man's significance in the ultimate scheme of things."[37] Finding a relatively stable point of reference allowed him to avoid the traps awaiting those political philosophies, which, engaging deeply in interpretations of history, were "compelled to flounder in the treacherous waters of passion, rivalries, projects, theories, and interests, most of them only imputed to whole governments and peoples. These are all second-hand, conventional, verbal factors."[38] This

---

33   LR1, 19.
34   LR1, 19.
35   DP, 55.
36   John Gray, *Post-Liberalism. Studies in Social Thought* (New York and London: Routledge, 1993), 29. Subsequently I refer to this source as PLIB.
37   McClay, "The Unclaimed Legacy," in GTACOUS, 133.
38   DP, 195.

opinion is related to Santayana's conviction about the material foundations of human history, in relation to which history as a narrative is bound to be marked by a degree of arbitrariness. To be sure, Santayana by no means claims that human nature is unchangeable and universally the same. It is subject to change and variation, but nevertheless reflection on human nature helps to establish a naturalistic framework for a political philosophy.

It is worth adding that Santayana's materialistic naturalism is not deprived of idealistic elements and is mitigated by the author's poetic imagination and language, whereby the whole receives more than a touch of subtlety and sophistication. However, in contrast to the label of an aristocratic or elitist thinker sometimes attached to Santayana, his endeavor in the field of political thought – if not in the views conveyed, then in intentions and methods – is democratic, dialogical and deliberative. One finds in his last work a human scale, references to common sense, and an unceasing effort to give voice to contrasting views. To emphasize the fact that his book is not addressed solely or primarily to specialists in the narrow field of political science, he declared: "I am content to stand where honest laymen are standing, and to write as I might talk with a friend on a country walk or sitting at a tavern."[39]

I find anti-dogmatism and eclecticism to be distinctive features of Santayana's political thinking and, hence, categorizing him has not been my aim. Nevertheless, by reconsidering the philosopher's ideas concerning such fundamental issues as freedom, justice, self-government, democracy, equality, and tolerance, the book obviously sheds light on Santayana's influences and political sympathies. Russell Kirk, in the already mentioned book *The Conservative Mind: From Burke to Santayana*, placed Santayana, next to a moderately conservative figure like Irving Babbitt, among "critical conservatives." These thinkers were concerned with a multifaceted crisis of modern culture, manifesting itself, among other things, in a religion of progress, a "sentimental equalitarian collectivism," the degradation of various standards of human perfection in the midst of a mediocre, materialistic uniformity, setting the ideal of an efficient, standardized mass production as the aim of human effort.[40]

One may raise objections as to whether the aforementioned critique is necessarily evidence of Santayana's conservative allegiance. Similar points of convergence may be found between his and the Frankfurt School representatives' critiques of modernity and capitalism. James Seaton, comparing critical essays by Santayana and Adorno, focuses on difference in tone, contrasting

---

39 DP, 33.
40 See: Kirk, *The Conservative Mind*, 365.

Santayana's moderation with Adorno's apocalyptic attitude.[41] What is important, though, is the fact that their criticisms are levelled at similar aspects of the cultural crisis they diagnose. The topic has also been raised by Daniel Moreno, who uses an umbrella term "Americanism" to cover a range of phenomena that constituted the target of Santayana's critique.[42] I think Moreno is right in claiming that, first, Santayana offers more than merely critical and deconstructive tools for understanding political reality, and, second, that he cannot be labelled simply as an anti-modernist thinker, even if one ascribes to him a certain conservative frame of mind.[43] I also wholeheartedly agree with Moreno's placing Santayana among the ranks of *"iconoclasts and noncomformists*, who were suspicious of anything established,"[44] such as Oscar Wilde, George Bernard Shaw, and – the best match, in my view – Aldous Huxley, the author not only of a famous dystopia but also of a bitter socio-political and cultural critique.[45]

Nevertheless, some of Santayana's sympathies and views contribute to the fact that he may be and has been recognized as a potential ally in the criticism of modernity from conservative positions. Jude P. Dougherty evokes Santayana's complaints about the crisis of Christendom and his reluctance towards the equalizing "spirit" of social democracy, which he finds "deadening" in relation to culture. He quotes Santayana's bold suggestion that to defend democracy efficiently one may want to "'deny that civilization is a good.'"[46] The main argument of Dougherty, being that Europe needs to find the way to recover its Christian identity, is further developed with the support of the views of Brad S. Gregory about the loss of a common moral orientation, involved in

---

41   Seaton, "Santayana as a Cultural Critic," in Flamm and Skowroński, *Under any Sky*, 115.
42   „Americanism" meant as an umbrella term, covering a broad spectrum of typically modern, socio-political, cultural and economic phenomena such as mechanization, the formation of mass society, uniformization, consumerism, propaganda, etc. Moreno, with reference to Santayana's private correspondence, points to the fact that he considered certain aspects of capitalism as "satanic". Despite all that, Moreno maintains, and I agree with him on this point, that ultimately Santayana was not an anti-modernist thinker. See: Daniel Moreno, "Santayana on Americanism," in Padrón and Skowroński, *The Life of Reason in an Age of Terrorism*, 103–114.
43   Moreno, *Santayana the Philosopher*, 97. Elsewhere in the same chapter, though, the author speaks of Santayana's "relativist frame of mind," see page 103. As for the conservative traits of Santayana's outlook, Moreno lists his criticism of democracy, his "organic" framing of social institutions and his enduring sympathy towards Catholicism (despite his atheism).
44   Moreno, *Santayana the Philosopher*, 95. My emphasis.
45   Aldous Huxley, *Brave New World Revisited* (New York: Harper & Brothers, 1958).
46   Jude P. Dougherty, "We are modern and want to be modern," *Studia Gilsoniana* 4:3 (2015): 241–249.

the legacy of the Protestant Reformation, Pierre Manent's ideas about the relation of European nationalisms to the emergence of "competing [religious and political] authorities," and Remi Brague's theory of Europe being "essentially Roman," where "Roman" is understood metaphorically, as a term describing a specific relationality towards other cultures. Even if Santayana's anti-dogmatism and relativism would prevent him, as I believe, from committing himself to the above perspective, some passages in his writings may indeed be used to support it. One comes there across a number of speculations about a universalism with a Catholic underpinning or an ideal empire modelled on the Catholic Church's hierarchy and order. Yet, the conservatism of these passages is diluted as Santayana speaks of a future evolution of a certain inclusive cultural and mental "quality" – the flexibility and ability of the Catholic mind, especially when infused with humanism, to tolerate and/or assimilate otherness[47] and the possibility of "the orthodox morality of the Church becoming almost rational morality, or human orthodoxy."[48] This sympathy of an atheist towards (his native) Catholic culture couples with his distaste for the modern and democratic desire "to organize, equalize, and train everybody, making them all unanimous."[49]

Returning to Kirk's classification of Santayana, it is a well-known fact that the author of *Genteel Tradition in American Philosophy* distanced himself from the New Humanism, of which Irving Babbitt was a representative, because of his reluctance to what he considered to be a doctrinaire anthropocentrism, part and parcel of the genteel tradition. Besides, Santayana's refusal to accept the New Humanists' or any other set of prescriptions for society and government was an expression of his intellectual independence. He nevertheless shared some of Babbitt's general views, to mention only their critique of romanticism, subjectivism, as well as their deep conviction about the destructiveness of human *hubris*. One should also mention a preference for continuity and steady reforms over revolution, even though Santayana would sometimes risk flirting with the idea of the latter.[50]

---

47 DP, 288–289.
48 DP, 157.
49 DP, 288.
50 According to James Seaton, "[i]t would be most unfortunate if the polemics of 'The Genteel Tradition at Bay' led to the conclusion that one must choose between Santayana and Babbitt." The ideas of the latter, in his view, exhibit "what is possible when Santayana's real insights are made the basis for intellectual and cultural renewal." See: James Seaton, "Irving Babbitt and Cultural Renewal," *The Imaginative Conservative*, 18 September 2016, https://theimaginativeconservative.org/2016/09/irving-babbitt-cultural-renewal-seaton-timeless.html.

Ultimately, Kirk admits that Santayana can hardly "subscribe ... to these venerable orthodoxies."[51] I would add that among the reasons why Santayana is a difficult match from the perspective of any orthodoxy is that he was a disillusioned humanist, an anti-dogmatic individualist, often conveying through his writings an attitude of a provocative moral ambiguity, while true and original conservatism is said to rely on prescriptions and authorities rather than private judgment, and it "rises at the antipodes from individualism."[52]

To give an example of the said ambivalence, in his final book Santayana puts into consideration the following controversy:

> while we certainly have neither the lights nor the strength of will to act always for the eventual good of all whom our conduct affects, ... it is better that we should blunder freely in love, in politics, and in religion, than that we should follow the prescriptions of external authorities, dubious authorities at best, which might save us a few knocks, only to lead us and the world, in their ponderous organized blindness, to the most hideous catastrophe. The art of governing mankind is difficult: until a true master of it is found, we may well prefer to try experiments ourselves.[53]

These words do not express Santayana's ultimate position. Exemplifying the aforementioned ambiguity typical of the philosopher's last book, they are meant rather to express the position of "the democratic mind" with whom Santayana dialogues and polemicizes in the book, just as he did earlier, in *Dialogues in Limbo*. Still, in my reading, this viewpoint is not at all alien to the author. It expresses honestly the radicalization of his deepest conviction about there being no absolute authority in politics or morals and no universal model of the best political organization. It also demonstrates how the conviction about the fallibility of human reason might serve as an argument in favor of liberty – one put forth already by the early liberals.[54]

To summarize this brief discussion about classification, while I find all the aforementioned, attempted comparisons and dialogues hermeneutically fruitful, I think any definite classification of Santayana's views is likely to turn out not only unnecessarily constraining but also elusive. The consistency and integrity of his outlook is not of a doctrinaire kind; rather, I would suggest, it is

---

51   Kirk, *The Conservative Mind*, 387.
52   Kirk, 211.
53   DP, 184–185.
54   See: John Gray, *Liberalism* (Minneapolis: University of Minnesota Press, 1986), 92. Subsequently I will refer to this source as LIB.

rooted in his deeper naturalistic commitments, as well as very few ideal "venerable orthodoxies" to which he voluntarily and spontaneously subscribed – such as the affirmation of diverse human accomplishment and what I call in this book his Apollonian individualism and humanism.

To refer, once again, to recent scholarship, Matthew C. Flamm, reconsidering the possibility of placing Santayana somewhere on the map of political allegiances, suggests that the thinker's attitude towards liberal democracy turns out to be more complex than it has been believed. While John Gray called Santayana one of the best critics of liberalism,[55] according to Flamm, "[t]he nuanced appreciation and sensitivity Santayana displays towards different models of democracy together with his pragmatic conception of government offer support to the idea that one should think twice about categorizing him flatly as a conservative."[56] Leaving classifications aside, Till Kinzel emphasizes the value of Santayana's "astonishingly comprehensive perception of the phenomena of political life."[57] John Lachs admits that Santayana's political writings are successful in revealing certain fundamental and universal aspects of the dynamics of the socio-political realm. Santayana is correct, according to the author, when pointing to all the more often ignored fact that "[w]hatever is done must be performed by men and women singly or in groups."[58] To use somewhat crude, naturalistic terms, we may say that what stands behind these individuals are psyches – "moving spatiotemporal region[s]"[59] being at the same time "moral substance[s]" and "the ultimate and only creator[s] of the goodness of whatever is good."[60] Yet, Lachs blames the thinker's relativistic individualism and deliberate detachment for leaving his readers without any moral compass, without any recommendation as to how they can orientate themselves and participate in the social world, let alone improve it. This kind of omission in a political philosophy, according to Lachs, makes for a serious failure.[61] This issue will reappear in this book. For now let me only say that even when one agrees that there are limits to the practical usefulness of Santayana's political thinking, one may still argue that the gain from enhancing one's *understanding* in this case is definitely more than just cognitive – it

---

55   John Gray, "Santayana and the Critique of Liberalism," in PLIB, 20–31.
56   Matthew Caleb Flamm, "Liberalism and the Vertigo of Spirit: Santayana's Political Theodicy," in Padrón and Skowroński, *The Life of Reason in an Age of Terrorism*, 130.
57   Kinzel, "Santayana, Self-Knowledge and the Limits of Politics," 95.
58   John Lachs, *Freedom and Limits*, ed. Patrick Shade (New York: Fordham University Press, 2014), 149.
59   Lachs, *Freedom and Limits*, 147.
60   Lachs, 148.
61   Lachs, 156.

is broadly humane and existential, and, as such, cannot be divorced from morals. *Understanding* politics as a form of gaining self-knowledge indispensable in the process of turning from mythically-guided politics to rational and ethical one has been the postulate of Plato.[62] If, in turn, the charge were that Santayana was not sufficiently pro-social, one might respond, with recourse to his individualistic naturalism, by evoking an explicit declaration of his intentions: "*What I wish to prevent is choking the human genius by social pressure.*"[63] As an additional comment to this, let me quote Daniel Pinkas's controversial opinion, in which, I think, there is at least a grain of truth: "especially in the later works, for better or for worse, his [Santayana's] primary aim is neither empirical adequacy nor conceptual clarity, but spiritual transformation."[64]

An important voice in the discussion about Santayana's thought as an *inspiration* for contemporary cultural and political reflection is Herman Saatkamp's inquiry into the thinker's cosmopolitanism. Saatkamp notes that it is precisely Santayana's moral relativism, grounded in his materialistic naturalism and drawing on the essential infinity of imagination and interpretation, that forms an environment for a cosmopolitan outlook. Regardless of Santayana's individualism, which may be a challenge from the perspective of a melioristic attitude towards the common world, the "hard core" of his philosophy corresponds with the idea that different people, representing different values, may live together without agreeing on values and preferences, provided that they share at least the willingness and the ability to communicate, understand and respect each other.[65] Ideally, diversity as a natural fact, allied with the virtue of understanding and appreciating otherness (which may be said to constitute "civility" as opposed to the blind and egotistic single-mindedness of "barbarism") may lead to the emergence of a set of *universally recognized interests and concerns*. Herman Saatkamp's reflections provide an additional incentive to reconsider the limits of Santayana's relativism and the way he problematized relations between politics and culture.

---

62   For more on this topic see: Cassirer, *The Myth of the State*, 74–83.
63   Letter to John W. Yolton, 27 Apr. 1952, LGS8: 440–441. My emphasis.
64   "One thing that we could say at this point is that Santayana often uses the term 'egotism' as the antithesis of the philosophical virtues he extols: humility, disillusionment, and detachment," continues the author. See: Daniel Pinkas "Egotism, Violence and the Devil: On Santayana's Use of the Concept of Egotism," in Padrón and Skowroński, *The Life of Reason in an Age of Terrorism*, 182.
65   Herman J. Saatkamp, Jr., "Santayana: Cosmopolitanism and the Spiritual Life," in *George Santayana at* 150, ed. Matthew Caleb Flamm, Giuseppe Patella and Jennifer A. Rea (Lanham: Lexington Books, 2014), 93–110.

While the present book does not aim directly to prove the "actuality" of Santayana's political thought, it does reveal its obvious – as I believe – relevance to the present time. In a sense, there is a mismatch between the notion of "actuality" and the universal "spirit" of Santayana's endeavor. One may even be tempted to speak – after Wilfred M. McClay – of a deliberate "unseasonableness" of it, keeping in mind that the opinion that Santayana's "thoughts were thoughts out of season, both in his time and in our own"[66] should be read metaphorically or as somewhat ironic. Nevertheless, rather than speaking of "actuality," I'd speak of a hermeneutic relevance.

One of the main aims of this book is to reconstruct and (re-)interpret Santayana's political hermeneutics. I attempt to curb systematically Santayana's thinking while preserving the structure of his own design, namely – 1) the dynamics between dominations and powers as describing the relational position of a given life or lives in respect to their true interests and with vital liberty in view; 2) the three, intertwining orders present in the socio-political realm: generative, militant, and rational. I describe this "structure" in the first chapter, devoted to the contours of Santayana's vision. The inquiry into Santayana's conception of human nature, condition and constitution allows me to illuminate the anthropological and existential pillars of his political ideas. I introduce, among others, the ideas of *negative anthropology, managing necessity*[67] (which I later enlarge into *managing necessity and harmonizing diversity*), and *governing life*, which provide a framework for my interpretation and, at once, are meant to illuminate the critical-hermeneutic potential of Santayana's political thinking. In the same chapter I discuss the twofold understanding of the very notion of "politics" held by Santayana, which, as I argue, is reflected in the dual nature of his endeavor in *Dominations and Powers*.

In the second chapter, I analyze the evolution of Santayana's ideas about freedom and liberty, with focus on the dilemmas and paradoxes involved in what the thinker calls "vacant freedom." This leads me to the conclusion that Santayana's considerations of freedom sharply reveal the fact that every conception of freedom contains a seed of servitude and no conception of freedom is impartial. Of all themes central for Santayana's political thought, that of freedom allows to illuminate in a most articulate manner the extra-political premises of this philosophy. It binds together his ontology, philosophical anthropology, elements of literary psychology, cultural criticism and reflection

---

66 McClay, "The Unclaimed Legacy," in GTACOUS, 128.
67 I introduced the idea of managing necessity for the first time in my essay: "Managing Necessity: Santayana on Forms of Power and the Human Condition," in Padrón and Skowroński, *The Life of Reason in an Age of Terrorism*, 28–42.

on socio-political issues. Moreover, it brings to light the threads of continuity – existing regardless of change – in his early and late works.

In the third chapter, in connection with the ideas of: 1) the state and society as sources of multifaceted servitude, 2) government as managing necessity, 3) liberty as constituted amidst limitations, I examine Santayana's vision of humans as thoroughly dependent beings, discuss the basic forms of human servitude and their political implications. These include the whole range of phenomena – from the fact of having a body and hence, natural needs, through social commitments, military service, ideal allegiances such as patriotism, to a problematic relation of man to technology. I employ, useful in my view, Santayana's distinction among three kinds of servitude: necessary, voluntary, and involuntary yet accidental.

The following, fourth, chapter is devoted to the theme of militancy – a generic term referring to the multitude of ways in which initiative, competition, strife and war manifest themselves in the socio-political realm. I discuss here, among other things, issues such as: forms of governmental oppression, economization of all spheres of life, the power of ideologies and propaganda, military conflicts. These phenomena have often been framed by Santayana in terms of re-barbarization, militarism, and tribalism. The diverse militant forms of human activity are judged from the perspective of their influence on the possibility of rational government and self-government and, thus, the attainment of what Santayana calls "the Life of Reason." The third chapter also features *a confrontation between a moralist and a cynic in politics*. This clash of attitudes belongs to what I consider to be the most interesting and deep insights in Santayana's political thinking.

Throughout the following chapters of this book (chapters five to eight) I gather and discuss – in a variety of contexts and with reference to other thinkers – the dispersed in Santayana's *oeuvre* pieces of his critique of liberalism, democracy, industrialism and communism. More specifically, in the fifth chapter I look at the problem, raised by Santayana, of the relation between the anthropological and cultural function of *arts*, as framed by the ancients, and the status of *work* as well as liberal arts in the contemporary world. Santayana was preoccupied, as I try to prove with reference to his and Ortega y Gasset's discussion of the modern art, with a phenomenon of a thoroughgoing alienation (to use Marx's term loosely) occurring between man and his activity. The following, sixth chapter, is devoted exclusively to the reconsideration of Santayana's inquiry into the fragility of liberalism and its unfulfilled promises. In chapter seven I discuss Santayana's ideas about justice, governmental legitimacy, equality, unanimity, the paradoxes of representative democracy, or, in other words, the ways democratic practice embodies and at once betrays the ideal of human self-government. I unlock Santayana's idea of justice with a double key: of harmony and charity. I address the issue of Santayana's universalist and cosmopolitan sympathies and look at the possibility of socio-political arrangements that are alternative to a democratic nation-state and, as Santayana speculated, might become all the more realistic option in the globalizing world. This topic is continued in chapter eight, the main theme of which is Santayana's changing views on communism.

In the final chapter, while summarizing major conclusions reached in the book, I explore broader contexts of the virtues Santayana extoled and the vices he reproached and ask whether they may be recognized as limits to his moral relativism. I also argue that one of a few overarching, though inexplicit, ideas that Santayana has conveyed in his writings on socio-political issues is that *culture is wiser than politics*. It seems to originate somewhere in the vortex of his philosophical commitments as well as personal preferences, which I frame in terms of: 1) a humble and self-critical humanism; 2) a modest and gentle individualism, which I call *Apollonian* and oppose both to social atomism and to a predatory individualism of power; 3) the primacy of culture over politics and the idea of not overestimating politics. Culture may constitute both a safeguard for humanity against the evils of politics and a source of betterment for the political sphere. Thus, upon my reading, one may find in Santayana an inexplicit incentive to depoliticize culture.[68]

Although the present book is not intended primarily to be a criticism of or a polemic with the philosopher, it does convey critical thoughts on specific ideas and tendencies that one finds in his thought. Furthermore, throughout this book, I refer to a number of thinkers, ancient and contemporary ones, whereby I continue the endeavor, undertaken in my previous work, to free Santayana's thought – which I find to be essentially dialogical – from a relative isolation, for which he was partly responsible himself, and partly was confined to by an accidental conspiracy of external factors. Some of the thinkers I evoke provide for a novel context in Santayana scholarship. Thus, I refer, among others, to Plato, Aristotle, Alexis de Tocqueville, the representatives of the Frankfurt School, Ernst Cassirer, José Ortega y Gasset, René Girard, Paul Ricoeur, Arthur

---

[68] Santayana never offered any explicit definition of culture. For the purpose of this study, I assume Santayana held a broad understanding of it, extending from a simple idea of shared practices and abilities, through Ernst Cassirer's theory of *animal symbolicum*, to Clifford Geertz's definition of culture as "an historically transmitted pattern of meanings embodied in symbols." Clifford Geertz, *Interpretation of Cultures* (New York: Basic Book, 1973), 89. Obviously, the said depoliticization of culture in the modern world can (and should) be only partial.

Schopenhauer, Arnold J. Toynbee, whom Santayana read extensively and by whose ideas, I'd suggest, he was modestly influenced, and John Gray – an interpreter of Santayana and a thinker whose ideas form, in my view, a fruitful hermeneutic dynamics with those of Santayana.

CHAPTER 1

Foundations and Contours

1.1 Dualities

Let me assume as a point of departure Santayana's remark coming from *Dominations and Powers* and concerning a twofold understanding of the notion of politics:

> The word politics has a nobler and a meaner sense, and it is only in the latter that most people use it [today]. It may mean what relates to policy and to polity – to the purposes of human cooperation and the constitution of society – or it may mean what relates to the *instruments* of policy only, as for instance to the form of government or to the persons who shall carry it on.[1]

The two senses imply two different approaches – a reflective and essentially philosophical one, and a technical and instrumental one, committed to finding practical solutions in the existing socio-political realities. The first one may either be limited to a critical elucidation of the status quo or it may aspire to setting ideal goals; the second is interested in increasing efficiency in the realization of practical aims. This is not to say that the boundary between the two senses is always sharp, or that they are disjunctive, or necessarily opposed to one another; they rather describe two different traditions and attitudes towards politics.

Santayana sees himself as subscribing rather to the first tradition. Like Plato, he associates politics with a form of self-knowledge. Like Aristotle, he tends to understand political science in terms of practical knowledge aiming at the good and happiness of individuals and communities, a kind of knowledge which he locates, at least partially, like Aristotle again, within the scope of ethics.[2] What is more, the nature of the practice and its end suggest, prescriptively, an intimate relation between political action and virtue. Correspondingly, Santayana insists that political action becomes an art. The critical part of his political thinking is motivated, not unlike Plato's *Republic*, by a discontent

---

1 DP, 164.
2 Letter to Sidney Hook, 4 June 1938, LGS6: 139.

with the existing socio-political practice and arrangements in the West, and, in particular, their cultural resonance. The discontent, one may speculate, may have prompted Santayana to engage in a larger project of illuminating forms of power in the human world with a set of morally and aesthetically informed criteria in view, which was finally embodied in *Dominations and Powers*. In this respect, Santayana's critical-hermeneutic endeavor, and still more so his speculations about an imaginary, rationally-governed, multi-national empire, bear a mark of Platonic inspiration, despite the fact that their philosophical conceptions differ fundamentally.

Among the dualities mentioned in the title of this section, there is a duality of perspectives that may be found in Santayana's political writings themselves. On the one hand, the thinker assumes the vantage point of an impartial observer, who attempts to describe the universal mechanisms or dynamics operative in the political realm. To achieve this aim, he proposes a *hermeneutics of politics* of sorts, embedded in his non-reductive naturalism and utilizing a set of categories that emphasize the inherent relatedness of the spheres of politics, culture, human life, and existence at large. This connectedness is reinforced by the fact that Santayana sometimes resorts to a loose and metaphorical analogy between self-government and governing others. This explanatory strategy, by the way, originates with Plato's analogy, undertaken later by Aristotle, between the order of the human soul and the organization of *politeia*. I see it as a way of appropriating Santayana's original naturalism for the sake of thinking politics, connecting individual well-being with the form of collective coexistence, justifying the significance of personal virtue in the political realm, as well as introducing the medium of culture as a sphere of negotiations between the individual and society. The large vista emerging from this eclectic philosophizing, involving elements of ontology, anthropology, psychology, phenomenology of everyday life, and cultural critique, produces – in accordance with the author's intentions – an effect of a drama of human affairs.

The other dimension of Santayana's undertaking, which remains in a problematic relation with the first, impartial view, is the idealistic or the normative one.[3] To be sure, unlike in Plato's case, Santayana's materialistic naturalism rules out the existence of any universal, eternal, and transcendent normative pattern that might be a source of reference for political practice. Neither a transcendental guidance, originating in human reason, is a viable option in

---

3 Daniel Moreno notes that the tension that emerges between these two perspectives makes an impression of a "calculated ambiguity," ultimately to be dismissed due to the fact that the spiritual, detached perspective has the final say in Santayana's reflections. See: Moreno, *Santayana the Philosopher*, 94.

the existential landscape sketched by Santayana, even if the assumption of the share of spirit (irreducible, 1st person consciousness) makes a difference in the makeup of the realm of human affairs, not least by the fact that it articulates the possible universality and persistence of a symbolically mediated human culture. The deficit of unconditional and certain sources of moral norms and judgments does not, in my view, readily condemn Santayana to a *sheer* moral relativism, especially in the field of politics, although from the strict perspective of metaethics, some kind of relativism has rightly been ascribed to him by critics and is evidenced by numerous passages in his texts.[4] I am inclined to interpret Santayana, in particular with respect to his political writings, which contain a prominent moralist thread, as a representative of value pluralism and a qualified relativism. The reader will find more on what I think to be the humanistic and constitutive limits of Santayana's moral relativism in chapters four and nine. Regardless of the issue of Santayana's relativism, he provides the reader both with the general criteria of judgment pertaining to the political realm and an imaginative horizon of an ideal *politeia*, being the principal subject matter of the third, final part of *Dominations and Powers* – "The rational order."

However, between his *hermeneia* of politics, his critical diagnosis, and the positive project there seems to remain a gap, which, as one might expect of a philosopher of politics, should be filled with at least a minimum advise concerning the amelioration of the status quo. Yet, this is what Santayana abstains from doing; there is no advice, let alone recipes, concerning practical solutions. Even though Santayana clearly and honestly states at the beginning of his treatise what the reader may and what they should not expect to find in it, the lack of practical advice has cost him some astute criticism back then and today.[5]

Now, the second, "moral" dimension of Santayana's political thought, consists itself of two threads. The first, present already in Santayana's earlier works, is of negative or critical nature and embraces, among other things, critique of some forms of militancy, industrial capitalism, liberalism and the associated critique of certain phenomena framed by him as barbarism, egotism, cynicism, worldliness, etc. The second thread, expressed in positive terms, is the already

---

[4] Santayana's approach in this respect has also been described in terms of value pluralism, expressivism and a non-cognitivist position. For a substantive discussion of this issue see, for example: Diana Heney, "Santayana on Value: Expressivism, Self-knowledge and Happiness," *Overheard in Seville: Bulletin of the Santayana Society* 30 (2012): 4–13. See also Santayana on his own relativism: DP, 300–303.

[5] An example of such criticism is John Lach's essay "Santayana on Society." See: Lachs, *Freedom and Limits*, 156–157.

mentioned Santayana's vague vision of a rationally governed state/empire. While the latter thread may well be considered an "experimental" addition to his political thinking, its first, hermeneutic, dimension along with the first thread of the second dimension, may be approached, in my interpretation, as constituting 1) a complete and self-standing project of a hermeneutic and critical illumination of the socio-political realm, concerned, first and foremost, with the position of the individual and their chances for completion in society; 2) a vital and integral part of Santayana's *oeuvre* as a whole, some themes of which reappear throughout a variety of his political and non-political writings, establishing an intimate connection between them.

At this point it merits mentioning that Santayana viewed the nature of his own work in political thought (in accordance with his philosophical "temperament") as predominantly critical. As mentioned in the introduction, he summarized his overall aim in negative terms, declaring that he wished to impede stifling the human genius by social pressure.[6] This statement, as I believe, is worth remembering, as it speaks volumes about the philosopher's principal motivation and the *spiritus movens* behind his political thinking.

I have started from the twofold understanding of the notion of politics evoked by the thinker and have drawn the reader's attention to the bidimensional character of Santayana's political thought. A reflection over *Dominations and Powers* may suggest to an inquisitive reader yet another kind of duality, a duality in tone and outlook. It is as if two impulses rivaled in Santayana. A disillusioned and pessimist one leads him to grant to humans a rather narrow margin of freedom and a very limited influence on the shape of political arrangements, let alone the course of human history, determined by impersonal, material trends and accidents, even though Santayana does not go as far as Plato, who said: "no human being legislates anything, but ... chances ... and accidents legislate everything for us."[7] The same "impulse" seems to make the thinker inclined to admit that there is more than a grain of truth in the Hobbesian vision of the origins of the social contract. This brief and rough description is, of course, a simplification and does not render the complexity and the nuances of Santayana's vision. The bleak outlook, nevertheless, prevails in *Dominations and Powers* – how different in tone from his earlier *The Life of Reason* – and this fact cannot be unrelated to the grim circumstances of the political landscape in the first half of the 20th century. A modest presence of a brighter impulse, though, should not escape the reader's attention.

---

6   Letter to John W. Yolton, 27 Apr. 1952, LGS8: 440.
7   Plato, *Laws*, 709 ab.

I see a ray of hope and even optimism, albeit very fragile, originating within Santayana's very naturalism. Insofar as psychic genius is alive and spirit, which conditions imagination and the common medium of human culture, is indestructible, there always is a chance for a revival. As one of the scholars noticed, Santayana "always rejected the notion that the triumph of trends or movements he opposed would lead to some final, ultimate catastrophe."[8] The revival, even after the darkest night, may be occasioned from beyond human powers, by the very natural course of things – the irresistible *change*. In this book I will explore both of these "impulses" and the way they intertwine. In my interpretation, the prevalence of the former one never results in the expulsion of the latter, no matter how disillusioned the tone of Santayana's final work may seem. Finally, one may speculate that the growing bitterness, affected by the exceptional historical circumstances under which the final book of Santayana was written, should have intensified the humanistic vein in him to the point that he speaks of "sins against humanity." For now, let me return to the fundamentals of the vision of politics that Santayana sketches in his last work.

1.2 Realms and Orders

The tripartite structure of *Dominations and Powers* is meant to reflect the preliminary "structure," being at once a hermeneutic framework, of the political realm as proposed by Santayana. It may be, by the way, read in reference to the natural/ideal distinction of *The Life or Reason*, and a very loose reference to the ontology of realms presented by the thinker in *Realms of Being*. Although acquaintance with the latter work is not necessary to benefit from reading *Dominations and Powers*, it may be of help for the purpose of a deeper analysis. Let me start, then, with a very sketchy overview of the main tenets of Santayana's general architecture of being.

The first in the order of importance is the realm of matter, which may be summarized as the generative force of reality, embracing the dynamic field of becoming and perishing. This realm of material events exists independently of human experience and perception, yet, "from the point of view of our discovery of it, [it] is the field of action."[9] The postulate of the realm of matter is a "compulsory assumption which I make in living; the assumption that I live in a natural world, peopled by creatures in whom intuition is as rife as in myself."[10]

---

8 Seaton, "Santayana as a Cultural Critic," in Flamm and Skowroński, *Under Any Sky*, 114.
9 RB, 189.
10 RB, 194.

The source of such basic "compulsory assumptions" that we find ourselves making spontaneously and prior to any reflection is a human faculty called by Santayana "animal faith."

The second realm, sometimes considered as expressive of the specificity of Santayana's philosophy, contrasting him, for example, from his contemporary pragmatists, is the realm of essence. In Kenneth Burke's reading of Santayana's "dramatism," while "matter is the scene in which our intuition is grounded, the essences which are the content of our intuitions become a scene-behind-a-scene."[11] Essences are infinite in number, "timeless ... self-identical forms of every degree of determination."[12] Every form is a manifestation of some essence(s), and every object of consciousness, if considered as a pure intuition of something, consists exclusively of essences, even if the ultimate aim of knowledge is acquaintance with existence, or, in other words, orientating oneself in the world. Thus, the human self, which in previous work I have described as a self- and world-interpreting being, may be compared, metaphorically, to a locus of an interplay between essence and existence, consciousness and knowledge. The imaginative, interpretive, and, at once, materially conditioned nature of the human self is important for us insofar as it has a bearing on the performance of human actors on the political scene, where they depend upon their ability not only to recognize, interpret and understand the world and their position in it, but also to persuade others and resist manipulation. Needless to say, susceptibility to illusion, (self-) deception, madness, and craving for a myth, implicit in Santayana's account of human constitution, makes the political dimension of human life precarious.

This brings us directly to the third realm – the realm of spirit. Spirit stands for consciousness and the first-person perspective, or, in some contexts, a conscious dimension of life. The idea expresses the philosopher's effort to save human consciousness from a naturalistic, materialistic and pragmatic reduction, a dominant trend in the twentieth century. Other than that, it articulates imagination, symbolic mediation, abstract thinking, and the transcending of any here-and-now, or, alternatively, dwelling *in* any here-and-now of an essence in contemplation, as faculties central for the humanity of humans. Santayana sometimes refers to spirit, metaphorically, as "impotent," a

---

11 Kenneth Burke, *A Grammar of Motives* (Berkeley: University of California Press, 1945/1969), 219.
12 John Lachs, "Santayana's Philosophy of Mind," in *Animal Faith and Spiritual Life, Previously Unpublished and Uncollected Writings of George Santayana with Critical Essays on His Thought*, ed. John Lachs (New York: Appleton-Century-Krofts, 1967), 255.

silent witness, or an observer, emphasizing the primacy of matter in initiating change.

The final, fourth realm, also expressive of Santayana's anti-reductionist tendency, is the realm of truth. Truth in Santayana's conception is an ontological category – an indestructible, eternal "register" consisting of the essences defining all occurrences past, present, and future. Truth thus conceived remains beyond the full grasp of humans, but it nevertheless may be seen as an ideal equivalent of the objectively existing, human-independent, material reality, and a tribune of sorts, in relation to which human cognition may be viewed as a certain approximation.

Now, what, if any, is the relevance of Santayana's ontology to his political thought? I'd suggest it is relevant in a couple of ways. Political reality is first and foremost a human reality, yet it is constantly threatened and corrected by the intrusion of an inhuman element. The depth and scale of this intrusion and the associated emergence of what I call – in previous work and here – *the sphere of human helplessness*, an idea applicable both to individual and collective life, may be accounted for with reference to the realm of matter. Next, there is Santayana's naturalistic conception of the human being (and self), influenced by Aristotle's conception of psyche as an organizing principle of life. Psyche is a material, dynamic seat of potentialities, subject to constant actualization in time, and a source of vital boundaries at once. A finite human being is at once a spiritual creature, capable of transcending the mundane reality of existence in fantasy and contemplation. But, in my interpretation of Santayana, consciousness (or: spirit), as a tool of imagination, supported by memory, intent, and animal faith, performs also crucial practical functions. Save for the fact that it facilitates sustaining a certain virtual image of oneself and other agents in a shared field of action, by enabling the production of tools, the generation and preservation of symbols, and idealization, it plays a fundamental culture-forming role. Finally, Santayana is a pluralist, "profoundly impartial with respect to being and existence" and his realms are "carefully designed to exhibit and celebrate such impartiality."[13]

Human self, particularly when considered in the light of Santayana's ontology of realms, is constantly challenged hermeneutically. This interpretive challenge, along with the fact that sanity is fragile and uncertain, makes political scene a favorable ground for chaos and manipulation, where actors occupy insecure positions and change roles unexpectedly. Keeping in mind all these general, pre-political or trans-political contours of reality, we may now pass to

---

13   Grossman, *Art and Morality*, 234.

the political sphere, which, as presented in *Dominations and Powers*, has its own dynamics, and where notions such as: will, needs, interests, contagion, necessity, virtue, self-government, etc. come to the fore. Relying on concepts and ideas provided by the thinker, I will shed light on this dynamics by illuminating its intrinsic interconnections and endowing Santayana's thoughts, whenever necessary, with some more clarity and emphasis. While doing this I will introduce elements of my own interpretation with the support of a few hermeneutic keys.

There are three orders, sometimes referred to as "stages," discerned by Santayana in the existence and development of socio-political units or agents, such as states, peoples, nations. The first one is *generative*, which, by the way, replaced "the natural order" of *The Life of Reason*.[14] It denotes a spontaneous, steady growth, the character and direction of which depend heavily on natural circumstances. It often dominates in, but is by no means limited to, the early stages of the formation of a community or a nation, when its fate is relatively independent of clearly political facts, such as codified wars, revolutions, or colonization. In the generative order, culture, religion, economic and liberal arts (Santayana's vocabulary), and political life are permeating one another, or rather, have not yet been separated and constitute the texture of people's common life, expressive of the specificity of their custom and tradition. As summarized by the author, the generative order is one "that grows up in itself."[15]

The second, *militant* order, called by the early Santayana "the free one," later – quite paradoxically with regard to its former name – is described by the author as "imposed on mankind in all sorts of contradictory ways by bandits, conquerors, prophets, reformers, and idealists."[16] As Santayana clarifies, the orders do not describe separate processes or forces, but rather are meant to express different types of socio-political *articulation* and the associated *moral results* produced in the course of history. It seems, then, that the orders connote a cultural, moral and psychological sense, rather than a strictly political, or that they echo an ancient, integral outlook, where clear boundaries between the political and non-political had not yet arisen. Thus, the militant order is meant to distinguish "the love of reforming the world from the total mutation that the world is always undergoing."[17] It manifests itself in countless ways,

---

14   A vague association may arise between the natural order and Aristotle's idea of the naturalness of the city. See: Aristotle, *Politics*, trans. and introduction Martin Ostwald (Upper Saddle River, New Jersey: Prentice Hall, 1999), bk 1, 1253a. The city is natural by virtue of the political aspect of human nature, the natural needs it springs from, and the fulfillment of natural ideals it serves.
15   Letter to Raymond Brewer Bidwell, 8 Aug. 1949, LGS: 8, 189.
16   Letter to Raymond Brewer Bidwell, 8 Aug. 1949, LGS: 8, 189.
17   DP, 177.

from scientific development to a fanatical militarism, the latter being a negative extreme. Interestingly, the pervasiveness of this order, is expressive – as all orders are – of certain threads in human nature, which fact evokes associations with the intimate connections, drawn by Plato in *The Republic*, in-between the parts of human soul, types of virtues, and political organization.

The final, rational order, formerly referred to as "ideal," needs to be distinguished from a rationalist utopia. It concerns a mature, reflective, and harmony-seeking phase, where moral and possibly, aesthetic, motivations of a disinterested, spiritual perspective prevail over or mitigate purely political ambitions, and what is sought is not domination but rather liberation of "all human interests, especially those that being ideal and harmless do not trample on one another and can often be pursued together, to the delight and enrichment of a rational mind."[18] A social order may approach its rational ideal during the time of peace, when "the exercise of government … is virtuously inspired and intelligently pursued."[19] A rational, competent, and virtuous government understands the real interests of the subjects and strives to harmonize the conflicting ones and conciliate them all with circumstances, of which it has a sound knowledge. The idea of rational politics is an extension of that of rational life, which "consists in those moments in which reflection not only occurs but proves efficacious … The limits of reflection mark those of concerted and rational action; they circumscribe the field of cumulative experience, or, what is the same thing, of profitable living."[20] What I call in this book, after Santayana, the Life of Reason, constitutes the ideal horizon of politics understood as an *art* of pursuing ideal aims in a way conducive to achieving "natural happiness." The capital "L" and "R" in the phrase emphasize its "eulogist sense to designate the happy maintenance against the world of some definite ideal interests," in accordance with Aristotle's understanding of human life as "reason in operation."[21]

The three orders overlap and their presence may be observed and experienced as intertwining. The generative order is unceasingly in the background

---

18   DP, 296. A rationalist utopia, from which Santayana distances himself, is often guided by a programmatic reluctance towards everything that passes for irrational, for example tradition and religion. Meanwhile, from Santayana's perspective, reason "by no means requires a man to set about making rational those things which are irrational by nature." See: DP, 295.

19   DP, 298.

20   Santayana, introduction to LR1, 2.

21   Santayana, Introduction to LR1, 2. Santayana usually uses capital "L" and "R" but he is not always consistent here. Subsequently I am going to refer to the life of reason using small letters "l" and "r."

of the militant one, the intensity and intrusiveness of which varies, while the rational order, or merely its promises, appear under favorable circumstances for a season, to recede, during turbulent and dark times, into the heaven of reflective minds. Regardless of this ideal, the existing specific political arrangements and feasible models of the best polity are largely dependent on natural and historical circumstances of a given people and their psychic "powers and passions, … taste or capacity for this or that form of association."[22] Still, Santayana accommodates within his naturalism the idea that "[i]n politics we may assume as roughly constant the physical order of nature and of human nature,"[23] which allows him to speculate about an ideal with some aspiration to universality.

Thus, while certain invariable and very basic traits of human nature may be roughly distinguished for the purpose of a political thought, Santayana, in the spirit of Aristotle, reminds that peoples and nations are dissimilar just as dissimilar are the convergences of natural environment and historical accidents that shaped them. *Alikeness of humans, then, and the dissimilarities between peoples coexist and this is something Santayana's philosophy takes account of.* The heterogeneity in question is rather persistent and cannot be neutralized by any theory, although it may be reduced in the course of history. With an exception of some universal ideas that illustrate, often clad in myths, certain insights into human condition and nature, theories concerning political practice are not resistant to the passage of time. On the contrary, we live in a situation of a tragic and "radical antinomy" between ideas and existence, an assumption justifying Santayana's anti-dogmatism.[24] The said disparity, though, does not imply that mind is altogether helpless in the face of reality. Despite constant change, nature exhibits enough regularities and continuities for the human mind to discern "approximately recognizable forms"[25] and even to rely on their constancy over time. In its lifelong education, with the support of science on the one hand and traditional human institutions on the other, it may acquire practical wisdom necessary for establishing a harmonious human coexistence of a limited scope and duration. All in all, Santayana's conceptual framework meant to grasp the specificity of the political sphere and the way it is conditioned existentially, articulates the intertwining of continuity and change, alikeness and difference. As such, it invites skepticism towards

---

22   DP, 5.
23   DP, 4.
24   DP, 61.
25   DP, 61–62.

any fixed theories that ascribe universal superiority and potential infallibility to any specific moral and political order, without implying, however, that all orders are equally welcome or acceptable. Moreover, the continuity and fluidity of orders describing the socio-political plane defy or dilute the significance of new beginnings and foundational acts in politics – be it revolutions or social contracts.

The three orders – generative, militant, and rational – perform the function of the tripartite thematic organization of *Dominations and Powers*, and form a kind of a background for another key idea of Santayana, namely – that of the interplay of dominations and powers. The elucidation of this and the associated ideas will allow me to introduce the reader to the core of the dynamics of political life as described by Santayana, the stakes of his vision and its hermeneutic capacity.

1.3   Powers, Dominations, and Virtues

Human life is always striving towards some kind of satisfaction, fulfillment or perfection. It thus has a specific direction, of which it is more or less conscious, and which originates in its specific psychic potentialities set in some environment. Yet, the possibility of their actualization, as well as the prospective completion or flourishing of a given life, is conditioned in multiple ways. It depends on this very life's integrity as well as external factors, while the boundary between the life's internal dynamics and influences from beyond is blurred. Fulfillment brings satisfaction and, under happy circumstances, may be the source of benefits for others; failure frustrates. Enabling individual lives to flourish along the lines of their native potential and in ways that harmonize with the flourishing of others is a possible criterion against which political practice should be judged.

Human existence inescapably involves what I call (the fact and experience of) *the sphere of helplessness*. The articulation of this constant allows Santayana to bring to light the tragic dimension of life. Ignorance, error and accident, as the ancient tragedians have revealed, frustrate even the most meticulous plans and the most certain undertakings. The higher the moral aspirations are, the more probable their clash with an indifferent course of events. But error and frustration *precede* human action. In Santayana's vision of a contingent world, unlike in those of a well-ordered cosmos and faultless teleology, it is nature herself that errs. "Failure, at least partial failure, is therefore everywhere; and there is really no such thing as *natura naturata*, in the sense of native potentiality realized, but only *natura denaturata*, or a jumble of potentialities all more or less distorted and baffled."[26] The irremovable inability to control life and circumstances in a satisfactory degree, a helplessness that no scientific or technological progress can remove, deserves to be recognized as part of human condition. "We are all born more or less lame and destined to a thousand difficulties and disappointments; our natures are partly diseased, disorganized, incapable, and inconsistent."[27] These realizations enter Santayana's political thinking and appear there as the ideas of necessity, fatality, and *nemesis*, while the whole intellectual endeavor of *Dominations and Powers* assumes an aspect of negativity, which couples well with Santayana's critical temper. All this, by the way, is not left by the thinker without some kind of an affirmative response, which, I hope, will emerge from the pages of the book. For now let me turn to the interplay of dominations and powers.

The sphere of politics, which is a moral sphere, may be described, to begin with, as a field of "forces," some of which manifest themselves as purposeful actions, some others as relevant but impersonal changes occurring in the world. Due both to human ignorance and the unintended consequences of human action, of which Santayana was, in my view, acutely aware, the boundary between the two remains obscure. From the viewpoint of each and every psyche that acts in the political sphere, and every group of psyches united under a banner of some interest and/or a shared identity, all relevant circumstances (called by Santayana collectively "powers"), are experienced as neutral, empowering, or inhibiting in relation to what they perceive as their interests, demands and ideal allegiances. In other words, some facts are favorable to the development of its potentialities, some obstruct it. While all of these circumstances are powers, the favorable and neutral ones count as powers, the frustrating and inhibiting ones receive the name of dominations. The more numerous and irresistible the latter, the greater the share of fatality in a given life. The relation between dominations and powers constitutes, as the author declares, the principal subject of his book.[28]

Both terms, descriptive of the duality of political experience, constitute a pair of complementary borderline concepts. What strikes the reader immediately is their relativity. It results from the fact that 1) the perspective assumed is that of an agent, who can simply be a poor judge, unable to recognize their interests and the condition of being empowered or dominated; 2) there is an ambiguity in the very distinction between dominations and powers, insofar as, in the long run and due to complex and unpredictable circumstances, being

---

26   DP, 181.
27   DP, 69.
28   DP, 1.

dominated may turn out to have been empowering, or, in other words, both conditions may enter into a sort of dialectical relation. This subjectivism and ambiguity, save for the fact that they are – to an extent – compensated by the notions of needs and interests, which aspire to objectivity, are not necessarily weaknesses of Santayana's vision. They may be viewed as honestly reflecting the transience and hazardousness of the political realm itself. Besides, the simplicity of the idea, supported by the analysis of the forms of domination developed by the author, may enhance the ability to think critically, and more specifically, to form a sound political judgment – an indispensable ability in democracy. Finally, the choice of this particular pair of terms as a hermeneutic tool for unraveling the intricacies of socio-political realm, couples well with Santayana's naturalism and his assumption – at once ancient and very modern – that politics is all about governing life.

Concerning the genesis of the terms in question, they are loose references to the powers, principalities, thrones, and dominions mentioned in a few letters of the New Testament.[29] These are heavenly and earthly authorities, sometimes presented as contradictory to one another, that strive to gain dominion over mankind. In Santayana's naturalized context they stand for all the circumstances, or capital "C" Circumstances, that forestall or foster human achievements; they complicate, and, to an extent, dethrone, the more severe, impenetrable, and tragic idea of fate. The title *Dominations and Powers* announces a reflection on politics and society that assumes the perspective of the interests of life, both individual and collective, which is viewed as contextual, entangled in a net of influences, inescapably subject to different forms of servitude, and challenged to a right interpretation of circumstances in its struggle for a chance to flourish.

The vision of life as a condition of having some potential and being torn in-between powers and dominations, though meaningful from a certain perspective on politics as governing life, may seem too one-sidedly negative, reductive, and untypical of Santayana, known for his attention to perfection and finite forms. And indeed, it turns out that a third party is involved in the dynamics. Daniel Moreno points out rightly that as soon as virtues come into play – and this requires the presence of the spiritual perspective, which is sensitive to excellence, beauty, and harmony – the relation becomes tripartite.[30] One may even risk an interpretation that, metaphorically speaking, it is *for the sake of virtues* that Santayana develops his reflections on society and politics. The

---

29　Santayana refers specifically to Colossians 1: 16. For other references in the NT see particularly: Ephesians 6:12 and Colossians 2:15.
30　Moreno, *Santayana the Philosopher*, 103.

meaning of virtues as assumed by Santayana, though, is anything but clear. Moreno, following some suggestions of the thinker, offers a poetic interpretation, calling them "harmonies and momentary perfections," possibly applicable to any occurrence, any power or domination indeed that presents certain qualities enjoyable from a spiritual viewpoint.[31] Accepting this understanding of virtues, in a political context I am more inclined towards other hints provided by Santayana, those that, in the vein of Plato and Aristotle, connect virtue tightly to human life in general, and politics in particular. Santayana says that "life itself is intrinsically a virtue in the body that posses it."[32] Among examples of specific human virtues he lists: intelligence, wit, kindness, poetic inspiration and the gift of good health. A relation between a power or a domination and virtue is made possible by "a human *capacity* to exercise power," meaning it is conditioned by psychic activity.[33] Rationality and wisdom, or: prudence, seem to be politically significant virtues. What is important, the influence of virtues extends decisively beyond the scope of individual life, radiating onto society, which "owes all its warmth and vitality to the intrinsic virtue in its members."[34] Obviously, the influence in question is not unidirectional, even if Santayana tends to articulate the suffocating and oppressive effect of society on the individual. He might regard Aristotle's view that "[o]nly in the city ... does man fulfill his potential for happiness understood as the life of action in accordance with virtue,"[35] as almost ironic in relation to the experience of modern times unless "city" is understood figuratively, as a culture, a spiritual community, or an ideal horizon. The notion of "virtues," insofar as it implies a spiritual vantage point, appears rarely in the book, admits the author, yet "the reader may feel them always silently hovering over the pages."[36] In the current book I interpret the silent presence of virtues – in the given context of dominations and powers – as constituting an ally of humans in the form of, first, individual genius, second, spirituality, and third, a realm more ineffable, yet larger, more universal and more lasting than any socio-political arrangement, namely – the human medium of culture, made possible on the one hand by virtue of human vitality, and, on the other, by the symbolic language of all conscious and sentient life.

---

31   Moreno, 104.
32   DP, 3.
33   DP, 3. My emphasis.
34   DP, 3.
35   Carnes Lord, "Aristotle," in *History of Political Philosophy*, ed. Leo Strauss and Joseph Cropsey (Chicago and London: Chicago University Press, 1987), 137.
36   DP, 3.

1.4 Human Nature, Condition, and Negative Anthropology

As a materialist philosopher, "an inquirer after the truth," Santayana feels compelled to consider "real events and real forces," and then to delve deeper, searching for their "causes and conditions."[37] Among those deeper factors some are accidental, and some others – and these are philosophically more interesting – may be associated with continuity, regularity, and recurrence, and, hence, predictability. The latter group of factors, as exemplified by human nature and condition, but also by predictable developments of certain types of sociopolitical configurations, constitutes at once the foundations and limitations of the political sphere (not of a political theory). Even if, as John Gray thinks, a theory of human nature may only be a prelude to a political philosophy, not its foundation,[38] a political philosophy neglectful of it, Santayana might say, is likely to be deficient and superficial; although, perhaps less deficient than one based on a "childish simplification of human nature."[39]

Human nature, Santayana thinks, which "has for its core the substance of nature at large and is one of its more complex formations,"[40] must remain to some extent unexplained, is modified by external circumstances and personal idiosyncrasy, evolves in history and during a lifetime, and is compatible with many alternatives.[41] Nevertheless, it manifests itself and, at least as a "functional unity," should be considered among the agencies controlling ideas and action.[42] Despite Santayana's rejection of an essentialist conception of human nature, an overview of his remarks on this issue allows to compose a list of traits and tendencies that he ascribes to the nature of humans, among them: plasticity, reason, (animal) faith, retention and repetitiveness (by way of memory, learning, habit, convention and ritual), mimetism or susceptibility to contagion, imaginativeness, reliance on symbols, desire for fulfillment and recognition, sociality and communication, tendency to idealization, projection, myth-making and superstition, an inclination to inner conflict and contradiction, susceptibility to illusion.

The human condition, in its turn, is related to what Santayana considers the most certain facts about humans – that human life has material foundations

---

37 DP, 3.
38 PLIB, 122.
39 DP, 201.
40 LR, 85.
41 See: DP, 23, 70, 71. See also: LR, 74–86.
42 LR, 79. Human nature manifests itself as "entelechy of the living individual, be he typical or singular." See: LR, 80.

and is finite, and that human cognition, unlike human aspirations, is inescapably limited. These facts cannot be evaded, they may be, at best, "circumvented" imaginatively, or their impact may be mitigated by science. Thus, understanding man's position in the political sphere involves the recognition of what I have called the irremovable sphere of helplessness and its material precondition in the form of multifaceted dependence, the potential fallibility of any human design, the phenomenon of the unintended consequences of action, related to what the ancients called *nemesis* and associated with man's greatest "sin" – conceit (*hubris*).

What is important, for Santayana *it is human condition more than the innate socia(bi)lity of man that constitutes the strongest social bond.* Plato located the rise of *politeia* in the necessity of satisfying human (material) needs.[43] Likewise, Santayana says, "human impulses convulse society, human necessities construct it."[44] It is difficult to understand Santayana's political thought, let alone appreciate it, without taking this idea into consideration. *The political sphere, then, as originating in and grafted upon necessities, forms a virtual space peopled with human vulnerabilities and aspirations, where forms of dependence and domination may thrive.*

In the part of the book devoted to the generative order of society (which is the only autonomous one, permeating the remaining two) Santayana tries to establish some rudimentary facts about human vital endowment and man's situation in nature and society. Two opposite, fundamental kinds of experience – will (as a modality of primal Will) and what Santayana calls "necessary servitude" are mentioned and illustrated with an example of a small child, who, "animated by primal absolute Will," for the first time discovers his physical dependence on other people and things and, hence, also his relative "impotence." Whatever stands in his way is a "non-ego," "an enemy to be conquered or ... an obstacle to be circumvented."[45] This is only a presage of the trials to come. Even if, under favorable psychological and social circumstances, the child becomes a happy adult, well adapted to his environment and able to recognize in obstacles "a formative, sustaining power,"[46] nothing can save him from the possibility of a confrontation, at some point of his life, with a situation that outgrows his ability of coping with difficulties, be it – to use the most obvious examples – a disease, a tornado, or a war. Existence is dynamic through and through, and nothing, no human orthodoxy, can prepare humans

---

43 See: Plato, *Republic* 369 b. See also: Wallach, *The Platonic Political Art*, 250.
44 DP, p. 5.
45 All quotes in this paragraph, DP, 61.
46 DP, 61.

for unexpected experiences, the source of which may be either themselves or the world. Human practical wisdom, desired as it is, may turn out to be insufficient, and what such situation teaches one is that sometimes only by resorting to a "critical self-knowledge" and capacity of spiritual transcendence one may, perhaps, save oneself by way of comprehension and acceptance. This is nothing other than a Stoic lesson of humility and spiritual autonomy. Unless will, responsible for the inner "thrust" animating man, is enlightened and curbed from within, it is likely to crash into and be overwhelmed by insurmountable obstacles.

The share of fatality in human life, then, means that some occurrences are experienced as unavoidable. Whether they are perceived as predetermined or as accidental and unpredictable, is a verbal matter. What is important is that certain facts concerning ourselves are simply there, almost offensive in all their unexpectedness, obstinacy, ugliness. The greater their inconvenience in relation to the direction of our efforts, the greater the sense of waste and the sacrifice they may enforce on us. They are part of necessity, the ancient *ananke*; science and technology cannot do away with necessity, although they may and do relieve humans from certain forms of it, shifting it, by the same token, into a different "location," another sphere of lived experience.

By way of digression, Santayana at some points seems to me to diminish the importance of the changes in the way people experience necessity, I mean changes owed to conscious, collective, human endeavor. The reason for his skepticism is probably his conviction about the price to be paid for some massive and hubristic interventions into the generative course of society. This is not tantamount to ascribing to Santayana a view that opts for conserving different forms of oppression as justified because they express an eternal law, an original sin, or allow to discharge the power of *ananke* in a predictable way. Rather, he distrusts utopian ideologies and endeavors aiming to transform the human world into a paradise. Not all melioristic efforts, though, are utopian and not all rebellions hubristic. Santayana tends to downplay certain initiatives and their achievements because of their presumed humane, cultural or spiritual cost.

As mentioned earlier, from Santayana's naturalistic perspective, the political sphere is an extension of the realm of human affairs. Just like human life at large, it is "hedged completely round with compulsory sacrifices. Yet they may be made gladly or as we say freely; for to be in harmony with necessity gives us a sense of freedom, which is the only freedom we have."[47] This articulation

---

47   DP, 66.

of necessity and sacrifice is part of what I call *a negative anthropology* emerging from Santayana's last book. In its light human beings in a socio-political milieu remind of a wellspring of unspecified yet nagging needs, a collective of potential lunatics endowed with imagination that can be easily inoculated with illusions and propagandized. These dreaming and often perplexed beings, in need of self-interpretation and self-articulation, are prone to social contagion and manipulation by arrogant individuals and factions driven by grandiose appetites for power and domination. There are a few sources of this pernicious negativity, some of which have already been mentioned. First, there is a caesura between existence and mind insofar as consciousness is peopled with essences only loosely related to material reality; second, there is the distinctively human ability of abstract thinking, which allows to manipulate absent objects and imagine counterfactual situations;[48] next, the hidden recesses of (material) will generate – often conflicting – desires and passions that need interpretation and rationalization, satisfaction or suppression; fourth, in the vein of Aristotle, humans are activity-oriented, achievement-seeking beings in pursuit of completion, which endows their life with an aspect of a "passage from prospect to realization."[49] While the fourth point carries in it a certain promise of excellence and fulfillment, taken together, all these sources of negativity in fragile beings – beings who bend under circumstances, strive to explain and assert themselves in the face of themselves and others, and whose condition is such that they have to pay the price for any choice they make and any action they undertake – turn the sphere of collective life into a potential battlefield, where actors, more or less deliberately, gain power by taking advantage of others' ignorance, insecurity, and helplessness. An actual political system does not have to be and should not be a direct manifestation of this condition, but unless it takes account of it, it risks an unexpected confrontation

---

48   The idea of humanity being profoundly marked by an aspect of negativity is shared by Santayana with a number of thinkers, to name only Aristotle, Hegel, Marx, or Heidegger. Its implications in Santayana's philosophy are, of course, distinct, especially in relation to Hegel and Marx, who conceptualize the said negativity in collective terms. Marx, for example, "uses" the idea of negativity as a springboard for the idea of human creativity and self-creation, the only limits of which are defined by the very fulfillment of an ideal form of humanity or a complete realization of human nature. There are, in turn, some similarities between the incomplete and indefinite *Dasein* of Heidegger, limited by the condition of "throwness" and doomed to an unceasing hermeneutic activity, and the existential insecurity of a human being torn in-between "animal" impulses and creative imagination, as pictured by Santayana. In both cases a human being copes with a pre-existing and obtrusive condition of being thus-and-so, expanded into an experience of manifold, socio-political dependence and servitude in Santayana's last book.

49   LR, 307.

with this grim and chaotic default mode. In other words, historical and human-specific factors may, and often do, contribute to the emergence of a brighter socio-political reality, but the phantom of the struggle for survival and domination, where human weaknesses and dependence are taken advantage of cynically, always looms in the background and should not be ignored under the threat of *nemesis*.

During nearly half a century when Santayana was writing his political essays and the treatise, historical circumstances delivered more than enough empirical data that confirmed rather than undermined these skeptical assumptions. To bring them a little further in the pessimist direction, not without Santayana's own guidance, one may say that civilization is a fragile, conventional stratum covering *an overpowering configuration, where one life survives and thrives at the price of another life's belittlement if not annihilation.* Hence, one comes across a grim conclusion, of which Santayana's sympathetic readers would rather forget, that "[t]he weaker life in any case perishes."[50] It is typical of Santayana, though, to see also a formative and constructive function of necessity. "Physical necessity and fate," he wrote, "when not conceived superstitiously, are therefore the true and only sure foundation for living at ease."[51] Yet, as understood already by Plato, if the necessity and fate are to provide sound foundations for human well-being, political practice must become *an art*, whereby it enables a human society to take advantage of the fact that "[n]ature, in the midst of these blind currents and continual partial catastrophes, manages to bring many happy possibilities to light; and approaches to harmony appear, here and there for a time, between the formative impulse of life and the balance of ambient powers."[52]

Having thus looked at the contours of Santayana's naturalistic hermeneutics of political reality via the lens of necessity, I feel compelled to add immediately that Santayana the moralist is far from deriving norms and ideals from the existing state of affairs or an imagined "state of nature" as a somber intensification of the human condition. On the contrary, even though Santayana accepts the basic assumptions of the Darwinian theory of evolution as true, he distances himself from its political and ideological implications, just as he does from political cynicism and *Realpolitik*. To anticipate certain ideas that will be discussed later in this book, if the ideals he prefers and endorses may be said to be derived from any "status quo," they are inspired by the

---

50 DP, 82. "Perishing" here is not synonymous with physical annihilation, rather it stands for different forms of oppression (or exploitation) debilitating the given life's development.
51 DP, 2.
52 DP, 2.

Aristotelian idea of human psychic constitution, where psyche seeks to actualize her potential endowment, while man, throughout his lifelong activities in the shared world, masters arts and acquires virtues, with some ideals in view. Once human well-being and completion are recognized as the highest good, the preferred principle of the organization of common life is that of pluralism enabling harmonious coexistence of diverse psyches and cultural patterns. At this point I also agree with Moreno's remark about the relevance of the spiritual perspective for the political realm.[53]

Let me summarize briefly the ideas of the current chapter. In the descriptive part of his work, Santayana draws on a sort of negative anthropology, which takes into account the limitations imposed on man by his condition and nature. Simultaneously, his vision of existence echoes a Heraclitean idea that in an omnipresent struggle everything exists at the price of something else. These existential invariables enter the sphere of politics, where they may manifest themselves in a variety of ways – from peaceful and mild forms of domination that arise in social organization in the generative order, to intentional acts of violence, such as wars, conquest, or colonization. The convergence of these factors, and the centrality of the idea that life involves struggle, dependence, and necessary sacrifice, has led me to propose the idea of *managing necessity* as a key for unlocking Santayana's conception of the political sphere and political activity. If government, as Santayana seems to have thought about it, amounts to governing life, it establishes and/or controls the relations of power and domination, where domination is nothing other than being in position to allocate necessity, or, in other words, to appoint the bearers of given costs and, by the same token, the beneficiaries of an established configuration. The question is how it is being done and with what purpose in view – "it is here that the great alternatives present themselves between the various forms of society, authority or political government."[54] Furthermore, to accommodate the moral dimension of Santayana's reflection, which, as I will show in the chapters to come, points in the direction of the protection of human variety under the conditions of pluralism, government as *managing necessity* must be completed with *harmonizing diversity*.

Meanwhile, the three intertwining orders composing the political sphere, and in particular the silent presence of the generative order beneath the bold

---

53 Daniel Moreno notices connections between *Dominations and Powers* and *Realm of Spirit* in terms of chronology (they were written more or less simultaneously) and the perspective of spiritual life. I agree this perspective is present in DP, but I am not sure whether it is dominant. See: Moreno, *Santayana the Philosopher*, 101.

54 DP, 82.

endeavors and the harmonies of the two remaining ones, bring promise of a beneficent continuity, relying on slow maturation, accumulation of experience, wisdom, and the idea that action, to be the source of benefit, must become an art. Now, armed with a synthetic picture of the premises and contours of Santayana's political thinking, let me take a closer look at his understanding of freedom, the experience and idea of which, next to that of necessary servitude, arises at the generative level of society.

CHAPTER 2

Liberty

2.1   From Cultural Critique to Political Thinking

An early version of the distinction between vital liberty and vacant freedom appears in an essay "English Liberty in America," which, along with "The Genteel Tradition in American Philosophy,"[1] may be said to constitute the finest example of Santayana's cultural criticism, some themes and ideas of which found their continuation in *Dominations and Powers*. Even though the ideas contained in these essays concern primarily American context, and as such have already been subject to research by other scholars, their relevance extends beyond historical and geographical topicality, and they may be considered as representative of Santayana's broader criticism of modernity. It is the latter possibility and its relation to Santayana's political reflection that interests me here.

First, let me take a brief look at the second of the above mentioned essays, "The Genteel Tradition in American philosophy." In it Santayana analyzes the mindset of the early 20th-century American elites, in particular the New England intellectuals, and arrives at a conclusion that it is characterized by a certain duality, the nature and origins of which he explains eloquently and not without humor while tracing the fate of Calvinism and its later discontents in America. The sense of a profound depravity of humanity, conveyed by Calvinism, faded away and was replaced with the optimism of Emerson, who elevated man to a privileged and harmonious position in Nature, which itself was a manifestation of the divine. While critical of what he believed to be the transcendentalists' error of mistaking the transcendental method with a philosophy of being, and of Emerson's romantic faith in the power of human genius, Santayana expresses sympathy with Emerson's "speculative eye," a contemplative aspect, representing "nothing except intelligence."[2] Santayana, with what I regard to be his somewhat subversive humanism, should have felt a kind of kinship with Emerson, who, like himself, preferred a vision over an

---

[1] In this chapter I refer to both texts as contained in the collection: George Santayana, *The Genteel Tradition in American Philosophy and Character and Opinion in the United States*, ed. James Seaton (New Haven and London: Yale University, 2009). I will refer to this source as GTACOUS.

[2] GTACOUS, 10.

argument in philosophy, and who endorsed a kind of poetic, imaginative individualism, rebelling against hypocrisy and suffocating convention. Santayana's formula "[o]ur dignity is not in what we do, but in what we understand,"[3] sounding provocative in the light of America's activist ideals, expressed his distance from pragmatism. He considered William James's religious naturalism and his overall outlook, informed by a pluralist openness and acceptance of diversity, to be refreshing and timely, and appreciated its ability to break "the spell of the genteel tradition."[4] Yet, he ascribed to transcendentalism and pragmatism alike an anthropocentric orientation, "inspired by the conceited notion that man, or human reason, or the human distinction between good and evil, is the center and pivot of the universe."[5]

Finally, Santayana charges both the genteel tradition and the dominant intellectual movements that rebelled against it with a sort of misguided exaltation of man and his action, embedded in an idealistic moralism. Genteel tradition, based on a self-delusion, "forbids people to confess that they are unhappy."[6] Addressing his California audience, Santayana speaks of it as "your tyrant from the cradle to the grave" and recommends the "primeval solitudes" of the natural world of the American West as a disinfectant from the "forced sense of your own importance not merely as individuals but even as men."[7] The said sense of importance, one might speculate, applied not only to American culture but also to the idea and attitude of American exceptionalism, of which Santayana was rather critical. Considering possible benefits flowing from the influence of American culture upon the world, he pointed to the flexible and inclusive practice of English liberty rather than the moralizing genteel tradition with its air of superiority and superstition.

A question may arise: Is what Santayana labeled "the genteel tradition" a purely historical and culturally-specific thing, or, perhaps, a recurrent and common phenomenon? In other words, has there been one genteel tradition or more? A possible way of understanding the idea of genteel tradition in universal terms is that it represents any deeply-rooted and lasting outlook that forms part of, in Santayana's words, collective "myth-making," a sort of collective self-delusion, a strategy of self-assertion in thought and action. In a psychological and anthropological sense, then, it may be recognized as a strategy of endowing the existence, identity, values, and interests of a single collective

---

3   GTACOUS, 10.
4   GTACOUS, 17.
5   GTACOUS, 19.
6   GTACOUS, 11.
7   GTACOUS, 19.

subject – be it a nation, a state, a group, or a class – with a particular meaning, importance, perhaps a mission among other agents.

Roger Kimball suggests that the genteel tradition may be understood as "the dominant tradition of establishment opinion, whatever it may happen to be at a given time." Santayana, in his view, managed to present "an anatomy of received opinion."[8] I would suggest that Santayana illuminated the way and the degree in which certain traditional ideas (and concomitant attitudes), often clad in new dress, continually exert effective, social, moral and intellectual pressure to the extent that they are able to swallow and transform any contrary tide. Not only a powerful social contagion but also a sort of unconscious inheritance is at play here. I agree with Kimball that the power of a genteel tradition should not be sought in "the substance of the governing structures" but rather in "the moralizing pressure toward conformity."[9] It is the latter that Santayana, at the turn of the century, thought to be more powerful and, for him personally, less bearable in the New World than in the Old. "The instinct and the ideal of uniformity are very profound in them [Americans]; if they are compelled to be rebels, they become propagandists, … and if they cannot conform to the majority they are not happy until they make the majority conform to them."[10]

The issue of freedom and liberty in a cultural context is one of the consistently developed themes in Santayana's *oeuvre* and resonates in his political ideas. In a couple of fine sketches, contained in the collection *Soliloquies in England and Later Soliloquies*, Santayana reflects upon different conceptions of freedom that have developed throughout the ages in the West. The Greeks, beneath the variety of outlooks they cherished, held a spontaneous conviction about there being "a single solid natural wisdom" to be discovered by reason and to be used as a foundation for the organization of the realm of human affairs in a way "necessary to set free the perfect man, or the god, within us."[11] Benjamin Constant famously distinguished between the ancient type of freedom, which consisted in the capacity and opportunity to participate in a collective self-rule, and the modern type, which stands for individual independence protected by law. John Gray notes that among the ancients the idea of

---

8   Roger Kimball, "Mental Hygiene and Good Manners. The Contribution of George Santayana," in GTACOUS, 179.
9   Kimball, GTACOUS, 179.
10 George Santayana, "Marginal notes on Civilization," in *The Genteel Tradition. Nine Essays by George Santayana*, introduction and ed. Douglas L. Wilson (Lincoln and London: University of Nebraska Press, 1998), 143.
11 George Santayana, *Soliloquies in England and Later Soliloquies* (New York: Charles Scribner's Sons, 1922), 167. Subsequently, I refer to this source as SiELS.

freedom was "applied as naturally to communities – where it mean self-rule or the absence of external control – as it was to individuals," yet in the latter case it connoted the right to participation in governing.[12] Already the Sophists, however, enjoyed early intuitions of individual freedom as autonomy, and Pericles, in his famous *Funeral Oration*, expressed "liberal, egalitarian and individualist principles."[13] Santayana, in turn, pays attention to a perfectionist aspect of the ancient understanding of freedom, the essence of which was assimilated by Christianity and preserved in its orthodox idea of freedom, the highest realization of which was sanctity. It was based on a definite conception of the human soul, its orientation towards salvation, meaningful in view of the assumption that "life on earth was ... abnormal from the beginning."[14] Both visions of freedom, with their demanding ideals of perfection, achievable for virtuous or ascetic minorities, were at a far remove from the modern understanding of it.

Thus, breaking free from the spell of those orthodox visions was natural both from the perspective of human diversity and that of a free spirit. Yet, Santayana fears that the modern "liberty to drift in the dark" may still put us at risk.[15] A uniform and lasting conception of human freedom may be unachievable, yet the ancients, he thinks, had a point in pursuing a certain definite idea of the conditions of human happiness in order to attain a judicious self-orientation. Besides, he doubts whether the liberal idea of freedom is a final destination of human moral inquiry. Rather, according to his assessment, people in the West have been suspended in a long period of transition and one may only hope that when a new morality is established, it will be "more broadly based than the old on knowledge of the world, not so absolute, not so meticulous, and not chanted so much in the monotone of an abstract sage."[16]

There has evolved, however, yet another idea of freedom, called by the thinker "German freedom." Rather than concentrating on the individualistic freedom of choice and enterprise, which it looks down upon, it professes that real freedom consists in a "compulsory service" perfectly integrated. Thus, the question of the relation between national and political sovereignty and individual autonomy arises. The idea is related to a vision of man as intimately connected to and thoroughly embedded in a larger social and national unit, which engenders its unique, intentional, dynamic and "all-inclusive" *Kultur* (not to be mistaken with culture) of a definite spiritual character.

---

12   LIB, 1. See also: PLIB, 21.
13   LIB, 2.
14   SiELS, 168.
15   SiELS, 168.
16   SiELS, 169.

An individual life becomes meaningful and free only when its own dynamics is attuned to and representative of the motion of the "polity." "So that, paradoxical as it may seem, it is only when you conform that you are free, while if you rebel and secede you become a slave."[17] Alluding to some unspecified theoreticians and propagandists of his time, Santayana notices that the idea grew ethnocentric and xenophobic. The intrinsic genius, according to this essentialist conception, is said to be "infinite inwardly, being capable of endless growth and modification by men of Teutonic blood, yet is limited externally ... in that it is not communicable to other races."[18] Wedding the sense of freedom to that of a nation and *Kultur* inescapably introduces the problem of the respective rights and claims of other nations and their traditions. Some versions of this vision, more explicitly inspired by Hegel, extend the purifying radiation of the German spirit and discipline to the world at large. One day, this expansiveness, warns Santayana, may turn into "a sinister claim to absolute dominion."[19]

Turning now to "English Liberty in America," the subject matter of Santayana's discussion here is not any theoretical conception of freedom, but rather *the practice of freedom as a matter of a certain political culture*, and, I would add, a mentality. Very different from the formerly discussed type of freedom, it is a kind of democratic liberty, the root of which "is free individuality, which is deeply seated in the English inner man," and which finds a favorable ground in the "spirit of free co-operation" existing in the United States.[20] Santayana keenly weighs the apparent drawbacks of being "crossed and biased by a large residue of social servitude" able to "warp the inner man and enlist him against his interests in alien causes" against the benefits flowing from the ability to cooperate with others against all odds, with a sense of genuine commitment, if not enthusiasm. The ability originates in English mentality, with "its reserve, its tenacity, its empiricism, its public spirit," and is actualized in America, where "each individual, being quite master of himself" is still ready for a cooperation among free people.[21] The remarkable fact about this phenomenon is that instead of there being a conflict between free individuality and social cooperation there is a mutual reinforcement. The democratic component allies with the liberal and individualistic one. "[I]f we consider human nature at large and the practice of most nations, we shall see that it is a very rare, wonderful, and unstable convention."[22] One assumes here that people's

---

17   SiELS, 170.
18   SiELS, 171.
19   SiELS, 172.
20   GTACOUS, 103.
21   GTACOUS, 104.
22   GTACOUS, 105.

interests are similar and compatible enough to make compromise possible, and a degree of unanimity is attainable by the price of suppressing individualism without annihilating individuality.

This description of English liberty in American context may evoke association with de Tocqueville's keen observations of the lights and shadows of the early American democracy. Like Santayana, de Tocqueville on the one hand appreciates the way the spirit of cooperation and the sense of public commitment contribute to the sustaining of both democracy and liberty in society, and, on the other, brings to the surface the leveling tendency and the domination of mediocrity inherent in such a democracy, which may result in the marginalization of talent and excellence, and, consequently, an impoverishment of culture. Even though in the essay discussed here Santayana only briefly remarks about this cost involved in the democratic practice, in his other works his criticism is sharper.

More specifically, de Tocqueville discusses what he calls "self-interest properly understood" as the way Americans combat the egoistic individualism (or rather, atomism) that the growing equality of conditions is conducive to. Americans de Tocqueville had the opportunity to observe, made themselves believe that it rested in the interest of everybody to curb egoism, be willing to make sacrifices in the name of others, and associate with others in defense of certain shared interests. He had no doubts that in the socio-political system he described, self-interest should become the predominant motivation and that it was understood in terms of material well-being. He noticed, however, that a certain reformulation of the idea of self-interest and its embodiment in daily practice might save society from the destructive results of atomization.[23] This insight belongs to one of the main ideas of the book, namely – that a "nation in which individuals lost the ability to do great things single-handedly without acquiring the capacity to produce them in common would soon relapse into barbarism."[24]

A reader of Santayana may have noticed that the praise of English liberty in America on his part is somewhat unusual given his critical temper and his advocacy of individualism, and not to be repeated in later works. He even concedes to the fact – although not without a grain of irony – that in the context of English liberty "the individual is neutralized; ... public spirit sustains him, and he becomes its instrument."[25] Like de Tocqueville earlier, he notices that

---

23 Alexis de Tocqueville, *Democracy in America*, vol. 2, trans. Arthur Goldhammer (New York: The Library of America, Literary Classics of the United States, 2004), 591, 599, 610–613.
24 Tocqueville, *Democracy in America*, 596–597.
25 GTACOUS, 106.

governmental offices in the United States are peopled with ordinary men rather than outstanding individuals, and this fact is not at all a hindrance to government's efficiency. His marvel seems sincere as the phenomenon he describes matches his preference for a harmonious equilibrium embodied in a tradition. Besides, a culture of an unforced, democratic cooperation, where "liberty is a method, not a goal,"[26] thus theorized and idealized by him, allows him to draw an opposition between this and other forms of collective sovereignty, where the idea of freedom is reduced to the particularistic interests of one nation or one religion, reinforced and absolutized by a set of dogmatic beliefs.

On a psychological plane, the discussed practice of freedom liberates and channels certain pro-social impulses latent in people in such a way that they work towards some common good. What is more, it constitutes a lesson of humility and the ability to give up part of one's own appetites when necessary. Its benefits, then, include both concrete improvements and further refinement of social cohesion and public spirit. The spirit of cooperation thus framed finds justification in Santayana's basic assumptions about multiple, conflicting impulses active in man, the vagueness and plasticity of human nature, and the need to accept an irremovable share of fatality. As long as the inner impulses are many, and often contradictory to one another, as long as man is a poor interpreter of his own interests, and as long as his needs are to some extent plastic, dependent on circumstances and adaptable to them, there is a good reason to believe that sacrificing part of one's own autonomy in the name of common interest may turn out better than deciding about everything individually. "In the end, adaptation to the world at large, where so much is hidden and unintelligible, is only possible piecemeal, by groping with a genuine indetermination in one's aims. Its very looseness gives the English method its lien on the future."[27]

James Seaton found it remarkable that Santayana, despite all his critique of America, including his skepticism about American exceptionalism and the growing imperialist tendencies, found English liberty to be a reasonable pattern that might be worth imitating on a larger scale and could possibly prove lasting.[28] There is a paradox in that Santayana's praise of English liberty, especially as exemplified in America, has something to do with his preference for humility and something that may be referred to as a fatalistic aspect in his thinking – features that made some of his views hardly acceptable in the United States, where pragmatic and activist ideals prevailed. Nevertheless,

---

26   GTACOUS, 105.
27   GTACOUS, 106.
28   GTACOUS, 167.

Santayana's assessment and interpretation of English liberty is all the more interesting as it is formulated by an outsider, capable of "the detachment necessary to see American life without first accepting its premises."[29] Santayana, a critic of the religion of progress, was not against the main goal of liberalism – securing and extending individual freedom. But his endorsement of British liberty, W. M. McClay observes, concerns something more particular – "a limited and culturally specific thing, built up patiently and unconsciously over many years through discrete and concrete actions taken, thereby taking on a modest and skeptical and empirical cast."[30]

His other writings, later essays and *Dominations and Powers* in particular, abound in criticism of democracy and liberalism alike, being evidence of the evolution of his socio-political views. However, leaving the history of Santayana's changing views aside, one may speak of an important, general distinction to be made between Santayana's advocacy of individualism, on the one hand, and his criticism of an "unlimited," egoistic individuality, on the other. When Santayana writes that it is wise "to limit oneself ... to establishing external relations, partial mutual adjustment, with a great residuum of independence," and when he expresses his conviction that "if you attempt more you will achieve less," he is consistent with his advocacy of self-limitation, or what he calls a "prudent instinct."[31] Empiricism, attentiveness to circumstances and flexibility serve common action better than dogmatism and fixed policies. Why is the former attitude wiser? The answer may be formulated in different ways, but the essential one seems to me to be: because it promises *"keeping the door open to a great volume and variety of goods, at a moderate cost of danger and absurdity."*[32] These words reflect Santayana's understanding of rationality, his prudence, and distrust of large-scale, abstract and dogmatic schemes of improving the world.

This being said, one cannot fail to notice that the usual sharpness of Santayana's criticism is not altogether lost in his interpretation of English liberty. He notes the paradoxical fact that, despite America's self-image as a land of freedom, "there is no country in which people live under more overpowering compulsions."[33] Compulsions are even more powerful than prohibitions, he notes, insofar as "what is exacted cuts deeper; it creates habits which overlay nature;" the compulsion of work, especially when it involves spending

---

29   McClay, "The Unclaimed Legacy," in GTACOUS, 129.
30   McClay, "The Unclaimed Legacy," in GTACOUS, 138.
31   GTACOUS, 106.
32   GTACOUS, 107. My emphasis.
33   GTACOUS, 109.

whole days at the office, is an example of "a narrow path left open to freedom as is left open in a monastic establishment where bell and book keep your attention fixed at all hours upon the hard work of salvation."[34] And yet, these compulsions did not annul the liberty at work in the America Santayana knew and described. He meant to show that the liberty in question – like any liberty – had its price.

All in all, Santayana points to the incompatibility of the spirit of English liberty with the alternative, "German" idea of freedom, which he ascribes to the practice of Prussian government, and describes as absolute, self-centered, and conveying fear of any external influence as a threat to the agent's integrity. For a follower of this model, English liberty may stand for an abandonment of the most impulsive pursuit of unconstrained freedom.[35]

Historically, according to Santayana, two great revolutions – the French and the Bolshevik – exemplified a warlike political practice and a misguided pursuit of freedom with no respect to its cost.

> Such is the inevitable practice of every prophet who heralds an absolute system, political or religious, and who pursues the unqualified domination of principles which he thinks right in themselves and of a will which is self-justified and irresponsible. Why, we may ask, are people so ready to set up absolute claims, where their resources are obviously so limited that permanent success is impossible …?[36]

Contrarily to this alliance of irresponsibility, dogmatism and will to power, the English mind, educated to seek "greater social harmony" tends to choose "the part of prudence."[37] The thinker ascribes to the English mind some of the Greek virtues and ideals – prudence, moderation, pursuit of social harmony – which,

---

34   GTACOUS, 110. Members of the Frankfurt school passed much more severe judgments on these tendencies in American society. Seaton notes that Herbert Marcuse considered them to constitute a kind of "totalitarian democracy." See: Seaton, "The Genteel Tradition and English Liberty," in: GTACOUS, 167. Santayana, elsewhere in his work, points also to other aspects of what was once named a "totalitarian democracy" by Jacob L. Talmon in his book *The Origins of Totalitarian Democracy* (1952), namely – a crisis of agency and the voters' illusory influence on government. Yet another "totalitarian" (using the term loosely) aspect of democracy is its aspiration to universality and superiority over all other systems, regardless of native cultures and traditions. See: Letter to Robert Shaw Sturgis, 21 October 1946, LGS7: 288–289.

35   GTACOUS, 111–113.
36   GTACOUS, 114.
37   GTACOUS, 114.

just like in Plato's *Republic*, exist in the people's souls and are dispersed in society and political practice.

This bright image, though, has its shadow side. There rise the discontents, those who are and feel disinherited, and unite under the banners of communism. As I will show in the subsequent chapters, Santayana's approach both to liberalism and communism varied and he would become increasingly critical of the former and sometimes, even if only exceptionally, more open to the possible benefits involved in the rising of the latter. In the essay discussed, though, he sees in the representatives of "international democracy" simply another face of an irresponsible radicalism, willing to "reduce everybody to forced membership and forced service in one universal flock, without property, family, country or religion."[38] He foretells that communism, with its rejection of the idea that private interest secures a sufficient degree of unanimity and cooperation, will become a major threat for liberalism. Communists, in his view, are wrong in that they "presuppose the universality of a type of human nature which is not English, and perhaps not human."[39] Both sides have a different conception of unanimity – English liberty assumes a partial unanimity of interests and a shared willingness to cooperate in order to attain common goals, communism pursues a more radical unanimity and equality as both its ultimate goals and the tools of the liberation of man. The former represents reason as moderation, the latter – as an utopian projection of a militant impulse. In short,

> the life of reason, like English liberty, is a perpetual compromise. Absolute liberty, on the contrary, is impracticable ... All the declarations of independence in the world will not render anybody really independent. You may disregard your environment, you cannot escape it; and your disregard of it will bring you moral impoverishment and ... unpleasant surprises.[40]

To transfer these considerations to the area of foreign affairs, Santayana notes that actors – nations and states – that seek to expand their external liberty are more likely to develop excessive discipline and organization at home, as well as engage in (self) destructive wars against one another and ideological crusades against worldviews other than their own. "This absolute liberty is the freedom of persons and nations 'to be just so,' to follow a master passion even in the teeth of nature and resistance."[41]

---

38   GTACOUS, 116.
39   GTACOUS, 116.
40   GTACOUS, 117.
41   John Lachs, "Understanding America," in GTACOUS, 152.

Let me note that Santayana conveys here an opposition between the "tentative and human," which is a favorable environment for the life of reason, and the "animal and absolute," where reason is treated merely instrumentally. Because, as I have stressed, impulses in man are many and conflicting, there is always a margin of ignorance informing human action, and "[i]n some human affairs context is all,"[42] the first option, which allows for "a harmony woven out of accidents" is more adaptable and promising in terms of a long-lasting harmony. Most importantly, the spirit and practice of English liberty is conducive to a peaceful coexistence of diverse groups and, as argued by John Lachs, may explain partly the fact that in America even "[t]raditional Old World Enemies live in relative peace with one another."[43]

To sum up, the essay discussed – being a tribute to flexibility, cooperation, compromise, and a moderate optimism in social and political life – expresses Santayana's appreciation of democratic pluralism and, at once, complicates the image of the late Santayana as an inveterate advocate of individualism, critic of democracy, and a social skeptic. Besides, given the broad meaning of the notion of individualism, it suggests one should reconsider what kind of individualism he defended, an issue I will return to later in this book. Now, using the categories of *Dominations and Powers*, the spirit of democratic liberty as described by Santayana originates in the generative order. It is traditional and specific, expressive of a set of silent assumptions that precede it as a form and an attitude of readiness to take the risk of democracy and to "acquiesce all the more readily in the result."[44] The share of violence in a democratic system embedded in such a tradition is limited and so seems to be the danger of the tyranny of majority of which de Tocqueville had warned. Decisions taken by such a government tend to ascertain and build upon what was established and agreed upon earlier and this is in accordance with Santayana's naturalistic contention that "[f]ree government works well in proportion as government is superfluous."[45] Santayana's reflections on English liberty express the thinker's appreciation for what might approximate, despite its many imperfections, a life of reason in the human world.

Now, typically of Santayana, he does not leave his readers with a mere apologia of one side only. At some point he suggests that the predicted failure of the proponents of absolute freedom is "a deep tragedy." Why is it so? Each form of life is entitled to its own ideal and this ideal may be an object of

---

42   Lachs, "Understanding America," 150.
43   Lachs, "Understanding America," 149.
44   GTACOUS, 108.
45   GTACOUS, 109.

appreciation by a disinterested observer. From the viewpoint of spirit and vital achievement, romantic rebels an heroes may be more likely to attain beautiful forms, be inspiring and fascinating in their integrity than "the dull broad equilibrium that may take their place."[46] However, "[t]he necessity of rejecting and destroying some things that are beautiful is the deepest curse of existence."[47]

2.2 Vacant Freedom and Vital Liberty

Let me now turn to *Dominations and Powers*, where Santayana's reflections on freedom reach maturity and assume the form of an opposition between vital liberty and vacant freedom. One may be tempted to compare it to the well-known distinction between positive and negative conception of freedom – such a comparison makes sense but what it reveals is merely a distant kinship. The categories proposed by Santayana are not specifically political; they are embedded in his naturalistic materialism, inspired modestly by Aristotelian and Stoic philosophies of life, and establish passages between an individual life, the socio-political realm, and existence at large.

When probing the ontological conditions of liberty, Santayana points to the fundamental "groundlessness [that] lies in the essential contingency of existence,"[48] assumed in his materialistic conception of reality. An opposite idea would be that of a necessary, wholly predetermined, mechanistic universe. The world is not fatal in this latter sense, even though living experience gives rise to an idea of fatality. By a capricious arrangement of things, a certain natural order arose, a system of repetitions, which makes life possible. In this plenitude of phenomena, exhibiting at once contingency and order, constancy and change, we find ourselves presupposing, by the power of tacit beliefs, called by Santayana animal faith, that there is "a contingent particular order of life potential in us, if we are able and willing to attach our private capacities to the opportunities that the steady march of nature happens to offer us."[49] Both the status quo of the world and our own vital order are,

---

46 GTACOUS, 118.
47 GTACOUS, 119.
48 DP, 49. In the context of his materialism, Santayana understands the notion of "contingence" in a classical way, namely – that an event that has taken place need not have occurred. For a brief explanation and disambiguation of Santayana's idea of material contingence and its relation to the idea of human insecurity see: Angus Kerrr-Lawson, "Rorty has no Physics," *Overheard in Seville: Bulletin of the Santayana Society* 13 (1995): 12–15.
49 DP, 50.

to a substantial degree, not of our own making but imposed on us. Thus, an "unfathomable non-ego dominates spirit in a man within and without, fitfully in the world and subterraneously in his hidden passions."[50] What is it, then, a question arises, "in man that can be free or enslaved?" Santayana's answer is clear and not at odds with a spontaneous human intuition: "the total aspiration of a man's animal nature, building up his spirit and becoming conscious in it."[51]

In order to understand the human pursuit of freedom and get an insight into the possible political manifestations of it, Santayana looks at the circumstances of the earliest experience of freedom in human life, sketching thereby an equivalent of an individual "state of nature." Looking at a newborn baby and its early development, he reaches a conclusion that a primary experience of freedom – like that of using one's voice (cry), moving one's limbs, or satisfying hunger whenever there is a source of food available – must be preceded by a sense of a need, an inner pressure or frustration. Only when one's basic needs are fulfilled may one cherish a sense of liberty, finding its fullest expression in play. Surely, man is first revealed as a creature limited by natural dependencies. "Liberty needs to be fed."[52] The sources of "food" lie outside, in the world around, and to access them is a challenge; it requires flexibility and risk-taking insofar as nature is dynamic and, to an extent, chaotic.

Of the human acquaintance with the world (and with oneself) Santayana writes the following:

> [O]n the scale of human perception and action, those hypothetical elements are unrecognizably fused or interwoven organically, so that the units distinguishable by our senses are compacted of innumerable invisible tensions, arrested impulses, and unstable equilibriums, established by fortune; as if every atom of our bodies were largely one of the hungry worms waiting to devour us. Therefore all our large human units, physical and moral, are tragically transitory, and our enacted wills comically cheated by our secret desires; for in society we act as persons with apparent spontaneity and initiative … [Yet] [o]ur own official wills are often false to our natures, not so much through hypocrisy as through blind habit and gregarious vagueness.[53]

---

50   DP, 64.
51   DP, 66.
52   DP, 36.
53   DP, 38.

The above words leave no doubt as to the precarious situation of an individual in nature and, at another level, a social and political actor among other actors, all assuming more or less arbitrary identities and roles. Not only is one's well-being, the very survival indeed, dependent on capricious and mysterious nature, but one's very self and nature are non-transparent, one's needs require interpretation and their fulfillment poses a challenge. Civilization and society, with their institutions, on the one hand, unlock some doors and serve to secure greater opportunity for survival and fulfillment, on the other hand, they introduce enormous complexity into the world, multiplying the sources of servitude and perplexity. But most importantly, the fact that the material mutability of the world can never be penetrated fully and subjugated to the light of reason makes human dependence all the more dramatic and has, time after time, shattered the "hope of the ancients, to build a city on a rock and defy the ages."[54] A valuable insight into the human condition is conveyed by the function of the chorus in Greek tragedy, "which represents the people, [and] is neither the agent nor the object in the action but only the spectator and moral judge of its course."[55]

This being said, let us not lose sight of the fact that for Santayana accepting limitations is a prerequisite for the life of reason in general and rational politics in particular. In fact, freedom originates amidst limitations. This idea differs from, for example, Hobbes' understanding of freedom as lack of obstacles on the path to the satisfaction of desires, which Santayana might associate with what he calls "vacant freedom" and oppose to "vital liberty." The latter articulates the relation between liberty and limits, and endows human finitude with a formative sense. This is the right moment to ask about the subject of vital liberty and the political subject in general.

The subject, in the most rudimentary and naturalistic sense, is an individual life or a psyche.[56] To experience vital liberty, which is a fragile equilibrium, means to reach integrity and harmony with the very forms one's life generates, the prerequisite of which is the recognition of and adjustment to circumstances. Vital liberty, when manifest in an achievement of something meaningful or beautiful, acquiring a virtue or mastery in some practical activity, may contribute to the common life. In fact, both its sources and influence transcend the individual. Given the mutability of nature and the multitude of

---

54 DP, 33.
55 DP, 405.
56 Collective subjects and agents in politics are perfectly possible and real by virtue of their influence and, sometimes, a common fate. However, their status remains derivative, their unity artificial and often short-lived.

terms and forms in which life may be experienced, understood, supported and organized, vital liberty requires definition and judgment. For these to arise, life must first be something given, a source of perspective and preferences: "There must be specific directions of growth, at least potential, for the living process to exemplify. Otherwise the emergence of life could never be discerned, not its progress measured, nor its varieties and perfections distinguished."[57]

Unlike Aristotle, by whose conception of psyche Santayana was inspired morally (the idea of life's self-fulfillment as an end in itself), the author of *Dominations and Powers* does not accept the teleological explanation of the dynamics of life.[58] Each psyche indeed carries some specific potentialities and determines partially man's abilities and preferences, but, save for the fact that these potentialities are obscure and abstract from the human perspective until they are discovered and actualized, they may change, derail, or atrophy during a lifetime. Psyche carries a hereditary material nucleus, but it is mutable. It is "determined afresh at each moment by the stimulations, inhibitions, ... or redirection which circumstances may impose ... The natural powers or primal Will of each individual will therefore vary, perhaps infinitesimally, perhaps radically, in the course of their manifestation."[59] With the help of shared, symbolic mediation of society and culture, the hidden powers are uncovered and named in the process of life, but only partially, while the possibility of their fulfillment is always dependent on the flux of ever-changing circumstances, which human language and institutions try to curb and stabilize. Additionally, life is intrinsically interconnected with the external world to an extent much greater than the ordinary human scale allows to see. It seems that not a *causa finalis*, but a capricious *material change* governs life. Let me evoke, once again, a phrase that conveys the haphazard character of psychic pursuit of fulfillment: "there is really no such thing as *natura naturata*, in the sense of native potentiality realized, but only *natura denaturata*, or a jumble of potentialities all more or less distorted and baffled."[60] One may also add that the completion of human

---

57   DP, 39.
58   According to the principle of *causa finalis*, life is naturally and internally directed towards its proper good(s).
59   DP, 59. The notion „(primal) Will," with capital letter "W," is explained by the thinker as follows: "by the Will that determines the good proper to any creature I understand the demands and potentialities of his [man's] nature, not of his consciousness ... Will, then, with a capital letter, here serves as a name for fundamental needs and capacities, not for casual desires or conventional judgments." DP, 422. Elsewhere, a slightly different explanation appears. The capital letter "Will" stands for a natural, universal drive, possibly unconscious, permeating human life. When this drive turns into a desire of some good, it becomes will in a psychological sense. DP, 41, note 1.
60   DP, 181.

life does not occur solely at its end or at an occasion of an achievement of a long-term goal, but – potentially – at each and every moment of joy, delight, creation, or contemplation.

Psyche herself is referred to by Santayana as a "mythical being," which means that her identity in the human world is conventional and she reveals herself to herself and to others in an imaginative, symbolic way, a disguise for something deeper and not fully intelligible. Still, psyches and their equally mythical counterparts – persons – stand behind the presence and visibility of actors in the realm of human affairs. In Santayana's attempt "to trace as faithfully as possible the generative order of things,"[61] it is assumed that agents in politics are psyches, not, however, in their "mythical" dimension, but in the material sense of their hidden vitality and a hidden self. If so, matters seem to be somewhat more complicated than in Santayana's initial assurance that a philosopher studying the political realm "need not trouble himself with truths deeper than conventional."[62] We read:

> There is a double force in repeating the old axiom that man is an animal. In the first place we… place man among the wonderfully various living creatures that feed, fight, and reproduce themselves … But there is a second implication … An animal has inward invisible specific springs of action, called instincts, needs, passions, or interests; and it is only in relation to these psychic springs of action that Powers and Dominations can be distinguished. The criterion in politics is moral; and the agent in politics is not man as he appears to the senses, but an inner proclivity to action and passion that animates him, and that I call the psyche.[63]

The distinction between the deep and the mythical psychic dimension introduces a meaningful complexity into Santayana's political hermeneutics, anthropology and psychology. In connection with his (non-reductive) materialism, the psycho-spiritual intricacies of his ontology that, in my view, echo in his political thought, and his idea of the human world as a theatrical stage, we are presented with two intertwining threads, "two concomitant yet strangely different streams"[64] operative in politics – the material one and the imaginative. One may risk saying that – in respect to our earlier discussion of

---

61   DP, 39.
62   DP, 3.
63   DP, 14.
64   DP, 15.

necessity and power-domination oscillation – the former describes, metaphorically speaking, the real cost-benefit outcome, the latter refers to the whole symbolic sphere of identities, images, ideologies and ideal allegiances of social and political life. The stakes and ultimate goals (*causa finalis*) in politics as it empirically happens to be concern primarily the first dimension, but the path to achieving them (*causa efficiens*) often leads through the second one. Hence, "[p]olitical ideologies are attempts to collect ... private murmurs into a chorus, so loud and imperative as to drown the concert of universal nature and turn it into an obedient accompaniment to the human voice."[65] Let me draw the reader's attention to the fact that the duality in question translates itself into problems similar to those Plato was concerned with, understood in terms of divergence between *logos* and *ergon* in democracy. Whereas the separation of the two threads is unclear and never definite, their very distinction, just like the distinction between needs and demands, is a powerful tool of criticism.

The definition of an agent in politics as sketched so far, with its emphasis on psyche as a source of potentialities and needs, is marked by a negativity of sort. "To feel needs is to feel separated from the good by some unfulfilled prerequisite to possessing it."[66] Needs and will, the latter as representative of the drive to satisfy needs and actualize potentialities, are expressive of *a profound state of deprivation and anxiety*, which creates a large margin for confusion and self-delusion in respect to the goods and ways of self-realization sought. Santayana warns that, in particular when politics is concerned, "self-consciousness is not self-knowledge."[67] The gap between hidden needs, potentials and interests and the way they are expressed in demands and articulated in political decisions is where dominations in modern societies thrive.

For Santayana powers and dominations – being moral categories – stand for, respectively, favorable circumstances and obstacles/inhibitions. These circumstances, though, include "powers" and "dominations" in a narrower sense. To have power is to be able to impose or undergo an intended change. Given the ability, will, and opportunity, one may exercise power, i.e., influence, grow, achieve, become, cause or do something in a desired direction. In Bertrand Russell's words, power is "the production of intended effects."[68] To dominate, in a politically relevant sense, may be interpreted as: to influence and prevail over other wills by means of direct or indirect coercion, taking advantage of

---

65   DP, 15.
66   DP, 40.
67   DP, 53.
68   Bertrand Russell, "The Forms of Power," in: *Power*, ed. Steven Lukes (New York: New York University Press, 1986), 19.

the potentiality someone else possesses, and, thus, often involuntarily, "offers." As living beings – precisely because we have needs and potentialities – we constitute a source of empowerment to others. This understanding of powers and dominations is relevant to the idea of governing the living and the negative anthropology which may be read in-between the lines of Santayana's political thinking.

In the sphere of politics the distinction existence – essence, present in Santayana's philosophy, becomes blurred insofar as ideologies and any other contagious mental "content" are employed as tools of persuasion and exert real influence. Modern politics, one may say, is where ideas and matter form tight alliances, be it in the form of ideologies. This being said, in no other sphere the distinction between ideas and existence becomes more glaring than in politics, where a consistent representation of an agent's material interests may involve masterful juggling with infinite numbers of apparently conflicting ideas, identities and symbols, as long as these fictions prove efficient in achieving goals, often by manipulating people's minds and vital resources.

Now, whatever one reveals, making it available to others in many different ways, is the resultant of one's vitality, personality, education, accumulated history, and social circumstances. The revealed and intelligible may well be only a fracture of one's hidden material potentiality. It is in the interest of each life that this "vital mechanism," the axis of which is primal Will, is enlightened by way of a lifelong *paideia* – education of the "soul." Enlightening and controlling one's will is a challenging process, part of self-government, and building resistance against unwanted dominations. For Santayana life is an organization, "an exercise of self-government" and of making sacrifices.[69]

Self-government involves discovering one's true needs, harmonizing will internally, and adjusting it to opportunity. What is the criterion of judgment in respect to one's needs? It seems to be a subjectivist one, namely – "[t]he true needs of a psyche would be those that, if satisfied, would free that psyche from moral contradiction."[70] Santayana, though, repeatedly stresses that man happens to be a poor judge of his own needs, interests, and circumstances, and a wise politician may do better in this respect insofar as basic needs are common, may be objectively assessed, and there is a layer of conventional morality shared by groups of people. Needs, however, are far from being constant. They evolve as life envelops and circumstances change. Meanwhile, "[t]he social world is more variable than any psyche can honestly be." No perfect adjustment

---

[69] DP, 241–242.
[70] DP, 43.

is possible, a margin of maladjustment and inadequacy is expected; besides, some needs are bound to remain unsatisfied and primal Will – "partly inhibited and partly distracted or entrapped."[71]

A few alternative reactions to this maladjustment emerge. First, there is an inflexibility in the form of either a simple stubbornness or an uncompromised idealism. The latter may result in martyrdom but may also evolve into an acceptance of circumstances and a change of heart towards some more practicable goods. Second, one may live a rather superfluous existence in the sense of avoiding any deep moral and intellectual commitments. Third, one may be a detached cynic, who, aware of the vanity of most of the temptations, "all equally gratuitous, might play the imposed game only for sport, laughing at his tyrant fate, and never risking his secret treasure, which would be his scorn of existence."[72] Finally, there is "the great lesson of conformity," when one sees that fighting for what is definitely beyond one's reach is exhausting and vain. A maxim to be considered in this case says that "[t]he best way to make things come about as you wish is to learn to like the way they have of coming about of their own accord when you give them a gentle push."[73] Even the last solution, though, being a "method of successful action and art," is far from being perfect as it involves partial smothering of spontaneity and genuineness.[74] An alternative to these attitudes rests in the only, in Santayana's view, *inalienable* freedom we have, namely – the spiritual freedom of transcending this world imaginatively. It is congenial to the conviction that "*there can be no real victory on the horizontal plane of flux and mutation.*"[75]

Santayana's idea of an achievable, individual human freedom, then, oscillates in-between vital liberty, which involves flexibility and compromise, but may require letting go of some of one's ideals and aspirations, and spiritual freedom, which always occurs at the price of partial detachment from worldly affairs. When it comes to the socio-political plane, the thinker mentions three basic meanings of freedom: freedom as power (the ability to act in accordance to one's will), negative freedom or freedom "from," and liberty, sometimes understood as a positive variety of freedom and equated with freedom as power. Liberty "seems to imply vital liberty, the exercise of powers and virtues native to oneself and to one's country."[76] Freedom from, in turn, by providing

---

71 Both quotations: DP, 43.
72 DP, 44.
73 DP, 45.
74 DP, 45–46.
75 DP, 46. My emphasis.
76 DP, 58, note 1.

security under the rule of law, is a pre-condition of vital liberty. As such, it stands for "freedom from the dangers of a *free* [natural] life. It shows us liberty contracting itself and bargaining for safety first."[77] Moreover, for the sake of his own political reflections, Santayana coins, as the reader already knows, the opposition between two types of freedom: vital liberty and vacant freedom, the latter associated with what he calls "liberty of indifference." Let me take a closer look at the latter, which, according to my interpretation, originates in a kind of *negative anthropological projection*.

In previous work I argued that in Santayana's ontology man finds himself as if stretched in-between two abysses – the nothingness of the inscrutable material potentiality and the ideal infinity open for the spirit. This condition of in-betweenness seems to me useful in explaining the origins of the craving for vacant freedom. It is born, on the one hand, in the experience of either an unbearable oppression or daily, tedious limitations, and, on the other hand, it springs from unfulfilled psychic potentiality, which, presumably – had the world been different – might be actualized in a myriad of ways. In other words, vacant freedom is a projection of a frustrated will craving for unlimited opportunity for self-assertion and satisfaction. In a socio-political context, it may become a source of egotist misconceptions, which disregard the natural limitations of freedom, to mention only human finitude and preexisting circumstances. They commit the error of "the moral illusion of free action without a definite impulse [and, one may add, a definite cost] in an existing world."[78] An illusion of a perfectly self-sufficient and autonomous agent and, as Bergson might say, of unconditionally free action implicit in the habit of thinking that things might have been otherwise, is involved. There is some truth in the idea that things could have been different given the share of contingency in history and the arbitrariness of any human order. Yet, the idea is abused when it implies that human action is determined solely by previous conscious deliberation, and its consequences embody the influence of an unconditioned human *fiat* on a plastic reality that awaits to be molded according to human wishes. This tacit assumption of a spectrum of equally available options open in front of humans, which is part of the sense of vacant freedom, is what Santayana

---

77   DP, 58, note 1. My emphasis. Santayana notes different origins of both terms – Latin in the case of "liberty" and, in his language, "Teutonic" in the case of "freedom." The distinction in meaning is not utterly clear, but he suggests that the former may be associated with a positive idea of freedom – freedom to something, and the latter – with a negative one, i.e., freedom from something. While "freedom" appears in usage both with "to" and "from," one does not encounter a phrase "liberty from." DP, 58, note 1.

78   DP, 47.

means by "liberty of indifference." There is a desire for (an absolute) freedom, unaccompanied by "a clear idea of what they [the agents] will do with their liberty when they have won it."[79] Longing for an unspecified space of freedom in politics easily turns into hatred of any aspect of reality that seems to be the source of limits and compulsion. It may, furthermore, be clad in an ideological dress. Meanwhile, questions, such as: what "will liberty bring to a free man" and what environment and tools "the liberated slave requires for the exercise of his vital liberty," remain unasked.[80]

A specific kind of liberty of indifference was conveyed by Christian anthropology and served as a justification for Christian morality and ethics. Man could be held fully responsible for the fate he prepared for his soul when choosing consciously between good and evil. It was assumed that man was well-equipped to be free to choose, that he could stand on a ground firm and neutral enough to be able to make the right choice. As the reader already knows, Santayana, emphasizing the fact of human finitude and dependence, questioned this tendency to overestimate human autonomy as grounded in free will and conscious decision.

Having said this, however, I don't intend to ascribe to Santayana a fatalism greater than he seems to have been committed to, which may easily be done due to his idea of impotent spirit.[81] Leaving aside the question of his alleged epiphenomenalism, from which he distanced himself at some point of his career precisely on the ground of his materialism, in a political context, as he clearly states, the intuition of the authorship of action is correct, even if it sometimes hides some misapprehension. *What is correct is that the self is indeed the center of decisions and action; the misconception lies in the equation of the acting self with consciousness, and of decision with a fruit of rational deliberation.* Santayana's point is to reveal

> the *inadequacy* of the conscious arguments crowding and disputing in the mind to cause or justify the decisions taken ... beneath that loud forum of sophistical pleadings there is a silent judge, the self, that decides according to its free will, contingently, and inexplicably ... Moreover, this

---

79   DP, 47.
80   DP, 58–59.
81   Spirit, or consciousness, does not cause things, it is impotent insofar as it is merely "a witness, involuntary and unprepared, of everything real and imaginary, good or evil that is ever experienced." It may, in contemplation or imaginative flights, transcend the reality of existence. It may also be easily distracted or deceived on its own, hyper-democratic terms of the equality of all essences as essences. See: DP, 55.

hidden self is, like every centre ... in nature, perfectly contingent in being groundlessly determinate; and to this profound characteristic of all existence self-consciousness bears witness in the conviction that a man is the author of his actions, and that his actions are free.[82]

It is assumed, then, beyond doubt, that psyches (individually and collectively), as natural centers of power and vital organization, are agents proper in politics. Rather than undermining the fact of human agency, Santayana aims to dispel those illusions about freedom that neglect man's natural basis and the weight of context.

What, if any, significance has the well-known idea of spiritual impotence by Santayana in a socio-political context? It may be viewed as serving to curb the illusions of humans about their power to change the world according to an intended plan. It may also support the following insights: 1) ideas themselves, unless embodied by sufficiently powerful psyches in the form of their directive imagination and supported by favorable circumstances, are powerless; 2) will, which, unlike spirit, is materially potent, is a seat of irrational trends, which may be misrepresented by their imaginative and verbal equivalents in the public sphere, whereby the non-transparency of the political realm is emphasized; 3) dogmas and utopias are likely to be betrayed by the course of things. However, it also suggests that 4) human life partakes in a realm which is not determined by material power and this fact, beyond doubt, has impact on individual hierarchies of values and culture. Last but not least, it may suggest that disengagement from politics is a serious option for idealists, artists and other spiritually-minded individuals, which does not mean that their activity is useless or insignificant from the perspective of society and politics. As for the second of the above points, will belongs equally to the sphere of material entanglements and to that of potential liberty. As a prelude to any further discussion of the ideal of the life of reason, and in connection with point four, let me say that *much, including the chance for vital liberty, depends upon the degree in which will is enlightened, intelligently curbed, and harmonized by reason, which is a path to wisdom.* Ideally, the principle of harmony, in the spirit of Plato, applies both to individual and collective human self-government. For its realization, though, it requires a reflective cultural environment, which draws on spiritual resources and facilitates – to refer to a useful idea by Harry Frankfurt – sharing higher-order volitions.

---

[82] DP, 53–54. My emphasis.

As for Santayana's attempt to wed freedom with limitations and virtues, he notes that if it wasn't for the fact of incarnation, which is a source of limitations, even spiritual freedom would not be freedom anymore,

> but absolute apathy and impotence ... Its proper freedom is liberation, disentanglement, parturition of its inner burden. For the spirit there is no question of choosing ... this or that fortune or love. Given existence, given fortune ... the problem for it is to digest, to refine, to dominate that existence, that fortune, or that love ... The inner liberty of spirit will not then be vacant but vital.[83]

Returning once more to the hypothetical, experiential origins of the idea of vacant freedom, Santayana evokes two scenes: that of a crying child, finding itself too long in discomfort, and Xenophon's story from *Anabasis* about ten thousand Greeks shouting *Thalassa, thalassa*, at the moment they saw the Black Sea, after a long and exhausting march from the depths of Asia. In both cases "[t]hey did not know what they want, but they find their condition insufferable."[84] Their cry is "a cry for freedom pure and simple, freedom wholly abstract yet unspeakably precious."[85] There is a noble element in vacant freedom to the extent that it is a distant echo of longing for a spiritual liberation. But in a political context similar ideas may be extremely militant, especially when accompanied by xenophobia and yet another ally – a "purge" kind of desire to make "to make a clean slate of society" or a nation.[86]

Along with the will to power, the mirage of vacant freedom is often at work in revolutionary movements, extreme forms of nationalism and imperialism alike. The exclusivist vice in nations and states claiming to protect their integrity and sovereignty may spring from a reluctance towards whatever is different. They "look on all others as nuisances or dangers ... [whose] territory should be annexed, the inhabitants assimilated, exterminated or reduced to slavery."[87] This primal and surprisingly persistent mode of political being is centered around a single ideal:

> infinite, vacant freedom surrounding a chosen way of life ... [It] has been loudly proclaimed by every militant religion, as to-day by the apostles

---

83   DP, 57.
84   DP, 57.
85   DP, 58.
86   DP, 49. My emphasis.
87   DP, 48.

of both kinds of democracy ...; and it is betrayed by the Soviets now in their continual demand for unanimity. In those who dislike to mention it, it persists in a secret unrest and perplexity at the existence of so many millions of blacks and of heathens.[88]

It cannot be excluded that when a state is highly developed and well organized, its domination might turn into a source of vital liberty also for the conquered peoples, perhaps a better one than those nations would be able to provide for themselves. Those peoples, however, might still want to, and have a moral right to, rebel against foreign domination in the name of liberty understood as freedom from oppression. Any attempt to bestow an apparently better order on peoples of different past, habits and institutions, must calculate the risk involved in ignoring the generative order and wishing – to repeat – "to make a clean slate of society."[89] This concerns both foreign conquerors and domestic revolutionaries.

A possible integrity of collective agents in politics, then, lying in the "wholeness and absoluteness of the Will,"[90] is morally ambiguous and must be mitigated by reason. Likewise, an excessively individualistic culture, as Santayana's analysis of English liberty shows, may be at odds with the idea of mutual reinforcement occurring between cooperation and liberty in democracy.[91] Hence, integrity should couple with self-limitation, the vehicle of which is humility. Santayana gives some clues as to the natural resolution of the tension between an assertion of vitality and humility in the following passage. I decided to quote it in its entirety, first, so as not to deprive the reader of the pleasure involved in an encounter with Santayana's poetic language, and, second, for a rare combination of insights that I find telling in respect to the overall texture of his thought:

> Were the soul humble before it was contradicted and chastised by uncontrollable circumstances, it would be a feeble and empty soul. Humility is strong and profitable only when it is the fruit of experience and of a

---

[88]   DP, 48.
[89]   DP, 49.
[90]   DP, 59.
[91]   This issue is nuanced. On the one hand, one finds in Santayana an advocacy of individualism in the form of intellectual autonomy and, sometimes, spiritual detachment. On another – one comes across a criticism of egotism, and excessive integrity leading to the inflexibility that may obstruct pluralism and cooperation. Paradoxically, while there appears in his writings also an appreciation of a robust vitality, in general Santayana praises the virtue of humility.

tragic contrast discovered and accepted between aspiration and destiny. Christian doctrine in this, as in much else, contains a perfect allegory of the truth. We must be born again, before we can enjoy true liberty or enlightened happiness. Our original unregenerate vitality was not madness – as solipsism would be – but only sin; not sin in yielding to any base or unworthy temptation, but that original sin of which Calderón speaks when he says that the greatest trespass of man is that he was ever born. It is the tragic sin of ὕβρις [*hubris*] or arrogance, in laying claim, by existing, on whatever we want, when nothing is really ours. The sin does not lie, as superstitious cowardice supposes, in willing this or that which is taboo, but in willing *anything* without leave. When leave is granted by fate, the love of life and of freedom is normal and noble … To primal Will liberty therefore seems a right, and is indeed an ideal that can never be surrendered. … Yet in the economy of nature there is no such thing as a right. Existence itself is an unearned gift and an imposed predicament. The privilege of more or less freedom is meted out to individuals and to nations temporally and unequally, not by any ideal justice or law, but by the generative stress of a universal automatism.[92]

There is nothing moral or just in nature, then. Psychic integrity of an enlightened kind is a promise of withholding the thrust of the "universal automatism" on the human level and responding to the impersonal universe with some temporary moral order, where sympathy may find expression and vital liberty be approached.

A political integrity, though, perhaps to the surprise of those who associate Santayana mainly with his famous dictum about forgetting history, need not involve

> [f]idelity to the past … if the man or the people has undergone a veritable μετάνοια [*metanoia*]; nor is absolute constancy in this new allegiance to be expected, except in the measure in which the conversion responds to all the ingrained needs and all the relevant circumstances of that person or that people.[93]

Also Santayana's attitude towards tradition is not as unequivocally supportive as some may be inclined to read him. Notwithstanding the fact that threads

---

92   DP, 63.
93   DP, 59.

of cultural continuity and historical awareness are vital both for personal and political integrity, each generation, he thinks, is "compelled to learn its lessons anew, and not to learn exactly the same lessons as its ancestors, but to forget their language and their gods in running after new idols."[94]

However, responding to an overwhelming fashion of associating freedom with change and reform, Santayana points to the fact that "[n]ature remains free to be constant."[95] He discerns between the actual lack of any "logical prohibition of reform or of variation" and an imposture of a constant change as necessary or at least highly desirable. Santayana illustrates humorously the latter idea with an assumption that "the sweetness of marriage would depend on the prospect of divorce."[96] Besides, sustaining relative stability in society is a kind of human remedy for the fact that existence implies "a continual variation and destruction in material things and utter moral disorder in history."[97]

Vacant freedom and vital liberty, although in theory opposed to one another, need not be discontinuous in real life. Their relation may be explained in psychological terms. Vacant freedom may be a moral consequence of the fact that psyche is at once mutable and capable of cumulative learning from experience. At the earlier stages of life, people find it easier to adjust the scope and ambition of their vital liberty to the reigning trends and actual opportunities. With time, as self-awareness, self-knowledge and knowledge of the world grow, they tend to become more selective, critical, and their idea of vital liberty – more specific. Thus, "the chasm between the mature demands of the Will and the path open to action" widens.[98] This is when frustration and discontent with society and the world at large arise. A similar situation may occur in a society where expectations fed by the lure of infinite venues for self-development and glorification of success clash with real opportunities. This may lead "public feeling … to identify liberty with rebellion."[99] Thus, as I will discuss in the chapters to come, the witnessed by Santayana deepening social inequality, standing in a glaring contradiction to the original ideals of liberalism, led to the radicalization of large groups of people. The promise of vital liberty unfulfilled engendered craving for vacant freedom, on which anarchist and revolutionary ideas could feed

---

94 DP, 62.
95 DP, 50.
96 Both quotations: DP, 50–51.
97 DP, 52.
98 DP, 60.
99 DP, 60.

2.3 Anarchist and Revolutionary Delusions

Santayana often voiced criticism of revolutions. Much as revolutionary impulse may be understood as natural "in a world false to its every promise,"[100] revolutions are dangerous experiments on a living substance. They may remove the most obvious impediments on the path to the well-being of some groups, yet they find it difficult to predict their own cost and their ideas about how to establish a better world are fallible.[101] The French Revolution was, in Santayana's view, preparing for something "hardly expressed with frankness before Nietzsche ... liberty absolute and forever empty; liberty without foundations in nature or history, but resident in a sort of prophetic commotion ... Hence the moral hatred of any view that recognized realities, or built upon them."[102] While Santayana's remarks about the hubristic aspect of some revolutions and the unacceptable human cost of their destructiveness are perfectly reasonable, his one-sidedness may provoke the reader to charge him with a deliberate underestimation of the scope and depth of injustice that preceded them. His effort to be an unbiased critic of society seems to desert him at some occasions. Having said this, one should note that much as Santayana's anti-revolutionary sympathies were evident, not all of his opinions were consistent in this respect. While his skepticism as to the moral condition of the political scene in the 20th century was growing, he became more sympathetic towards revolutionary trends. Let me also note that Santayana's ontology and his political anthropology provided him with democratic essentials he could resort to. One was his idea of there being a profound equalizer at work in the world, namely – the human condition and the necessary servitude people pay to natural and artificial dominations. Collective suffering from domination, insofar as it was unnecessarily high and inflicted by impostors, might bring about – justifiably – a revolutionary wave. Reversing Santayana's own words but retaining his logic, reality is dynamic through and through, and even if, in principle, relative constancy is better for the flourishing of mankind, there is no logical prohibition for a revolution to occur when a status quo is felt to be unbearable.

In his brief discussion of anarchy, Santayana, consistently with the method and style of his philosophizing, first sheds some light on its cultural and psychological premises and only then, and in very general terms, on its political manifestations. The idea of anarchy is where two other – that of vacant freedom and that of militancy – converge. Politically, anarchy stands for either an

---

100 DP, 55.
101 DP, 60.
102 DP, 224.

absolute individual freedom in the state of lack of any legal authority or, in international relations, the absence of any authority higher than nation-states. Santayana brings to light and puts into scrutiny some contradictions and paradoxes involved in an *anarchistic impulse and imagination* finding expression in the already discussed, vague, yet militant, idea of absolute freedom, which is conditioned, on the one hand, by an experience of limitations and oppression, and, on the other, by the ability of human imagination to transcend any concrete circumstances. Human existence implies a "virtual self-transcendence of intelligent action,"[103] which allows to envisage oneself in an altogether different context and design a possible path leading to the realization of this vision. In this flight of imagination, though, some circumstances tend to escape attention, enriching the dark recesses of ignorance.

"Mankind has always been unhappy, more unhappy perhaps when submissive and pious than when rebellious."[104] Rebellion may be viewed as a dignified and self-assertive response to misery. It is when rebellion turns into hatred of anything established, such as history, tradition, excellence, truth, reality as such, that Santayana quarrels with it. Such a destructive or deconstructive idea of freedom disregards the fact that liberty is conditioned too, it is "not a source but a confluence and a harmony."[105] In other words, it is a final accomplishment, a long awaited equilibrium that comes into being after much effort is put into establishing a harmonious internal and external organization.

This being said, the idea of absolute freedom from oppression, even if only a fantasy of spirit, retains something of its nobility. Especially when it is an intuition contributing to the idea of tolerance and respect for other living being. But, ironically, the existence of those "other beings" happens to be the first obstacle for the advocates of radical freedom. "We are drawn away violently from irresponsible play to a painful study of facts and to the endless labour of coping with probable enemies."[106] Liberty thrives when there is peace; war, by way of confrontation with bare necessity, brings slavery. There is a major contradiction within the anarchical idea of absolute freedom since to establish and sustain a peaceful coexistence, an "eternal vigilance," moral and material *discipline*, and virtue are needed. The canonical principle of not interfering with the freedom of others imposes itself. Is not discipline, by the way, by definition a violation of absolute freedom? Once a relatively harmonious organization of life is established, it may turn out that liberty is actually already there,

---

103   DP, 239.
104   DP, 236.
105   DP, 237.
106   This and all the remaining quotations in this paragraph come from: DP, 238.

liberty to pursue some goods, to follow a chosen path. But liberty thus understood is not exactly synonymous with what is commonly understood today – since Josiah Berlin's classification – as positive liberty. Rather, it turns out to be, first and foremost, *a disposition*.[107] When illusions of absolute freedom vanish, what remains is "[l]iberty to follow the golden rule: whereby our free hearts are at once sobered and transfixed in their inmost affections."[108]

Still partly unsatisfied with this resolution, Santayana questions the above "orderly" idea of liberty as unacceptable or even deplorable for truly "free spirit[s]." Perhaps living dangerously, always spontaneously, and in the present is closer to their ideal? This is where the vista of "a paradise of anarchy" opens, where peace, if it were meant to be, would have to assume the form of "the perfect insulation of each life and its utter irrelevance to all others."[109] Freed from morality, these imaginary, uprooted atoms wouldn't be bothered by any idea of truth either. They would be free to "pursue gaia scienza which is not knowledge of anything but pure composition. Yes, ... [they] would become *too free to think*."[110] This, obviously, is an impossible scenario in a world where all living beings are dependent.

The idea of being "too free to think" is perhaps worth remembering for its wisdom and wit, but there are more important reasons why ideals of absolute freedom, politically, are not simply unrealistic but dangerous. The above visions are abstractions. A perfect freedom for all is possible only in an ideal world, where there is no material friction and all beings are self-sufficient. In the political realm it is will, not pure spirit (which has a sort of inalienable freedom at its disposal anyway) that strives to assert itself. "The disruptive force in society is not that of understanding, but that of some political passion."[111] And it asserts itself among material, mortal beings, whose interests are likely to be affected by the expanding freedom of some. This is where freedom becomes militant, it allies with desire and power, turning into an aggressive self-assertion. Freedom in the political realm is no more innocent. It yearns for space, time and resources. It may be egotist, imperialist, experienced by others as violent domination.

---

107 Santayana's conception of liberty here gets close to Charles Taylor's reformulation of Berlin's idea of positive freedom in terms of "exercise freedom." See: Charles Taylor, "What is wrong with negative liberty," in *Philosophy and the Human Sciences. Philosophical Papers*, vol.2 (Cambridge: CUP, 1985), 211–229.
108 DP, 238.
109 DP, 239.
110 DP 239. My emphasis.
111 DP, 240.

Santayana seems to be right when saying that "[a]t the level of complexity at which thought and laughter are possible, to exist means to be distinctly organized, localized, contrasted with other things, and conditioned by them. It means to have a mock freedom only."[112] This implies that any socio-political conception of freedom is always biased. Specific rights and liberties may be pursued and won to alleviate some dangers and burdens that are recognized as unbearable, arbitrary, excessive, unjust. But life does not cease to be an exercise of self-government, meaning that a degree of control and organization is inherent to it. From an individual perspective, this brings us back to the formula of the liberty to follow the golden mean. The question is how to achieve an equilibrium between self-government and subjection to external authorities, or between autonomy and servitude to society and the state. Liberty, personal and political, implies finding relative comfort among frictions. The "rebellion of Lucifer was essentially a suicide: reducing himself to free spirit he reduced himself to nothing. Real powers are always definite, or they would not have definite results."[113] As for collective life, any conception of freedom, realized under given circumstances, has some shape, the contours of which are expressed through law and customs; in other words, it manifests itself in a certain type of coexistence with others and in relation to authorities. Thus, it imposes restrictions, requires some type of organization and discipline, whereby it cannot help favoring individuals of certain dispositions and outlooks more than some others. In a libertarian society, for example, where freedom is based on the pillar of private property and free market competition, a specific type of individuals, namely – those endowed with entrepreneurial skills and who value material goods highly, is undoubtedly privileged as far as self-fulfillment and power accumulation are concerned, and it is them that are going to enjoy the libertarian freedom in a fuller degree than some others, who may well experience enslavement. As for anarchy, discussed by Santayana, while the anarchist thought has a respectable tradition, and empirical examples of communities existing without legal authority or social structure are known, it is clear – both in literature and the real life examples – that the survival and stability of an anarchic social establishment requires a remarkable civil, mental and external discipline, and a specific moral orientation. To conclude, if Santayana's main point is that no actual freedom can satisfy the anarchistic impulse, he is convincing. Likewise, he is insightful when claiming that *any conception of freedom carries an implicit*

---

112   DP, 241.
113   DP 241.

hierarchy of types of servitude within. By restricting some of them, it may, sometimes unintentionally, create or strengthen other forms of dependence. Reading Santayana may enlighten one's understanding of what these other forms are or may turn out to be.

CHAPTER 3

Servitude

> Society suffocates liberty merely by existing.
> DP, 65

∴

Santayana's investigations into the nature of liberty and freedom are paralleled by a reflection on servitude, by which he means the whole variety of human dependencies – from the most natural and universal to the most artificial ones. Assuming the human experience of limitations as his point of departure, Santayana grounds the idea of liberty in the existential fact of servitude, or, to use a broader category, in the human condition. This approach, part of what I call here Santayana's "negative anthropology," allows him to 1) analyze the ways in which the already mentioned sphere of human helplessness becomes a target and a bargaining chip in politics; 2) shed light on misconceptions present in some interpretations of freedom; 3) articulate a balanced and realistic approach to the question of negotiating between liberty and subjugation. Contrarily to what it might initially suggest, however, let me remind the reader that Santayana's purpose is to prevent "choking the human genius by social pressure"[1] rather than to suppress human spontaneity or creativity. Let me take a look, then, at Santayana's reflections on the forms of human servitude.

Three kinds of servitude occur in the human world: necessary, voluntary, and involuntary yet accidental.[2] The last kind is easiest to identify – it is slavery in the literal sense of the term. It occurs when one person is against their will reduced to an instrument in another person's hands and is deprived of the "privilege of terminating that servitude at will," while the other person, the master, could live without the slave.[3] This is the most extreme violation of the principle that "each man is by nature an end in himself and sufficient unto himself." In Aristotle's idea of natural slaves, there is an "inconsiderate haste in asserting that whole classes of men are capable of no [free] activities," and the

---

[1] Letter to John W. Yolton, 27 Apr. 1952, LGS8: 441.
[2] DP, 73.
[3] DP, 77.

whole theory "sins against persons" when it denies them "prerogative to spiritual freedom."[4] Yet, Aristotle's theory is revealing to the extent that it concerns the arts and the status of man's labour. Both forced work and work that is merely instrumental and for which there is no slightest internal justification turn man into a slave. "[A]ll instrumental and remedial arts, however indispensable, are pure burdens; and progress consists in abridging them as much as is possible without contracting the basis for moral life."[5]

For heuristic reasons, Santayana turns to yet another kind of "slavery," where one of the parties is non-human. Insofar as human relations are based on pure interest, the economic life of society reflects some aspects of the fate of farm animals. Moral judgments in this respect depend on the changing "criteria of benefit and injury involved in living," or on the standards of governing the living, one might add.[6] The provision of basic security may be a powerful argument for moving from the natural slavery in a jungle to a more civilized sort, even at the price of being caught in a net of irresistible dependencies and sacrificing one's vital powers in a foreign service. The organization of slavery and brutality of exploitation, however, may vary greatly, depending on historical, cultural and economic factors, and the most drastic mechanisms of its execution may be delegated, with time, beyond public visibility, to be performed "by less familiar and more hardened officials."[7] It is possible, then, that the enslaved creatures prefer the dangers of the jungle than the perfectly organized "butchering." A feeling of brotherhood in craving for freedom may arise, with time, amidst both the slaves and, sometimes, the system's officers of lower rank. But another reaction is possible too, when those who have been born under a totalitarian kind of slavery and indoctrinated properly, eagerly make the sacrifice of their lives for the sake of an elusive higher goal.

With the development of civilization, a new form of slavery, slavery to technology, partly replaces and marginalizes (or simply relocates) the earlier, more primitive forms of it. In this kind of relation, the boundary between mastership and slavery becomes blurred. Human mastership over technology means control over "a greater physical force, with an even more exact manifestation of your own will and purpose."[8] Potentially it is a rewarding and beneficent form of mastership, especially when widely accessible. Concomitant to it is spread of literacy, efficacy-oriented organization of society, and a slow but

---

4   LR, 306.
5   LR, 307.
6   DP, 74.
7   DP, 75.
8   DP, 77.

steady reduction of the most drastic forms of poverty. Both custom and law change so that they may provide support and rationalize the new, healthier, better organized, more systematic and disciplined kind of society. Civilization, more clearly than ever, seems a path of no return.

Within the new system both human needs and potentialities are taken into account scrupulously as belonging to a larger economy. It is man because of whom and thanks to whom all this machinery is set into motion. However, man's position is ambiguous and "we must never forget that among the raw materials of industry the most important is man."[9] A "terrible responsibility," rests on man's shoulders at the time of this unprecedented dependence upon – if not slavery to – the rapidly developing technology. It resembles dealing with a time bomb. Moreover, humanity is fully mobilized, as "[c]ivilization will require and must enlist every human being in its perpetual service." There is a moral obligation in it too – "[t]o hang back would be treason and would deserve death. ... to the perfect order of society all men, even their leaders, must be slaves in soul and in body."[10] Not all aspects of technological progress, then, serve the emancipation of man. Traditional forms of slavery have been replaced by new, collective, milder, and more acceptable ones, as if fulfilling, thus, the master-slave dialectic. This, by the way, does not mean that the former have altogether disappeared. Rather, they have been relocated beyond public visibility. The very phenomenon of slavery to technology reveals the unreality of the vision of a complete human mastership over technology and questions the very possibility of taking responsibility for its evolution and impact on the social world.

A reflection on the relation between man and technology is set in a broader context of modernization as part of civilizational progress. Modernization entails prospects of some emancipatory social changes, such as bridging deep social inequalities, securing equality of all in front of the law, providing common education, liquidation of oligarchy, if such existed, and separating the state from the church. Santayana notices that some of these emancipatory, pro-egalitarian changes are accompanied by the rise of less explicit, sometimes introduced imperceptibly, anonymous forms of subjugation and instrumentalization of persons, serving, for example, the omnipresent requirement of efficiency. What is more, the accountability for the scope and direction of the changes underwent by the world under the influence of technology seems to outgrow human competence. The results of the expected social emancipation,

---

9   DP, 77.
10 All the remaining quotations in this paragraph: DP, 77.

though precious, are insecure for at least two reasons. First, the development of technology offers the possibility of gaining enormous economic and military advantage to predatory agents, endowing them with unprecedented opportunities of dominating others, whether they be located within nominal governments or beyond, in some hidden centers of power. Second, if social and economic emancipation is not accompanied by other forms of progress, society may be formally emancipated, yet morally and intellectually degraded. Even though one may charge Santayana with fostering certain anti-modern sentiments, his purpose is to shed some light on the unintended consequences of modernization in the form of anonymous yet irresistible human servitude to a "system."

Another, the most rudimentary of the three forms of servitude is necessary servitude. It is nothing other than the discussed in this book share of necessity in human life, manifesting itself as a sphere of helplessness – mutable yet irremovable, regardless of the powers one is able to accumulate and the freedom "from" that is secured to one. It is servitude to nature, owed to the fact that – to say the least – we are mortal beings. Among striking and persistent examples of a collective manifestation of necessity, relevant to the socio-political plane, one may list, on the one hand, disease, aging, and the concomitant issues with managing public health in highly developed countries, and, on the other hand, the phenomenon of hunger in the third world and beyond, both natural and one caused by human intervention, to mention the Great Famine in Ukraine in the years 1932–33 as one of the most shocking and literal examples of politics *via* necessity. At the time of writing the present book the world is experiencing yet another tête-à-tête with necessity – in the guise of Covid-19 pandemic. Nothing illustrates better Santayana's conviction about the latent possibility of an unexpected material tide to correct excessive optimism and carelessness, and distract our long constructed state and sense of well-being, bringing our helplessness into full light.

The fact of "necessary servitude" has long preoccupied philosophers of politics, who weaved natural necessity into their conceptions of the state, showing the way in which it is tamed, neutralized or transmuted. Thus, Thomas Hobbes tried to illuminate the social contract with reference to the state of nature. Humans, fearful of death, used their intelligence to organize themselves and create a more livable environment. The state itself was a necessity, replacing another, more ruthless and deadly kind of necessity. For John Locke, in turn, nature had a more human face for it already contained and conveyed, via humans themselves, basic guidelines as to how people should arrange a better, social world for themselves. The state was an option, not a necessity. Starting with Plato and his metaphor of reason "persuading" necessity in *Timaeus*, the role and fate of necessity in different conceptions varied accordingly to the position and power ascribed to human reason in relation to what may be considered as non-reason. Philosophers of the twentieth-century, especially those associated with the critical school and hermeneutics of suspicion, have been particularly sensitive to the issue of necessity, often without calling it so *expressis verbis*. Ideas like "bare life," governing the living, *homo sacer*, biopolitics, political sovereignty as the right to wage war and announce the state of emergency, the idea of governing via manipulating human sexuality, all allude, in a more or less direct way, to the ideas of necessity and human negativity as understood in this book, often looking at the state via the lens of the forms of coercion and exploitation. Santayana's reflections on the forms of servitude in *Dominations and Powers* may be said to prefigure some of the aforementioned ideas and may enter into a dialogue with them. However, Santayana's political thinking can by no means be reduced to similar ideas. To say the least, his humanism and the ideal of the life of reason – to the extent that they challenge the horizon of "bare life" – defy such reduction.

All in all, necessary servitude implies the potential for controlling social life through the biological premises of this life and its very survival. It permeates the institution of the family and human work, both being a means of securing basic needs. But in both spheres, with the support of economy, culture, and laws, the share of necessity may be partly alleviated or transformed into another kind of servitude – a voluntary one. In the large sphere of what Santayana calls servitude to society, the boundary between necessity and choice is unclear. Other than that, Santayana certainly believes that man is a social being, but he immediately points to the fact that the very society that supports the individual suppresses him even to the point of destroying what is the best in him. This sensitivity to the destruction of individual potential reflects both Santayana's humanism and his defense of a subtle, non-exclusivist, individualism.

Santayana, according to my reading and as I mentioned briefly in the first chapter, accepts the basic scientific tenets of Darwinism and does not ignore them in the descriptive layer of his political thought, but as a political thinker *is neither a representative nor an ally of any form of social Darwinism*. He admits that man is naturally inclined to selfishness and his rationality serves primarily his self-interests. These features belong to the core of human individuality, even if in the process of its formation they become overgrown with other, sometimes contradictory, inclinations, passions, habits. Altruism and readiness to sacrifice are not absent from the scope of man's attitudes but they are occasional and in the time of crisis tend to be overshadowed by a profound selfishness. Selfishness, the unreliability of virtues learnt but not integrated, and, most of all, narrowness of moral imagination, impact the quality of political life too. Santayana writes of an average politician: "[a]s to what might prove pleasing to others in the long course of their experience, he is incapable of appropriating or of conceiving anything so complex and ambiguous."[11] The question is to what extent and in what ways man's inclination to selfishness determines the shape of society and culture and the forms of servitude suffered by its members. The project of eradicating selfishness from social organization, undertaken in the 20th century by the communists, turned out to be an inhuman experiment with tragic consequences. A solution of sorts to this problem may be found in the idea of enlightened self-interest and the already discussed ethos of English liberty. Yet, we are talking of a long tradition of a political and legal culture, which is a local and, probably, a transitory model. Nevertheless, Santayana pays attention to the standards of excellence as conveyed by culture and the personal virtues of the governing class, which, for the sake of satisfying our craving for classification, may be included in the set of the conservative traits of his thought.

Having relieved man from the burden of some harsh material trials, society has surrounded him with a net of conventional, suffocating burdens – "the necessary cradle of the individual."[12] Since "[e]ndless alternatives are compatible with human nature,"[13] all customs are arbitrary and their origins accidental. Yet, customs and myths form a lasting and powerful structure capable of endowing common life with definition and integrity, while, at the same time, narrowing down the margin of individual freedom. A custom originates in a public experience of a crisis and its accidental solution that have impressed public imagination with a lasting "reflex," forming an inclination to repeat the act under similar circumstances. The most deeply ingrained customs, and, as René Girard would add, those that arose in most dramatic circumstances, become rituals, the origin of which is usually associated with mythological events. Human myth-making, Santayana thought, is an expression of a primitive rationality in the face of lack of scientific knowledge, but also a poetic, allegorical representation of existential truths like the one about humans living at the mercy of nature. From a political perspective, persisting customs, as part of native tradition, may become significant in many ways. They may obstruct reform but they may also support people in resisting the power of a temporary, cruel regime or arbitrary law, or, at least, let them endure without perishing. Thus, customs may form a kind of protection against the caprices of the political realm. There is, however, something "primitive" in the powerful

---

11   DP, 72.
12   DP, 64.
13   DP, 70.

hold that customs have on men. Santayana has no doubts about there being "hardly any degree of constraint, cruelty and ineptitude, which may not characterize custom."[14] People who live unreflectively, self-content and immersed in the cyclical temporality of rituals, both those public and private, delight in their slavery, often becoming indifferent, blind, if not hostile to otherness and change.

Among other major sources of servitude are economy, the nation, and the state. In his critique of industrial economy, the ripe development of which Santayana witnessed, he points to the fact that it relieved the power of tradition, while providing "new instruments and fresh occasions for artificial demands and unnecessary subjections ... exactions, compulsions."[15] As for the state, the greatest abuse on its part and the sacrifice it imposes on the people is a "blood tax" in the form of military service. Since government's duty is defense, "this defense will often be preventive defense, that is to say, timely aggression."[16] The institution of a nation-state, which Cassirer regarded to be based on a constructed myth, introduces a powerful, partly artificial allegiance, which happens to be conducive to the resurrection of tribalistic passions, namely – an allegiance to one's nation and its political sovereignty. Here Santayana tries to see both lights and shadows of the phenomenon. Patriotism is a form of natural piety and may be conducive to achieving personal and social integrity alike. As an ideal loyalty, it may inspire, and has inspired throughout history, virtues, noble feelings, a sense of belonging to a greater whole, and remarkable achievements in different areas of human activity. Patriotism opposes egoistic individualism and emphasizes the fact that certain areas of common existence are issues of public concern – something, according to Santayana, overlooked by the liberals.[17] Patriotism stands for "being sensitive to a set of interests which no one could have if he had lived in isolation, but which accrue to men conscious of living in society, and in a society having the scope and history of a nation."[18] Rational and beneficent patriotism, or, in other words, patriotism in its noble from, would involve veneration and tenderness towards the vital influence of the past, expressive of the idea that a kind of "sanctity hangs about the sources of our being, whether physical, social, or imaginative."[19]

---

14   DP, 70.
15   DP, 68.
16   DP, 424.
17   "It was the vice of liberalism to believe that common interests covered nothing but the sum of those objects which each individual might pursue alone." LR, 168–169.
18   LR, 168.
19   LR, 167.

This attention to the past that formed a national and/or religious community, though, should not turn into a "ritualistic shadow of the past. ... a retrospective religion."[20] Neither should it become a competitive patriotism, expressive of a sectarian and militant attitude. A *rational patriotism* would imply an allegiance to a government only if it happened to be representative of the general welfare of its subjects. Just as piety may be extended over the whole humanity, such a government might also be "an international benefit" as a potential good model of governing for others. Ideally, then, patriotism, as an expression not only of a natural piety but also of reason, "should extend over a wider field," beyond local allegiance, and "embrace ideally what really produces human well-being," including other nations, civilization at large, and even humanity.[21] It is important to note, then, that *rational patriotism* – a modern and at once ancient (Stoic) idea – overcomes locality and ethnocentrism, and connotes an idealistic, spiritually- and future-oriented attitude, an ultimate realization of the ideal of the life of reason. Thus, patriotism, while it retains an aspect of piety, evolves along the line of Santayana's orders – from a generative and militant phenomenon to a rational one.

The thinker's cosmopolitan sympathies, more evident in his reflections on patriotism than elsewhere, along with his personal and theoretical reluctance towards different forms of exclusivism, prompt him to consider patriotism as it empirically happened to be at that time a "great curse," a potential source of xenophobia and of endless wars – war being, except for some rare situations, a "servile art."[22] In *The Life of Reason* Santayana shares with the reader his farsighted intuitions concerning tensions between globalization, governance on the level of a nation-state and democracy.[23] He criticizes patriotism as a "perfervid artificial" allegiance, which in the contemporary world too often tends to be at odds both with the changing individual and universal human interests and "the industrial and intellectual solidarity of mankind, every day more obvious," to the influence of which patriotism itself – he expects – may one day succumb.[24] Nationality, as a natural fact, should not be ignored. Yet, rather

---

20   LR, 164.
21   LR, 161. See also: LR, 261.
22   LR, 310.
23   A century later Dani Rodrik, in *The Globalization Paradox*, wrote: "[W]e begin to understand what I call the fundamental political trilemma of the world economy: we cannot simultaneously pursue democracy, national determination, and economic globalization." See: Dani Rodrik, *The Globalization Paradox* (New York and London: W.W. Norton & Company, 2011), xii.
24   LR, 124. The issue of this conflict would reappear in *Dominations and Powers*, where Santayana sounds more skeptical about the effects of globalization.

than becoming a fetish and a source of domination, it should be treated "only [as] a starting-point for liberal life."[25] Meanwhile, in an essay "The Intellectual Temper of the Age," which I consider insightful and still actual in our day, Santayana observes that patriotism has become a

> public, intrepid illusion. Illusion, I mean, when it is taken for an ultimate good or a mystical essence, for of course nationality is a fact … It is right to feel a greater kinship and affection for what lies nearest to oneself. But this necessary fact and even duty of nationality is accidental; like age or sex it is a physical fatality which can be made the basis of specific and homely virtues; but it is not an end to pursue or a flag to flaunt or a privilege not balanced by a thousand incapacities. Yet of this distinction our contemporaries tend to make an idol, perhaps because it is the only distinction they feel they have left.[26]

Likewise, an allegiance related to patriotism (and, sometimes, nationalism) is loyalty to a given faction or a clique within one's country. It is justified only if it serves realization of some policy, otherwise it is a factor corroding the quality of socio-political life in democracy, discouraging potential virtuousness, and condemning disinterestedness and the love of truth to exile. Not exclusively

> a private and speculative side of our being … chafes under social servitude; it is also our moral conscience that actual society offends. Local loyalties condemn the spirit to injustice and overwhelm it with the ignominy of taking sides selfishly, for one's self against everybody else, for one's family, country, party, or religion against all others.[27]

In case of a modern empire, in turn, patriotism tends to be artificial because it pretends to unite two different sentiments: local love of home and "the pride of empire."[28] The second postulate contaminates the first, which may be spontaneous, with a set of arbitrary, usually militant interests and is disseminated among masses of people, who do not share either a home or a nationality. Santayana thinks the idea of an empire "has perhaps outlived its function" except it should be an empire of a different type, one that is governed

---

25   LR, 167.
26   George Santayana, *Winds of Doctrine. Studies in Contemporary Opinion* (London: J. M. Dent & Sons Ltd., 1913), 6–7.
27   DP, 66–67.
28   DP, 279.

rationally and motivated by an ideal of a peaceful coexistence and common interests rather than by patriotism.[29]

Finally, there appears the domination of mass society over its individual members, or in other words, the domination of quantity. The crowd is an irrational wave influencing the individual by contagion, coercion, and inertia alike. The domination exerted by society on its own members may be said to be "purposeful" only to a limited extent and in a degree in which a given society recognizes the direction of its institutions and laws and is capable of controlling them. Everything that is beyond the sphere of social self-awareness renders servitude to society more profound and involuntary.

> Quantity overpowers, and the irresistible crowd may cut us off from the very society which we might have liked and might have flourished in. The crowd compels us to adopt its language, manners, morals, and religion; and it is a rare freedom in human life when even a slight personal originality in any of these matters ... is not crushed at once by universal obloquy and persecution. This is not because the public is wicked but because it is the public.[30]

The problem of unwanted and destructive influence of society on the individual and the attitude of socio-political disengagement that may be assumed in response to that has been a universal philosophical problem and has reappeared from antiquity to the present day. Benjamin Constant proposed that the modern idea of liberty, as opposed to the ancient, champions individual independence, which embraces the freedom from political engagement.[31] But even a community-oriented thinker like Plato, whose concern was persuading excellent individuals to contribute to the constitution of *politeia*, admitted that under some circumstances disengagement is an understandable and even the right option.[32]

---

29   DP, 280. See also: DP, 402.
30   DP, 64–65.
31   Benjamin Constant, *The Liberty of Ancients Compared with that of Moderns* (1819).
32   See: Plato, *The Republic*, 496a-e. See also: Plato, *The Laws*, 770e. In the first case Socrates speaks of a minority of noble individuals: "they have seen sufficiently the madness of the many, and that no one who minds the business of the city does virtually anything sound, and that there is no ally with whom one could go to the aid of justice and be preserved. Rather ... one would perish before he has been of any use to the city or friends and be of no profit to himself and others. Taking all this into calculation, he keeps quiet and minds his own business – as a man in a storm ... stands aside under a little wall. Seeing others filled full of lawlessness, he is content if somehow he himself can live his life pure of

Santayana speaks of two basic attitudes assumed in the face of politics in the state of crisis and its corrupting influence. "The individual may elude the feeling, though not the fact, of subjection to society either by a willing conformity or by a mental reservation."[33] The first way, the way of conformity, is accessible to majority; the second and rare one, personally preferred by Santayana, is that of detachment. To be sure, Santayana is far from recommending the latter to all. The secret of the "mental reservation" mentioned by him "is not so much obdurate self-possession or stoicism as secession."[34] Science, literature, humor, religion and arts, he notes, "afford so many social sanctuaries to which you may escape from ordinary society;" you may even "abuse your country, and may migrate mentally, if not materially, into another world."[35] The literal or imaginative (inner) emigration, then, allows for a devotion to one of the non-political havens offered by culture, where one may thrive, not at all unproductively, while still contributing to the common good. It is quite obvious that this solution is viable only insofar as culture remains relatively free from politicization. *It is this freedom from politicization, or, in other words, disinterestedness of certain areas of common life that is an inexplicit yet vital postulate of Santayana's political thinking.* The aim is securing cultural and intellectual resources important not only for the attainment of vital liberty but also – in an indirect way – for a more conscious participation in a democracy, or, in other words, individual and collective self-government.

There seems to emerge a third way, let me call it "the middle way," one of moderation, selectivity, and refinement. It involves negotiation between conformity, ideal allegiances, and detachment. Yet, even this moderate attitude only rarely brings real satisfaction. From an existential perspective, none of the three options does. The necessities one decides to accept or even to like and then to build one's vital liberty upon do not deliver one from the necessity of choice, which is potentially tragic. As if echoing the complaints of Wilhelm Meister, Goethe's hero, who breaks away from his social environment and destiny, while striving for authenticity, Santayana says:

> The servile thing is not that we must fight and die – it is noble to accept that physical necessity. The shame is that we do not fight or die under our true colours. We neither assert ourselves with perfect integrity, nor

---

injustice." The source of this quotation is: Plato, *The Republic of Plato*, 2nd edition, trans., notes, and interpretive essay by Allan Bloom (Toronto: Basic Books, 2003), 496a-e.
33   DP, 65.
34   DP, 65.
35   DP, 65.

abdicate with perfect content; so that we are enslaved both in living and dying: enslaved to accidental coercions suffered against the harmony of our total nature, and enslaved to the general order of destiny which we have not the elevation of mind to observe philosophically, and to turn to spiritual uses.[36]

Having discussed examples of human servitude and its sources, as well as their ambiguous function in human life – constructive and suppressing at once – Santayana ends on a warning note, which is part of his critique of modern society. He thinks the prevailing ideologies of his time, the common denominator of which is their quantitative and instrumental orientation, make the fatal mistake of neglecting the individual and leaving the issue of broadly understood education (*paideia*) to the impersonal mechanisms within these systems. To quote the philosopher:

> foolish governments and philosophies in our day sometimes try to get on without reconciling the individual. The result sooner or later, is disaster; their constituency deserts them with a wonderfully sharp and sudden revulsion of feeling. Converts, infidels, and revolutionaries have bad memories and worse tempers. To justify their apostasy and heal the wounds it may have caused they require the balm of libeling their past and lording it over their new surroundings. They are the founders of the worst tyrannies.[37]

Different large-scale, socio-political and economic schemes – part and parcel of the militant order – that aim at the transformation of society, often under a banner of the liberation of man or universal wealth, treat man as a raw material, a means to an imagined brighter future. Thus, people are recruited to serve interests they don't understand and scarify their lives in endeavors of unknown costs. Their self-government and individual autonomy turn out to be fictitious, the future of democracy is put in peril.

---

36   DP, 67.
37   DP, 73.

CHAPTER 4

Militancy

4.1 Sources and Forms of Militancy

Existence is marked by "a universal dominance of crime"[1] and war is older than any political organization. War is not an essentially political phenomenon, even if politics is essentially militant. The essence of existence, according to Heraclitus, consisted in an unceasing conflict. Existence is "a blind and involuntary war … It should never be forgotten by anyone who does not wish to be deceived about this world and about the place of life and morality in it."[2] Already a child strives to dominate its surroundings and make them obedient to its will. Save for the fact that humans find themselves engaged in countless struggles with their environment, they are also subject to internal conflicts, personal "civil wars" between contrary desires and beliefs, which are among the sources of militancy. Aware of the limitations of similar analogies, Santayana nevertheless says of these inner conflicts that they are "reproduced on a larger scale in society and in rivalry of nations."[3] As succinctly phrased by him, "[y]et it is precisely this joint awareness of the passions, with the need, but hardly the power, of reducing them to harmony that renders human life *de iure* rational and *de facto* tragic."[4] Santayana, by the way, tends to see human life in terms of a tragicomedy or a tragic farce, whereby he follows in the footsteps of at least a few representatives of Spanish literary tradition, such as Miguel de Cervantes, whose *magnum opus* embodies a similar intuition, and Lope de Vega, one of the greatest Spanish dramatists, who argued about the superiority of tragicomedy, among other dramatic forms, in representing reality.[5] From this perspective, the political realm is a public stage of passions, vain efforts, betrayed ideals, and comic failures.

In the militant order, which manifests itself in a myriad of ways and in nearly all spheres of human activity, including economy, philosophy, religion,

---

1 DP, 228.
2 DP, 178. This, Santayana notes, was asserted in different ways by Heraclitus, Lucretius, and Darwin.
3 DP, 428.
4 DP, 374.
5 Lope de Vega, *The New Art of Writing Plays* (1609), trans. William T. Brewster, introduction by Brander Matthews (New York: Dramatic Museum of Columbia University, 1914).

historiography, art, politics, and military operations, man is willing to be the master of his own fate and, often, to dominate others by persuasion and coercion, by reforming and conquering. Thus, turning from an involuntary mechanism into a deliberate effort to dominate, conscious of its enemy as embodied by "all dissenting forms of existence … [,] war becomes intentional, self-righteous, and fanatical."[6]

Militancy, as *modus operandi* of will, on the one hand contributes to civilizational progress, and, on the other, generates self-destructive mechanisms in the very civilizations the development of which it had accelerated, and the impoverishment of the very cultures it had once vivified. It is not militancy in itself but certain aggressive forms of it, labeled by Santayana as barbarism, militarism, tribalism, or acquisitive vice (greed) that he quarrels with in his writings. Once an absolute condemnation of rivalry and struggle is recognized as the standard of virtue, he thinks, it "draws the ladder up after it as it climbs; and the earth remains altogether abandoned to the less sensitive sort of virtue that begins with the will to live."[7] What bothers Santayana, then, are social and cultural results of a long-lasting domination of certain forms of militancy, which may involve, among others, the suppression of liberal arts (i.e., those identified by spontaneity and free function), the marginalization of spiritual life, the rising of extreme economic inequalities, the instrumentalization of human activity, as a result of which "nothing will be done for its own sake or enjoyed in its own fugitive presence."[8] These phenomena, sometimes justified as the inevitable price of political sovereignty or material progress, impoverish culture and weaken both individual and social resistance against unwelcome forms of political domination. Besides, a predatory sort of militancy is at odds with Santayana's humanism and seems to him to be unworthy of a human being, "who has long walked in the path of reconsideration, repentance, and the desire for union."[9] Santayana sometimes sees culture in terms of a tension between what he calls "polite humanity" and "brute humanity," being, perhaps, an inexplicit reference – with an opposite vector of sympathy – to Nietzsche's distinction between the Apollonian and the Dionysian element.

---

6 DP, 179.
7 DP, 228.
8 Santayana, introduction to LR1, 8. In the same passage fanaticism is famously defined as follows: "Fanaticism consists in redoubling your effort when you have forgotten your aim. An earnestness which is out of proportion to any knowledge or love of real things, which is therefore dark and inward and thinks itself deeper than the earth's foundations-such an earnestness, until culture turns it into intelligent interests, will naturally breed a new mythology."
9 DP, 228.

Unbridled militancy misses the wisdom necessary to recognize the conditions of human well-being and set them as guidance for political action. Militancy, which originates in human will, receives definition and direction in imagination. Ideas conveyed by art, religion, science and philosophy may be employed as a means of rivalry and domination in politics. Ideas guide the directive imagination of humans, evoking passions that are far from innocent. "The militant motive is rather political; and imagination helps only to render this motive clear and communicable."[10] Intellectual militancy need not always be idealistic or positively dogmatic. It may manifest itself in a negative way, through a skeptical or empiricist doctrine, precisely by way of its indiscriminate refusal to "bow to any alien power or admit the existence of any hidden thing."[11]

The Sophists were militant in their rebellion against the oppression of tradition and convention. The early Santayana appreciates "the personal independence" and "the brave humanity" of those who made man the measure of all things and the "the happy freedom of the Greeks from religious dogma [that] made them the first natural philosophers, [and] their happy political freedom [that] made them the first moralists."[12] But decades later, Santayana, whose humanism has been put to the test of the turbulent twentieth century, notes that the Sophists may have overlooked the anthropological function of the myths they dismissed speculatively. These myths were spontaneous and almost unconscious creations of human imagination, conveying some of "the vital secrets that might lie beneath the surface of events."[13] This, by the way, is in line with how Santayana conceives of religion in naturalistic and symbolic terms, but there is a change in the thinker's relation to what he calls religious myths. While at the turn of the century he tended to approach them as obstacles on the path to rational life, in *Dominations and Powers* he seems to be somewhat more cautious about emancipation from religious tradition, just as he seems less convinced about the futility of thinking in metaphysical terms. His conclusion is that a skeptic's speculative success may happen to be, anthropologically, a Pyrrhic Victory. This is due to the fact that the dismissal of old myths may lead – and it usually does – to the creation of new ones such as the worship of sense data, facts, or language. "Blind to this fact, both ancient and modern critics have made a metaphysic out of appearance, and have thought themselves enlightened for being deceived only by the most artificial

---

10   DP, 192.
11   DP, 192.
12   Santayana, introduction to LR1, 11.
13   DP, 192.

of illusions."¹⁴ The new myths, when they become a dominant ideology, may turn into a *cultural tyranny*. The late Santayana, in the spirit of the Frankfurt School, believed a complete enlightenment impossible. Humans adopt myths as sources of overarching paradigms organizing their worldview. Such myths may be called militant by virtue of their very power over human imagination and action. A myth may be beneficent and wise when it produces "concretions in arts and morals," without enslaving human imagination, impairing understanding or adaptation.¹⁵ As one learns from a letter to Sydney Hook, Santayana thinks the Catholic doctrine might fulfill these requirements insofar as it "virtually transmits a wise conception of human virtues and vices and a wise mood." If taken literally, however, "it is fanatical and repressive" and has been used by the Catholic Church as a tool of persuasion and coercion. Thus, he contrasts two interpretations and two applications of the same doctrine – the imaginative and spiritual one against the militant. When the "illusion" created by the dominant myth is "incomplete," porous, and approached as metaphorical, it serves humans better as it leaves room for autonomous thinking. "[The] integrating dominant organization and myth will have to … fit the impulses and capacities of the age … and need not prevent free thought in those really capable of thinking."¹⁶

Myths and other thought-organizing paradigms precede and limit any political establishment. So do local customs and traditional social institutions, which often happen to be more respected and integrated by society, and, hence, more powerful than law. Agents of political authority only rarely are the inventors of coercion – "[by] the time a law is established, an organ for enforcing it already exists in the strong right arm of the legislator."¹⁷ The generative order of society, of which we are talking here, is compared by Santayana to a natural language, which is shared, quite unreflectively, by the whole people.

> [L]arge questions of policy and of human ideals are settled behind the politician's back by the growth of social institutions … all arise and are virtually in operation before a law or an explicit agreement consecrates or defines them; and the history of politics is accordingly reduced almost entirely to the compromises and transitions between ruling interests when they conflict openly and threaten a civil war.¹⁸

---

14   DP, 193.
15   Letter to Sydney Hook, 6 June 1938, LGS6: 139–140.
16   All quotations in this paragraph: Letter to Sydney Hook, 6 June 1938, LGS6: 139–140.
17   DP, 78.
18   DP, 79.

Government, then, appears as an extension, a complication of, and an intermediary in these processes. Initially, it represents an inherited status-quo, being but a late stage in the generative chain.[19]

Whereas the generative order, with its inertia, never ceases to influence politics, in the militant order government seems to be "always an evil and sometimes also a good, as war is."[20] It may assume a form of an unending conquest, "a chronic raid," a tool of "raising taxes and soldiers," a despotic regime.[21] In such a case, more than in others, it is evident that "a government's [criminal] origin has nothing to do with its legitimacy."[22] But even a foreign government founded on conquest or a domestic absolutism, when representative of some virtue, may happen to be able to define "the commonwealth it tends to preserve" and act on behalf of its interests in ways that are defendable rationally.[23] It also may, with time, develop in a direction of a democracy or a republican "individualism" founded in citizenship. Metaphorically speaking, it is this rationality armed with some ulterior moral horizon that, under favorable circumstances, may "redeem" the violence of the government's origin and the coercion of which the government necessarily is a vehicle. Besides, these reflections lead one to note, once again, that national sovereignty is not a priority in Santayana's political thought.

An example of a destructive influence of government's militancy on culture, may be an imposition of a formal linguistic uniformity on a variety of dialects.[24] Government, acting in the name of uniformity, which helps it to

---

19   See: LR, 120.
20   DP, 79.
21   LR, 121.
22   LR, 122.
23   LR, 120. There may even be one benefit related to being subject to a foreign tyranny insofar as "[o]ne distant universal enemy is less oppressive than a thousand unchecked pilferers and plotters at home." LR, 125.
24   These reflections merit comparing to those by Toynbee on so-called *lingua franca*. The British historian writes: "If we now proceed to examine the causes and the consequences of the transformation of local mother-tongues into oecumenical lingue franche, we shall find that a language which wins this kind of victory over its rivals usually owes its success to the social advantage of having served, in an age of social disintegration, as the tool of some community that has been potent either in war, or in commerce. We shall also find that languages, like human beings, are unable to win victories without paying any price; and the price a language pays for becoming a lingua franca is the sacrifice of its native subtleties." Arnold J. Toynbee, *Study of History*, one-volume edition (New York and London: Oxford University Press, 1947), 468–469. In another interesting remark we read: "In disintegrating civilizations ... we are apt to see languages ... waging internecine wars with one another and conquering, when victorious, wide dominions at their discomfited rivals' expense." Toynbee, *A Study of History*, 467.

secure a greater authority to itself, may "kill" a language along with the whole microcosm conveyed by a given oral and/or written tradition that evidences the cultural evolution and specificity of a community or a region. This is one way of suppressing cultural heterogeneity and autonomy of a (minority) community. Likewise, philosophy, culture, religion, and, one may add, science, become "national" and are employed "in the service of trade and political conquest."[25] Whatever may be the benefits of these processes, and there surely are some, they occur at the price of weakening – at least temporarily – human and spiritual immunity against the vicissitudes of politics. Whether the benefits outstrip the costs is to be assessed only in each particular context.

One of the definitions of government assumed by Santayana, a disillusioned one and matching the first, empirical, understanding of politics in terms of *Realpolitik*, is: "[g]overnment is a modification of war, a means of using compulsion without shedding so much blood."[26] An important passage follows, which I will quote for it conciseness and clarity:

> All government is therefore potential war; and if this threat and the ability to use force disappear, government ceases. In the country for instance, in which laws are not enforced, there is to that extent no government. Those who fancy themselves in power are simply one or more social philosophers editing precepts for the public; the public admires these precepts, and the philosophers' function is fulfilled. But if this academy employs an armed force to arrest and eventually execute or mulct anyone who does not respect their edicts, then they are a government; and to take people prisoners, to kill and despoil them are acts of war. Every government is essentially an army carrying on a perpetual campaign in its own territory; it is always up in arms against actual or possible faction – called illegality or crime.[27]

---

25 DP, 81.
26 DP, 79. Compare to Max Weber's definition of the state and politics: "a human community that (successfully) claims a monopoly on the legitimate use of physical force within a given territory." Thus, the state is "the sole source of the 'right' to use violence. Hence, politics … means striving to share power or striving to influence the distribution of power." Max Weber, *Politics as a Vocation*, trans. and introduction by H.H. Gerth and C. Wright Mills (New York: Oxford University Press, 1946), 4.
27 DP, 79. In the light of this idea of government in action, justice becomes a priority if the citizens' well-being is not to be altogether lost sight of. This idea of government is, of course, at a far remove from the Platonic ideal, where "war is not politics by other means (Clausewitz); nor is politics war by other means (Foucault). For Plato if politics is simply another manifestation of war or war a manifestation of politics, the polis is on the road to self-destruction or defeat." See: Wallach, *The Platonic Political Art*, 253, note 82.

Government is responsible for the defense against enemies and waging wars, which, by the way, tend to converge – too often against the interest of the governed – in "preventive defense" or "timely aggression."[28] Nevertheless, this is one of the functions that confirm governmental authority in a most pronounced way. "War is impossible without a virtual government and government without a virtual war."[29] Insofar as government secures peace, it may be referred to as "latency of war." Government may not be an absolute necessity, but its disappearance would probably invite more chaos and more wars. By way of a similar, paradoxical reversal, Santayana alludes, ironically, to governments and leaders (being sources of laws) as being relatives with, or heirs to, criminal element, sometimes by the right of their distant historical origins, sometimes by their function of force administration, or by a simple psychological affinity. The "romantic criminal," the "sentimental bandit" "is a monarch or a general or the founder of a colony, or of a great business enterprise. Sometimes too he is a revolutionary leader, an enthusiastic humanitarian. He is not robbing and murdering for his own benefit."[30]

In Santayana's materialistic hermeneutics of politics, the boundary between the inhuman, physical necessity and the necessity imposed by governments turns out to be vague, as evidenced by his analysis of tyranny. The term "tyranny" has two senses – rhetorical and legal-historical. According to the first one, a government or a regimen is tyrannical insofar as "they trample upon many other people in many unnecessary ways."[31] Tyranny in this sense, from the perspective of a good government, is a grave mistake, even though a degree of oppression never disappears completely from *any* government's operation. Machiavelli, whose views Santayana often contradicts, was prudent to place the interest of Italy above the interests of local tyrants. "It is the absence of solid intelligence that renders governments cruel to their subjects and fatal to themselves."[32] From a legal point of view, in turn, tyranny stands for an absolute government that has usurped power by *a coup d'état*. The turnover involves the abolition of former privileges, the disestablishment of the ruling class and the existing elites. This might happen to be, under such "admirable tyrants" like Caesar or Napoleon, a welcome change, the beginning of a happier order.[33]

---

28 See: DP 424.
29 DP, 82.
30 DP, 213.
31 DP, 220.
32 DP, 426.
33 DP, 223. Santayana mentions here also his contemporary leaders that "may be smoothing the way for socialism, and establishing it in a form less hostile to tradition than a revolution could be," having in mind, most probably, Mussolini.

Nevertheless, Santayana emphasizes, there are deeper processes that the change is expressive of. Probably, were it not for this or that concrete tyrant, the change would have occurred anyway, in other circumstances, by means of other human agents, allied, more or less (un-)consciously, with some material tide. "Behind the visible tyrant stands an invisible one."[34] The same rule obtains for the metaphorical "tyranny" – the sacrifice people are forced to suffer under any government. The remarks about the "invisible tyrant" testify to the late Santayana's controversial tendency to diminish the weight of human agency in oppressive regimes by incorporating them into a bigger picture of mysterious material tides.

The above idea seems to express a degree of fatalism hardly acceptable for readers attached to more affirmative vision of human agency and responsibility. However, it may be somewhat hasty to charge the thinker with a profound fatalism. As mentioned earlier, at the outset of his treatise, Santayana clearly states that human psyches are agents in politics. This is in accordance with his conception of psychic freedom.[35] In the course of his reflections, he sheds light on the limits of this agency but never discounts the idea. One may say that this strategy, helpful in revealing the potent militant and hubristic threads in the Western culture, belongs to his critical repertoire. A "look from beyond" has traditionally been assumed by philosophers, sociologists, cultural anthropologists and historians, from Hegel, Marx and Spengler to Toynbee and Girard, all of whom were explaining political phenomena in terms of larger processes to which human agents are subject. By tying the realm of human affairs to an inscrutable material dynamics, Santayana introduces into this realm an inhuman and partly unpredictable element; the presence of the generative order, in its turn, emphasizes human embeddedness in history and culture.

Having said this, one may still note that emphasizing the influence of subterranean and unconscious forces on major socio-political changes, as Santayana does, may have an eviscerating impact on the moral and imaginative power of the people to oppose what they consider unjust and harmful in an unbearable degree.[36] To refer to a real-life example, an enormous

---

34   SP, 221.
35   Angus Kerr-Lawson distinguishes between psychic/vital and moral freedom in Santayana and points to the fact that none of them makes appeal to indeterminism. The former type is assumed in the latter kind of freedom, which involves a sense of authorship of action. Angus Kerr-Lawson, "Freedom and Free Will in Spinoza and Santayana," *The Journal of Speculative Philosophy, New Series* 14, no. 4 (2001), 247.
36   Among Santayana's contemporaries, John Dewey accused Santayana of " 'kneeling before the unknowable.' " See: Thomas M. Alexander, *The Human Eros. Eco-Ontology and the Aesthetics of Existence* (New York: Fordham University Press, 2013), 228. Beth Singer

faith in the meaningfulness and efficacy of a common, grass-root initiative, as well as a sustained effort at the level of practical organization, were needed to fight communism – which, to be sure, was experienced by majority as a condition of enslavement – and bring about the desired change in Poland in 1989. While Santayana might have been right that a deeper material "wave" was there to "feed" the people's conscious efforts, this makes no difference at all to the facts of the social plane, namely – that the mass "Solidarity" movement and the so-called bloodless revolution leading to the desired change, which *many well-wishing skeptics had considered impossible*, required precisely an unmitigated courage and faith in the possibility of *causing* it; in other words, it required a powerful directive imagination, a sense of authorship, supported by a conviction of moral legitimacy, leaving aside the countless material, daily challenges that had to be coped with. This is only to say that the perspective of subterranean forces, leaving aside the fact that it may complicate – in a meaningful way – a hermeneutic and existential plane of Santayana's political thinking, morally is a doubled-edged blade. It is in this context that John Lachs pointed to the weaknesses of Santayana's political reflection, without robbing it of a hermeneutic and critical value. I think Daniel Moreno is right too when saying that:

> Santayana professed not to lead any effort against artificial social systems, but rather simply to point out their nature and await their own eventual collapse. In the same way as when he identified fallacious human projections, he did not expect them ... to disappear without more of them occurring. The profound naturalism that characterized his thought approximates fatalism at this point: if certain societies make place for themselves and become established, it is because the sufficient conditions were given for them there, whether they happened to be spontaneous or artificial.[37]

---

    suggests that in the light of Santayana's materialism, "[p]olitical action ... is reduced to the status of a process, rather than being an art ... This position of Santayana's is paradoxical, in view of the importance he places on reason and art." Singer, *The Rational Society*, 14. I agree that Santayana's materialism poses a problem of agency, but I disagree with the claim that this should lead to the general conclusion about Santayana denying political action the status of an art. Rather, I would say that political action may and should aspire to become an art, which happens when the two senses of politics distinguished by Santayana converge.

37 Moreno, *Santayana the Philosopher*, 94.

The way Moreno looks at the issue reveals yet another important feature of Santayana's political thought, which I discussed earlier, namely – the dynamics formed by the categories of nature, spontaneous (usually synonymous with the generative) and artificial (usually connected to the militant aspect of human activity) orders, and facticity. While Santayana tended to value the quality of naturalness positively, facticity was something value-neutral and unworthy of admiration. I am inclined to think, then, that it is his materialism even more than naturalism that makes his (supposed) fatalism legitimate. Santayana, though, was not always consistent in his use of concepts, so my intuition is but a loose speculation.

Coming back to the issue of tyranny, great changes usually do not originate in political deliberations, even though ideas are by no means irrelevant. "The art of an intelligent tyrant, like Lenin, is to read the signs of the times, [and] to jump into the breach."[38] Santayana does not say that Lenin was not the author of his actions or was merely a victim of something he did not understand. Indeed, many people fell victim to the crude militancy, the fanaticism, and the degradation of the humane element that blighted the endeavor he represented. And Lenin might have fallen victim too – to the illusion of his own power and the tragic illusion of the possibility of an efficacious, human-controlled plan of the overall correction of the human world. Rebels, Santayana admitted, are sometimes right in their rebellion against some arbitrary and oppressive status quo, "but they are probably wrong in thinking their own heresy less arbitrary, and not likely to be oppressive in far more important respects."[39] The particular case of the Bolshevik Revolution and its aftermath confirmed this intuition.

In chapter two I remarked briefly on Santayana's habitual reluctance towards revolutions. As for his view of the French Revolution, Santayana, consciously or not, followed into the footsteps of Edmund Burke, a thinker he respected.[40] He criticized the Revolution indiscriminately, as a work of destruction, led by fanatics, haters of any orthodoxy and discipline, who did not recognize that Christianity and feudalism were natural stages in human history, and, rather than reforming them, wanted to erase them and establish a liberty "without foundations in nature or history."[41] Like Burke, Santayana thought of the revolutionaries as speculators, driven by "a desire to have everything their own way," blinded to particular circumstances by theories modelled on an extreme

---

38   DP, 221.
39   DP, 222.
40   Santayana mentions Burke only once in DP, as an example of a "noble mind," someone capable of preserving intellectual autonomy in the middle of political faction. See: DP, 389.
41   DP, 224.

case.[42] All in all, it was characteristic of Santayana to distrusts revolutions for two reasons. First, revolutions often involve a wholesale negation of past achievements, disrupting any beneficent continuity, and, second, the harm involved in the destructiveness of revolutions tends to outrun the benefits they bring. Reflecting on his own ideas and their reception, he wrote:

> My naturalism and humanism seemed to them [Santayana's liberal readers] to give carte blanche to revolution: and so they do, if the revolution represents a deeper understanding of human nature and human virtue than tradition does at any moment; but, if we make allowance for the inevitable symbolism and convention in human ideas, tradition must normally represent human nature and human virtue much better than impatience with tradition can do.[43]

While he would probably allow for some exceptions from this rule, one may say that sometimes Santayana's attachment to what he calls the generative order seems to be motivated by a fear of anarchy, and, as generalized as it is, clearly enters into conflict with some other of his ideas. Let me also note that, given Santayana's gift of a penetrating criticism, not devoid of social sensitivity, as evidenced, for example, by his essays on liberalism, one might expect from him somewhat more rigorous and impartial assessment of the circumstances of the French Revolution. This is something, I'd suggest, he could have done without the need to change his fundamental sympathies and convictions.

To conclude, let me note that the idea of militancy, the most emblematic manifestations of which involve government, reform, revolution, economic enterprise, and war, is a hermeneutic and critical tool serving to define the sphere of human initiative in the world that pertains to politics, yields itself to criticism and requires criticism. Militant action may draw on the generative order or rebel against it, try to ignore or destroy it. The militant order may engender the rational one and let itself be guided by it, or inhibit, deviate, and subjugate it. Reflection on and criticism of different forms of militancy are

---

42 Harvey Mansfield, Jr., "Edmund Burke," in *History of Political Philosophy*, third edition, ed. Leo Strauss and Joseph Cropsey (Chicago and London: Chicago University Press, 1987), 691. For a relevant piece of criticism by Burke see: Edmund Burke, *Reflections on the Revolution in France*, ed. William B. Todd (New York: Rinehart & Co., 1959), 69–78.

43 George Santayana, "Apologia pro Mente Sua," in *The Philosophy of George Santayana*, ed. Paul Arthur Schilpp (Evanston, Illinois: Northwestern University Press, 1940), 559.

meant to enlighten human will as to its motivations, entanglements, perspectives, and long-term consequences of human undertakings.

4.2   War and Wars of Imagination

"Between sensation and abstract discourse lies a region of deployed sensibility or synthetic representation. ... called imagination."[44] Militancy, born in will, acquires definite forms in imagination and this is problematic because human imagination is "extraordinarily fertile and redundant."[45] Unless controlled by an integral personality mediated by cultural and social checks, in falls easy prey to unquenched desires, delusions, and manipulation. Gaining self-knowledge, knowledge of the world, attaining a sane and coherent interpretation of one's position and prospects in the world – all these provide ample opportunity for failure. One's cultural and social environment may soften but also deepen the disorientation. Politics, where interests collide and actors are engaged in determining other people's fate, is likely to be the source of deceit and abuse. On a more abstract level, one may compare each psyche to a unique, embodied "point" on a map of universal radiation, a vital center, where energies converge and are transmuted in a way that is supportive or destructive from the perspective of a given incarnate being and other beings that happen to be within the range of its influence. Humans, as individuals and as groups, imagine, translate and channel these fluctuating configurations into languages and structures expressive of a powers-dominations context, where any fact or thing may be ascribed a meaning.

Needless to say, these interpretations are inescapably local and biased. This is where the broad field of politics extends. Its middle name is "ambiguity."[46] It is fueled by will and imagination, its stakes and results always concern interests and real powers at work. Politics oscillates in-between honest representation and deception, legitimacy and usurpation, virtue and vice. If Santayana thought monarchy might inspire hope for a good and rational government, it was because a monarch – under happy circumstances – might constitute a well-integrated, virtuous, competent, and transparent center of control – a challenging combination for a democratic kind of representation, especially when competing parties and factions engage themselves and their supporters in endless *wars of imagination* and *plays of ambiguity*. Thus, democracy, especially in the time of crisis, becomes a seedbed of bifurcating, chaotic militancy,

---

44   LR, 303.
45   DP, 191.
46   DP, 183.

perhaps leading to the formation of some sort of post-democratic oligarchy, or, worse, totalitarianism.

Collective imagination, like public opinion, is like a no man's land, a prospective battlefield, waiting to be conquered and colonized for a season, even for a moment. Human life, however, is not a no man's land. When treated merely instrumentally, dominated and exploited, its loss is real, irretrievable, often irreparable. The discrepancy between the fluidity and ambiguity of the public sphere and the fragility and preciousness of the lives of concrete individuals is what makes politics a sphere of all imaginable abuses and a great test for humans. This explains Santayana's repetitive references to virtue and moral sanctions in politics,[47] as well as the introduction of the horizon of vital liberty, which may be seen as constituting a sort of "categorical imperative" for a modern political imagination in the time of peace. The idea of vital liberty is meant to grasp a specifically human interest and, as such, it may provide limitations and suggest directions for political action. To frame a bolder idea, let me say that *a government that in its goals and operations fails to protect vital liberty or suppresses it in unnecessary ways, sacrifices the true human interests to defend some other, arbitrary ones*. Morally, such a government undermines its own legitimacy.

A democratic partisan system offers ample opportunity for wars of imagination to multiply. Their medium, and victim at once, is language, which intrudes into the interplay of will and imagination, grafting there artificial interests and demands. It is possible because will, unless enlightened and disciplined, is blind, and imagination, which is susceptible to manipulation, "inclines man often to folly and sometimes to crime."[48] Thus, man may be inclined to desire illusory goods, someone else's goods, or ones that would not satisfy his true needs; in other words, he may be enlisted in the service of false ideologies and alien interests. Militancy arises both between agents supporting competing narratives and within man, in the "the indecision or self-contradiction of animal Will in pursuing distractedly incompatible goods at the same time."[49] It is as if desire and imagination – the two outlets into infinity – betrayed the fact of incarnation and the sense of finitude, both of which carry a promise of peace

---

[47] In this context, the following understanding of the term "moral" is worth taking into account: "Morals ... are an economic discipline by which the human psyche learns to accept the conditions of life, while transforming them as much as possible in its own favour." DP, 190. A moral sanction, then, would refer to the limits and conditions of the said accepting and transforming reality with regard to interests, including rules for defining the very interests.

[48] DP, 183.

[49] DP, 183.

to human self by letting it "be content in each case with special virtues which its organs and its world are capable of realizing."[50]

Human will, then, may be called the "raw" or "naked" agent in politics. It fights its battles under different banners and in different socio-political configurations, affecting bodies and imagination, sometimes straining them and playing one against the other. In a (post-) democratic milieu it works through confusion and persuasion, its trusted allies being the power of contagion, the desire for identity and recognition, fear of disease, poverty, and death. Imagination attaches appetites to will, appetites that may cost a lifetime of vain effort and in the end bring despair rather than satisfaction. As Daniel Bell noted, social, cultural, and economic factors may bend imagination "purposefully" towards contradictory ideals, such as asceticism and immediate consumption, at the same time. Santayana emphasized that while material security is the basis for vital liberty, an impression that material prosperity is man's highest goal and warrants man's well-being is an illusion or a half-truth at best.

It merits to evoke, once again, de Tocqueville's ruminations on democracy. A sympathetic observer of the American democratic practice, he was at once a friendly critic, able to discern potentially dangerous tendencies inherent in a democratic society aspiring to the equality of conditions. One of them was its passion for material well-being. He noted that the change from an aristocratic, static social organization, where material well-being was a question to a large degree determined by birth, to a democratic and liberal one, where nominally everyone had a chance to become rich or fall into poverty, caused in people certain insatiability of appetites and constant restlessness. Material concerns dominated people's imagination, and the only outlet left for the suppressed spiritual needs of some was religious radicalism. Tocqueville blamed equality for making people "unreservedly surrender their hearts, their imagination, their lives" to the pursuit of some goods and "lose sight of those more precious goods that constitute the glory and grandeur of the human race."[51]

Whereas Santayana shared this insight with Tocqueville, he was critical of a system where social status was inherited. Neither did he cherish illusions about an alleged moral excellence of hereditary aristocracy, even though, as I will show in the seventh chapter, he believed that some kind of social hierarchy, if expressive of just principles and embodied in just institutions, could be of benefit to society as a whole. Despite his decisive dismissal of Plato's political utopia, one may trace an inspiration by the Platonic ideal of social harmony

---

50 DP, 184.
51 Tocqueville, *Democracy in America*, 621.

in the early Santayana of *The Life of Reason*, who says that an aristocratic society "might be a perfect heaven if the variety and superposition of function in it expressed a corresponding diversity in its members' faculties and ideals."[52]

The potential precariousness of democracy seems to be deepened by the (*de iure*) importance of private judgment on which political choice is said to depend and the (*de facto*) prevalence of public opinion. The latter meant for Santayana social control by irrational and ephemeral forces, centered around capricious views, not grounded in a genuine quality debate. Public opinion, notes César García, had a "gag effect" on individual liberty and intellectual autonomy.[53] Yet, private judgment posed problems too. Despite the fact that "[t]he maxim that every man is the best judge of his own interests recommends itself by its simplicity and the air of honest and good sense," Santayana suggests it may be misleading. What is the scope of one's interests? Do they include (potentially infinite) interests of one's closest others or even the interest of one's country? Do they concern primarily material wellbeing or rather moral and spiritual condition? And what "if such ulterior interests are included, does … [one] remain the best judge of what is best also in those perhaps indefinite careers?"[54] The issue of the scope of interests immediately directs our attention to the question of man's inescapable ignorance, pertaining to – here Santayana is thoroughly democratic – everybody (although not in the same degree), including sages and experts. Other than that, to understand one's interests, it does not suffice to

> know what we want; the crucial points are whether the present circumstances render it obtainable and whether we have the means of securing it. On both these points, in the political field, the ordinary man thinks little and gets that little wrong.[55]

This being said, Santayana does not dismiss either the private judgment of the average man or an expert's opinion. In an ideal world governing might be executed by a single, virtuous, experienced and knowledgeable individual, or a

---

52   LR, 132.
53   César García, "Santayana on Public Opinion," *Overheard in Seville: Bulletin of the Santayana Society* 23 (2005): 23–27. The author compares and finds similarities between Santayana's views on public opinion, which he regards as insightful and timely, with those of Walter Lippman, Santayana's student and the author of the well-known book *Public Opinion* (New York: Harcourt, Brace and Company, 1922).
54   DP, 184.
55   DP, 185.

group of individuals, truly understanding the needs of the people and willing to represent them, with the support of experts. But in the concrete reality of his times, he sees no actual alternative to reliance on private judgment. "The art of governing mankind is difficult: until a true master of it is found, we may well prefer to try experiments ourselves, and run our chances in detail".[56] This, however, brings us back to the problem of knowledge and reliable, established authorities, to the opinions of which one might resort safely.

In this respect, the liberal democratic (and capitalistic) environment, despite the fact that information is plenty and within easy reach, and experts multiply, engenders confusion. In the contemporary world certain tendencies described by Santayana have been radicalized. The number of "'authorities' to tell the average man what he should think and attempt to do, if he wishes to prosper" is out of any proportion and while knowledge is fragmentary, these authorities are "often technical, and at odds among themselves."[57] Experts specialize in narrow fields and may be ignorant as to the broader context of what they profess and the possible effects of its application. Besides, a valuable piece of advice by reliable experts may sink in the ocean of demagoguery.

This more or less acute state of confusion – usually revealed fully only at a time of crisis – is conducive to the flourishing of sectarianism, where "each self-confident authority or sudden fashion attracts plenty of adepts" for whose "perplexed mind and empty heart" it becomes "a refuge from apathy and a social bond."[58] Ideologies,[59] if skillfully crafted, fitting into the existing

---

[56]   DP, 184.
[57]   DP, 185.
[58]   DP, 185.
[59]   The term "ideology" as used in this book combines two types of meanings, as distinguished by Raymond Geuss: the descriptive and pejorative one. First, it stands for a system of beliefs, usually forming a world-view. Second, it seeks to change the way of life and influence action. Third, along the line of the Frankfurt School's approach to ideology, it misrepresents some aspects of reality, socio-political in particular, in order to serve particular interests of some group(s). Emancipation from delusion, then, would constitute the main aim of a critical school's program. As Geuss notes, such criticism must be based on an assumption that agents that are subjects to ideology have some *"real" or "true" interests* that may be uncovered. Obviously, in Santayana's philosophy this condition is met already at the level of the psyche being a natural agent in politics. See: Raymond Geuss, *The Idea of Critical Theory. Habermas and the Frankfurt School* (Cambridge: Cambridge University Press, 1981), 4–15, 45–46. Santayana uses the term "ideology" very rarely but when he speaks of false and/or artificial worldviews dissipated by propaganda and meant to affect beliefs, attitudes, and action, he clearly means ideologies. Interestingly, Santayana emphasizes the key function of idolatry in such "artificial" sets of beliefs, which makes it akin to myth. Idolatry usually consists in attributing "dramatic and moral qualities to diffused natural agencies." Secular religions, such as worship of progress, power, or nature

socio-cultural patterns and addressing some actual material concerns – a real inequity, claim, fear, or ambition – may easily penetrate the imagination of the many and gain followers. Thus, they are capable of polarizing societies and the world. "[I]t is by contagion that mankind is most easily, radically, and perfectly educated."[60]

No particular solution is offered to this problem, as it is probably assumed that no universal one exists, other than perhaps the generally advocated by Santayana sanity. Knowledge itself, insofar as it is expressed in ideal terms and claims to be the knowledge of the facts of existence, "implies a literal and immeasurable ignorance, mitigated by a constant possibility"[61] of practical verification. The application of knowledge, in turn, requires sanity. The latter seems to consist in sound judgment, attentiveness to circumstances, respecting the fact that there is an external world peopled by others, a degree of common sense and moderation, the ability to learn the lessons of experience. Under favorable conditions, sanity may aspire to wisdom. Pure speculation in human affairs, without reference to some experience and virtue, may be a misleading guide, an "ignorant and spiritually dangerous course."[62]

With regard to political context and the desired soundness of opinion there, one is advised to distrust public opinion, which is a treacherous medium and subject to endless "contagion ..., hearsay, exaggeration, misunderstanding, and artificial excitement."[63] More trustworthy seem to be judgments of an autonomous, competent and experienced individual, who has let himself recognized as someone "able to embody his convictions"[64] and act consistently in the public realm, with emphasis on concrete institutional solutions that are able to gain adherents, rather than engaging in the bloating of public opinion. The reliance on virtuous individuals' judgments rather than those of the public connects Santayana, once again, to the Platonic tradition. Let me note that while his criticism of the dangers related to the power of public opinion seems justified, Santayana would have been more impartial had he stressed the fact

---

       may be understood as ideologies in a very broad and abstract sense. See for example: DP, 15 and 216. See also: Daniel Bell, *The End of Ideology* (Illinois: The Free Press of Glencoe, 1960), 369–375.

60   George Santayana, "On Public Opinion," in *The Birth of Reason And Other Essays* (New York: Columbia University Press, 1968), 102. I will refer to this source as BR. Elsewhere Santayana speaks of fashion that "it produces innovation without reason and imitation without benefit." See: LR, 236.

61   DP, 189.
62   DP, 187.
63   DP, 188.
64   DP, 189.

that, as George Orwell notes, certain fatal, political mistakes, mistakes of great "magnitude can only be made, or at any rate they are most likely to be made, in countries where public opinion has *no* power."[65]

Now, Santayana finds an average politician in a democracy untrustworthy. "Everything in the politician's mind represents the real world, except his politics."[66] To start with, politicians tend to either manipulate history or fail in their interpretations of it. They are both poor historians and poor prophets. It is important insofar as politics often seeks justification and legitimacy in history and visions of the future. Politicians try to weave current events into the texture of this or that alleged historical continuity. Meanwhile, "[t]hat which really determines action, and thereby the course of history, is the combined momentum of all the bodies and psyches concerned."[67] The materialist idea of a "combined momentum," especially when associated with a vision of a multi-centered universe, although not developed further by the author, seems to discount those linear and universalist conceptions of history that are teleological or eschatological, as mental illusions. Santayana rejects also a dialectical vision of history as it "inspires the rhetoric of demagogues" and "only perpetuates profound misunderstandings."[68]

Study of history is bound to be imperfect, but it may at least exemplify an honest effort at approximating the truth, when unbiased, disinterested, critical, ready to accept fragmentariness, attentive to the details of material culture, social institutions, habits and traditions, "the scattered bits of self-revelation" conveyed in past artistic achievements.[69] In Santayana's era this modern approach to history was not yet popular. "Not one political philosopher or prophet that I know of, not one speculative historian" writes Santayana, "has dared to chart the ocean on which he sails."[70] Unwilling to admit contingency and discontinuity, "[t]hey can see the universe only in the likeness of a ship, and its history as the log of voyage. They cannot conceive the wisdom of Aristotle (so little a historian and so much a humanist) when he said that the arts have been lost many times and re-established."[71] As for politicians in their daily practice, unless an abrupt material turmoil disrupts their sense of security, they may cherish a very superficial sense of temporality as merely sailing over "the waves of opinion," and elude

---

65 Orwell, "James Burnham and the Managerial Revolution," 179. My emphasis.
66 DP, 194.
67 DP, 195.
68 DP, 197.
69 DP, 195.
70 DP, 195.
71 DP, 196.

themselves that "they would sail safely for ever."[72] The reader will find more about Santayana's opinion on the politicians of his era in chapter seven. At this point the conclusion is that the instability and superficiality of the democratic milieu, where public opinion constitutes the political medium, in a sense corrupts politicians – hardly any politician can be "a true statesman, because a true statesman is consistent, and public opinion will never long support any consistent course."[73]

Let me turn now to the issue of propaganda – a form of modern militancy, common in mass societies, consisting in "intentionally controlling the movement of ideas by social agencies"[74] – the power of which suggests that not only impersonal material trends but also ideas may codetermine the course of history. Propaganda embodies the force of persuasion used by concrete agents, members of a government, a party, or a sect, representing some interests. Propaganda is effective in a degree in which it finds a proper propensity in its human targets and its messages are somehow attuned to people's concerns and expectations. It usually contains reference to concrete circumstances which it manipulates by embedding them in a made-up narrative. Unlike in the case of honest communication, which concerns interests in no need of aggressive dissemination, "the great fertilizer, for artificial convictions, is the appeal to irrelevant interests."[75] The effectiveness of propaganda depends also on the language used, and increases when the ground has been prepared by launching its fragmentary forerunners in the guise of catchy, snappy formulas, perhaps even new, emotionally loaded words, a newspeak, that find resonance in society.

A rational government is aware of its own limitations. It by no means aspires to influence, let alone dominate, all areas of human activity. Propaganda, we should add, breaks this principle, as it sometimes strives to hoax and enroll people for whole new visions of reality, often centered around an imagined enemy, a scapegoat, an illusory obstacle on the path to a better future. In such a case propaganda serves an ideology. Propaganda may be partisan, in a democracy, or governmental, in an autocracy; yet, the most complete form of it occurs in totalitarian regimes. Propaganda seems to be a common element for all these systems, even if it functions somewhat differently and its potential power varies accordingly to circumstances. In a globalized world, propaganda works beyond borders and even beyond the specificity of this or that political

---

72   DP, 197.
73   SiELS, 185.
74   DP, 199.
75   DP, 199.

system; it can be channeled effectively in the most shrewd, hidden ways, unlike anything one might commonly associate with propaganda.

Santayana presents propaganda as an activity contrary to the generative order of nature and a means of domination proper to fanaticism bent on suppressing or erasing contrary interests and outlooks. The said political fanatic is "a tyrant on principle, and often a hypocrite in practice,"[76] intent on pushing through his own vision of reality. Even if aware of the harm and injustice involved in the cost, he nevertheless considers it subordinate to his schemes, which he carries out as if vice could be transformed into virtue by serving a higher goal. Interestingly, Cassirer considered a modern political leader to be a synthesis of an (archaic) *homo magus* and a (modern) *homo faber*, "the priest of entirely irrational ... religion," which he propagates, though, "very methodically."[77] Both Santayana's and Cassirer's reflections on propaganda and fanaticism had surely been inspired by war propagandas and the totalitarian propagandas of communism and Nazism, which they witnessed during their lifetime. Santayana charges leaders, governments, and regimens in question with fanaticism, misanthropy, squandering the art of government, and, sometimes, resentment resulting from the very fact of having suppressed the humane aspect of the self. The moral "impurity" of a fanatical endeavor is mirrored in its propagandist *modus communicandi* – "loudness and repetition, eulogy, ... affections, self-interest, and vilification, ... hypnotic compulsion" meant to "deflect and canalize the spontaneous course of ideas."[78]

It should not escape the reader's attention that Santayana's philosophy offers a review of human and socio-cultural factors that may potentially limit the effectiveness of propaganda. Autonomous thinking, personal integrity, the presence of trustworthy authorities, traditional institutions, even a variety of forms of spiritual life, constitute a natural counterweight in relation not only to the ideologization of life, the tool of which is propaganda, but also to an excessive penetration of life by public opinion. A similar, protective function against totalitarian temptations as well as against xenophobic ideologies may be played by a pluralism of ideas and a reasonable distrust towards unreflective unanimity, provided that there remains a set of values or, at least, standards of common life, shared by all.

Yet another factor of resistance, the most natural and common one, is worth mentioning here, namely- the vital mutability, spontaneity, and unpredictability of each psyche. No dogma, particularly when artificial and grafted upon

---

76   DP, 200.
77   Cassirer, *The Myth of the State*, 282.
78   DP, 200.

human psyche by way of usurpation, may be said to be totally safe. Hardly any rigid machinery of socio-political organization, even when supported by a well-organized propaganda, is likely to function without the silent cooperation of its host – the individual, whose "name is legion."[79] The awareness of this fact has made tyrants and dictators of this world sensitive to any individual sign of resistance, rebellion, or even a slight difference of opinion. Authoritarian and totalitarian systems, as a few authors of anti-utopias had predicted, introduced clever mechanisms of coercion via group self-control and verification, such as forcing employees or, simply, citizens to inform proper services against their colleagues and compatriots, collective responsibility, appointing prisoners as guards in concentration and forced labour camps, etc. The history of the twentieth century abounds in such examples, and they need not refer exclusively to political systems but also corporate and bureaucratic environments. The truth about an individual posing a threat to a system also resonates in contemporary attempts to introduce a "social points" system on a large scale. *Santayana's insights into this sort of unarmed, human resistance and his sense of the need to support it, perhaps underestimated today, belong, in my view, to the unquestioned highlights of his thought.*

Let me now return to the issue of war. Contrary to what some critics may claim, even though the idea of struggle or war plays an important role in his political thinking, Santayana is not, by any means, an eulogist of war! He acknowledges the actual and persistent presence of different dimensions of war in the human world, tracing its transformation, trying to discern virtuous elements within traditional militant cultures, and contrast them with contemporary, predominantly cynically run, wars. These reflections, where his distinction of the two ideas of politics – the "ancient" and the "modern" – echoes, lead to a conclusion that the divorce between war and chivalry paralleled the disconnection of politics and virtue. Furthermore, and more importantly, one may infer from Santayana's ruminations that it is the primordial phenomenon of war, as embodied in politics and economy, that tries to dictate the rules to the whole culture, contributing to what he calls a moral confusion and, ultimately, nihilism. As I will show in what follows, however, Santayana, assuming the position of a discontent, while engaging in a general polemic with his chosen, emblematic cynics and nihilists – Thrasymachus, Machiavelli, and Nietzsche – remains himself in a position of moral ambiguity.

In his overview of the forms of militancy, Santayana addresses war also in its most conventional sense of armed conflict between enemy nations or

---

[79] DP, 202.

states. Already in *The Life of Reason* one finds criticism of militarism, which he considers to be a prominent manifestation of barbarism. One reads about "shameless assertions" about the alleged beneficence of war for a society or a nation, while, in fact, wars have proved to be the most exhausting, wasteful and hindering human experience.[80] Arnold J. Toynbee commented on the situation of his generation in the following words: "we have learnt, through suffering, two home truths. The first truth is that the institution of War is still in full force in our Western Society. The second truth is that, in the Western World under existing technical and social conditions, there can be no warfare that is not internecine."[81] Santayana, alluding to the reality of his days, notes a deepening rift between the publicly declared anti-war sentiments, embodied in the newly formed international initiative of the League of Nations, and political reality – "at this very moment the laws of war have collapsed, and peoples glare at each other in absolute hate and terror, like crouching beasts in the jungle."[82] He then contrasts contemporary, "criminal" in their cynicism, wars with historical ones, which he tends to idealize, although not as naively as it might seem at first glance. At the time Santayana was writing *Dominations and Powers* he witnessed the unprecedented rise of militarism and could rightly say that to manufacture weapons had become "the most competitive and crucial of arts in human society, and never more so than it is now."[83] The transformation in the nature of war, which began already at the time of Napoleonic wars, has also been noted by other thinkers, such as Santayana's contemporary, the already quoted Arnold J. Toynbee, and, more recently, by René Girard.

---

80   LR, 126.
81   Arnold J. Toynbee, *War and Civilization*. A selection from *A Study of History*, selected by Albert V. Fowler (New York: Oxford University Press, 1950), 3. Analyzing the history of modern Western wars in terms of a process of intensification, in which he is similar to Rene Girard's idea of the escalation of war, Toynbee distinguished two phases, divided by "an intervening lull ... The first bout consists of the Wars of Religion, which began in the sixteenth century and ceased in the seventeenth. The second bout consists of the Wars of Nationality, which began in the eighteenth century and are still the scourge of the twentieth." The second phase, according to Toynbee, "which has not ceased in the twentieth [century], has been keyed up to an unprecedented degree of ferocity by the titanic driving-power of two forces – Democracy and Industrialism-which have entered into the institution of War in our Western World in these latter days when that world has now virtually completed its stupendous feat of incorporating the whole face of the Earth and the entire living generation of Mankind into its own body material." Toynbee, *War and Civilization*, 4, 9.
82   DP, 205.
83   DP, 89.

Historically, remarks Santayana, wars often had something to do with duel – the defense of one's sovereignty, liberties, rights, or dignity was at stake. Sometimes both sides simultaneously felt the urge to struggle because of the collision of their incompatible interests. Cruel as they could be, historical wars, at least nominally, invoked justice, respected enemy's rights, and used to have rules and limits. There was a connection between war and the spirit and idea of chivalry. Toynbee thinks there were good reasons for the worship of military virtues insofar as they were "virtues in every walk of life. Courage ... is a cardinal virtue in every action to which a human being can set his hand-or hers."[84] Such virtues, however, were cultivated predominantly by societies that perceived war as part of natural necessity rather than something controllable by humans. In modern times, wars started to be treated either like a sort of royal sport, such as hunting, or as part of a divine plan and an exercise of the noblest human virtues – an idea promoted by the nineteenth-century Prussian eulogist of war, Hellmuth von Moltke. But the intended resurrection of chivalry, notes Toynbee, was fake. Mussolini's and von Moltke's militarism were radically different from "the innocently archaic 'military virtues' of the Chevalier Bayard. ... never [to] be recaptured in our Western World by the heirs of Frederick's [the Great] and Napoleon's cynicism."[85] Likewise, Santayana thinks courage is noble if understood as a form of rational perseverance, a "steadiness under risks rationally taken."[86] Courage associated with bravura, a bellicose, audacious, warlike attitude, though, is closer to vice in politics than to virtue.

In the final parts of *Dominations and Powers* one finds *an upright condemnation of war*, which "in its sheer malice is the worst disorder possible," "a sort of subterranean chaos, sometimes bursting through the crust of civilization."[87] In accordance with the spirit of the final part of the book, which is that of the rational order, Santayana interprets war in terms of order. Since the enemy in war is faced as an embodiment of crude necessity, each of the belligerents, through mobilization, tries to strengthen their own internal organization while disrupting the order in the rival ranks and/or territory. There is an "irony in it, heightening and concentrating order here, in order to produce anarchy there."[88] In civilized wars the conquered country's population is spared and chaos is soon replaced by a new order, imposed by a peace treaty, perhaps under a new government. Under this interplay of organization

---

84   Toynbee, *War and Civilization*, 12.
85   Toynbee, *War and Civilization*, 23.
86   LR, 127.
87   DP, 439.
88   DP, 439.

and chaos, though, there is a "deeper disorder, some suicidal madness in the human race."[89] Except for rare cases of absolute necessity, when war is clearly the only form of defense, *all attempts to rationalize war are shallow and dubious in face of its costs*. Santayana thinks there is no truly rational justification for war, which in most cases is an irrational display of "self-hatred and self-contempt: ... *a deep, dark impulse to challenge and to destroy everything that has the impertinence to exist.*"[90]

A question arises – can wars in the human world be avoided or are they rooted in the nature of things? Santayana replies by questioning the very alternative contained in the question. Like Heraclitus, he assumes that conflict in the material world is unceasing. But this principle holds for a certain abstract level of description. The right question from the political perspective would be: "Need the forces that decide the course of history take the form of armies advancing to capture or to destroy one another?" The answer is "surely No."[91] Humans as rational beings do have the potential to reflect on, judge, foresee, and prevent war. What prevents them quite efficiently from taking full advantage of this potential are passions and lack of knowledge. But empirical evidence of the repetitive phenomenon of war does not allow one to infer about its future inevitability with absolute certainty. The passions and ignorance standing on the path to peace have sometimes been and may be subject to modification. In fact, as mentioned before, government as such may be described as a modification of war. The problem is that the world is incredibly complex, governments are many, and reason can hardly dominate universally over passions attached to rival interests. Nation-states happen to be engines producing artificial allegiances and, relying on contagion and herd instinct, inspiring peoples against one another. "[N]othing endears itself so much to us as that for which we are making unreasonable sacrifices."[92] At this point, Santayana clearly blames "artificial units" called nation-states for waging most of the modern wars fought by humans. Were these "units" disarmed, which, in his view, might happen spontaneously either by division into smaller local communities or by merging into empires, "wars of that character and on that scale would be rendered impossible."[93]

There would still exist some natural collective agents, though, moral or economic. Many wars are fought in defense of moral, religious, spiritual

---

89   DP, 439.
90   DP, 440. My emphasis.
91   DP, 441.
92   DP, 442–443.
93   DP, 443.

traditions. But they are legitimate only when purely defensive, which is rarely the case, insofar as allegiance to one's religion is often accompanied by a sense of superiority and a desire to expand, which, in Santayana's language, counts as fanaticism. Economic factors, potentially able to curb belligerent tendencies, were nevertheless frequent causes of war in the world full of rivalry for colonies, resources, routes. Santayana does not exclude that wars on economic grounds could and should be restricted by international authorities and treaties, but thinks that a global, peace-oriented economic organization would not prevent other bellicose factors (historical, psychological, moral) from coming into play unless "a central universal government, self-aspired and autocratic, always ready to wage it with overwhelming force" were established.[94]

Santayana links the transformation of war with the rise of modern political cynicism. His reflections lead to two conclusions concerning culture. First, by becoming purely materialistic and instrumental, war lost any connection with virtue. Second, the disappearance of chivalry was accompanied by a change in the perception of death. At this point it merits quoting Santayana:

> When death is habitually defied, all the slavery, all the vileness of life is defied also. It belonged almost to the pride and joy of life to hold life cheap, and risk it, and be coolly indifferent to losing it, in defense of the least of one's rights and liberties. A smiling and mystic neighbourliness with death, as with one's own shadow, intensified life enormously in the dramatic direction ... and it concentrated the whole gamut of human passion and fancy within one hour ... In contrast with that freedom and richness we can see to what a shocking degradation modern society has condemned the spirit.[95]

While I do not personally support the point of view conveyed in the quotation above, I nevertheless see how Santayana's words fit into his general criticism of a culture where virtues are overshadowed by a preoccupation with security and comfort. "We don't know what we love, or if we do we don't dare to mention it. ... [w]e do not talk of justice but of interests."[96] The reduction of life's affirmation to a fearful holding on to personal security is accompanied by the will to immerse in the crowd – we are "afraid of standing alone." What seems to be the belittlement of human individuality and the flattening of living experience, resulted, in his view, in a growing dissatisfaction of humans

---

94   DP, 444.
95   DP, 207.
96   DP, 207.

and their seeking for a material compensation. Desire has been given a quantitative articulation, reflected in mirages of growth and accumulation, whereby the negativity of humans has been brought to daylight. "We have become very numerous … [and] encouraged a great many of people to wish themselves very rich … And we need our neighbour's land and markets and colonies … so as to be able to expand a little, and to breathe. For as it is, we are dreadfully crowded and insecure and unhappy."[97]

The above mentioned elements of cultural criticism, voiced in psychological terms, make the rationale for Santayana's advocacy of individualism become clearer. The alternative seems to be between personal integrity and a hollowness overwhelmed by unquenched desires. One may even speak of a controversial alternative, which challenges some commonly made, at least since Tocqueville, associations, namely – individualism *or* atomism, where the latter is understood as a crisis of individual autonomy. Finally, Santayana's psychic individualism may also be opposed, although the opposition in this case seems less obvious, to the individualism of an abstract cipher, as phrased by John Gray in his critique of a Kantian thread in what he calls new liberalism.[98] In other words, the individualism Santayana proposes may be seen as an alternative in relation to two models of the reign of militancy – that of single, predatory agents competing in the socio-economic field, and that of an atomized society, possibly under a totalitarian regime. One may also say that the individualism in question is an extension of Santayana's naturalism and the idea that each individual is the sovereign, associated with a normative assumption that each life is lived for its own sake. A people, a nation, a state, an empire, can be sovereign but only in a derivative sense.[99] Whereas in the generative order, the individual in his self-government, tends to be more dependent on, and affected by, culture and society than this or that government or political regimen, in the militant one this dependence may be reversed and the individual becomes a "hostage" of this or that tyrannical government. Rational order, if ever realized, would work towards harmonizing the operation of government with individual self-government.

However that might be, in Santayana's naturalistic frame of thought, the individual is inescapably social and embedded in culture, but – under regular circumstances – never to the point of society or the state fully overtaking the

---

97   Both quotations: DP, 207.
98   John Gray, *Enlightenment's Wake* (London and New York: Routledge, 1995/2007), 6.
99   César García associates Santayana's individualism with a Spanish or Latin individualism, accompanied by a distrust towards public opinion and the reality of large, collective subjects. See: García, "Santayana on Public Opinion," 27.

status of the sovereign and the judge. In an imagined multi-cultural *politeia*, which I will discuss in the eighth chapter, this margin of personal sovereignty is manifest in everybody's right to secession from their cultural, religious or "moral society."[100] The actual transfer of sovereignty from individuals to collectivities is barred – in a crudest and most upright sense – by biology and human psychic constitution. Conceptions of negative liberty and human rights draw on this intuition and expand it. Yet, in the era after Foucault and Agamben, a corrective is needed here. Under inhuman and undignified rule, it is via biology, or, in other words, through human body, that individual sovereignty may be abolished and individual potential wasted, exploited, or taken advantage of. This may happen by way of compulsory military enlistment, imprisonment, torture, control of access to medical care, forced work, but also in more subtle and non-transparent ways. Political agents make use of the fact that, to remind a grim remark by the author, "[t]he weaker life in any case perishes, but it may perish insensibly, by being transformed rather than annihilated."[101] As evidenced by the text of *Dominations and Powers*, Santayana was acutely aware of this fact.

4.3 The Limits of Relativism and Moral Ambivalence

The above reflections on the human fate under noble or inhuman rule are associated, in one way or another, with the main problem of Plato, namely – the relation of political practice to the good. A set of alternatives in this respect revealed itself in the ancient thinkers' (and poets') writings to reappear over the course of centuries, under different guises and in different circumstances. Thus, the views of Callicles and Thrasymachus prefigured, in Santayana's eyes, those of Machiavelli – an emblematic modern political thinker. Yet, the late modernity posed a new challenge – a major change in the character of actors ("recognizable units") and the scope of their action, occurring as part of the process of globalization, the formation of mass society and technological development. Political reality became more complex and liquid, and political practice was often reduced to *Realpolitik*. Machiavelli, as Santayana saw him, introduced a notable and deliberate omission, soon to become notorious, namely – neglecting the importance of deliberation and the choice of ends in politics in favour of increasing the efficacy of means. Machiavelli and his

---

100   See: Letter to Bruno Lind, 5 Jul. 1951, LGS8: 368–369.
101   DP, 82.

recent followers could be insightful and honest in their approach to facts, but they "confuse[d] the natural history of politics with rational government."[102] Thus, it is implied that "what is done is right, and what is not done is wrong."[103]

Cynicism is contained in the assumption that since the majority of people are prone to evil, anyone wishing to come out on top or have it their way, must be evil sometimes too, even if he is morally sensitive enough to see the evil. There may be some truth in this advice, notes Santayana, but what should alarm us is the fact that it is taken for granted that a worthy individual wants to succeed and dominate in the evil world rather than, for example, try to make it better or withdraw. *From the perspective of human culture, it is a mistake to trade its ideal allegiances for rather mediocre and base desires and to announce publicly that fulfilling them is a new and universal standard of perfection.* Once a culture assimilates this message, what remains to do is working on improving the efficacy of means.

Machiavelli "seemed to assume … that it is better to be a wicked prince than not to be prince at all."[104] Of similar assumptions in the modern times Santayana says that:

> it is just these hasty or false ideas that *the worship of evolution* introduces into ethics; for it is then taken for granted that to survive is the mark of excellence, and that the will to dominate is the basis of morals. But the will to live could be the basis of morals only for a brute that had not discovered that he was mortal, and must ultimately fail in that blind effort; an effort which is no doubt the occasion of much bravery and many labours, but also of many crimes. Meantime, the only rational aim he can pursue is to live in the best possible manner while he does live.[105]

The phenomenon of political cynicism taken for granted "has been aggravated in our day by the demoralizing influence that optimism and the worship of evolution exerted in the nineteenth century."[106] Meanwhile – and this is Santayana's moralism in the most explicit form – the aim of government is not, or at least not exclusively, to preserve the state or the quantitative growth of society, but rather – "to redeem human life from vanity and barbarism."[107]

---

102   DP, 209.
103   DP, 209.
104   DP, 209.
105   DP, 209–210. My emphasis.
106   DP 209.
107   DP, 210.

This is a problematic statement. First, given Santayana's naturalism, virtues and ideals can be hardly sustained and liberal arts cultivated unless a relatively safe and nourishing vital foundation is secured. Second, a government thinking that it is entitled to "redeem" the souls it represents sounds like a dogmatic government, unless "redeeming" is a sheer metaphor. What Santayana speaks against, as I read him, is the overwhelming domination of the idea of power accumulation, which overshadowed and displaced alternative ideals and models. It was a certain conspiracy of trends that Santayana feared and identified as a wave capable of washing away, indiscriminately, much of the beauty, virtue, and wisdom achieved in the past, along with certain ways of experiencing and cherishing life and the ability to accept finitude.

Santayana's brief ruminations on the long-term influence of Machiavelli's theory on politics find counterpart in a lucid and well-argued summary of "Machiavellism" by Ernst Cassirer. The author assesses the isolation of the political world from other areas of human existence, ethics in particular, as highly perilous. Its consequences, however, were fully exposed only much later, in the nineteenth and twentieth century – an era when the technical means of committing political crimes were becoming all the more efficient, and dictatorships – all the more brutal. "Machiavellism showed its true face and its real danger when its principles were later applied to a larger scene and to entirely new political conditions … Now we can, as it were, study Machiavellism in a magnifying glass."[108]

In his honesty, though, Santayana the moralist confronts his *alter ego* – a disillusioned skeptic. Trying to see through the human impulses standing behind cynicism in politics, he considers a possibility of a nobler, though, perhaps, not fully conscious, motivation hidden therein. He speculates about a "morally sound insinuation" present in *Realpolitik*, namely – that when conventional morality loses its grip on humans, then a natural, authentic *virtù* may shine. Should that be the case, though, the "naturally admirable" quality should not be associated with anything animal or wild, nor should it occur "at a prodigious expense of cruelty, labour, sorrow, and remorse."[109] The criterion for a natural

---

[108] Cassirer, *The Myth of the State*, 140–141. Cassirer admits that the said consequences were probably not intended and not even foreseen by Machiavelli himself. He postulates, then, distinguishing between Machiavelli and "Machiavellism." Nevertheless, "[n]o one had ever doubted that political *life* … is full of crimes, treacheries, felonies. But no thinker before Machiavelli had undertaken to teach the *art* of these crimes." Cassirer, *The Myth of the State*, 150.

[109] DP, 210.

excellence would be its affinity with the best part or the best version of human nature, which could be recognized only by sages. Such a complete knowledge of human nature, though, is unattainable, and any moralist's convictions, if imposed universally, are likely to be misguided.

Ultimately, however, Santayana cannot remain blind to the fact that this argument works against all conventional moralists more than against their rebellious critics. It also sheds a new light on our creators of "wicked heroes" – Thrasymachus, Callicles, Machiavelli, and, of course, Nietzsche. I find it notable that Santayana does not shy away from accepting and even embracing an irresolvable moral ambivalence here. He asks about the alleged wickedness of these figures – was it merely conventional, "or was it something that these philosophers themselves in their hearts felt to be wicked, but which they had the effrontery to welcome nevertheless ... [because] [t]hey were out for mischief."[110] Santayana thinks it was the latter. Psychologically, they loved "rising on stilts of insolence above the vulgar crowd," but even this contempt (or misanthropy) did not, *could not*, exclude the possibility hiding in the background – "the smart of some veritable deep injustice, or the light of a better world shining through all this impatience."[111] Interestingly, Santayana seems to have believed, even if only inexplicitly, in a ray of light proper to human nature. He admitted it rarely, but, as I will try to show in the final chapter of the book, he believed that pure wickedness was something inhuman. Moral ambivalence, in turn, was all too human. He also held a conviction that the power of convention, though sometimes seems so strong that it strikes us as an automatism unworthy of a human being, should not be overestimated. Human subjection to it "is greater in words than in thought, and greater in thought than in action."[112] In the light of these ruminations, Nietzsche, asserting the centrality of will to power, might have been bold enough to be honest.[113]

Nevertheless, having assumed the role of a moralist critic at this point, Santayana is compelled to come up with a clearer conclusion. And it turns out to be a disillusioned and a bitter one. Nietzsche and his followers are all too

---

110 DP, 211.
111 DP, 211.
112 DP, 221.
113 For more on Santayana's ambiguous relation to Nietzsche see: Lydia Amir, "The Democritean Tradition in Santayana, Nietzsche, and Montaigne," *Overheard in Seville* 38 (2020): 74–78. For an analysis of Santayana's early criticism of Nietzsche see: Katarzyna Kremplewska, *Life as Insinuation. George Santayana's Hermeneutics of Finite Life and Human Self* (New York, Albany: SUNY Press, 2019), 170–175.

human in their rebellion. Once their ideas start to dominate, and "[t]he oracular Zarathustra, become[s] prime minister," they will become conservative too! "If their domination lasts they will have established a social order on the same old foundations of physical necessities and human accidents; and they will proceed painfully to unravel the rights and wrongs of their new experiment."[114] As if by way of the law of *nemesis*, some bold actions will turn out to have opposite results to what was intended. When the humane element is trampled by megalomania and arrogance, "the misguided hero, like ... Macbeth, will lose his soul in gaining a sorry world, and his wishes, once attained, will horrify him."[115]

The heroes and the winners in Macbeth's "sorry world," and in ours, are the aforementioned "romantic criminals" or "bandits pure and simple" – self-assertive, greedy, merciless towards their enemies. Unlike the chivalrous ones, they say: "[t]he wise, the efficient, the ultimately kind policy is to attack the weak. Then the struggle will be brief, the victims few, and the settlement decisive."[116] This, in Santayana's vocabulary, is a manifestation of a rebarbarization of society and culture, where notions such as "barbarism," and, occasionally, "savagery," are used metaphorically and stand for a predatory kind of militancy, a common domination of "crime," resurrected in a new, more threatening form due to the technological power it now has at its disposal.

Interestingly, Arnold J. Toynbee, with whose work Santayana was well acquainted, and, probably, modestly inspired by, considered the emergence of archaistic and barbarian elements in culture, art in particular, as sings of civilizational decay.[117] According to Toynbee's general theory, the following phenomena parallel the dissolution of a civilization: the weakening of the creative minority (the spiritual elite) and its turning into a dominant, coercive minority, the emergence of an internal, "alienated proletariat," and an "external proletariat," consisting in warlike barbarian bands, being the future conquerors of the governing minority and potential members of the new, universal church that is to be founded by the "internal proletariat." In the era of civilizational dissolution, individuals are attracted mimetically to certain "resurrected" cultural themes, commonly associated with the rude, the "primitive," the violent, which, by the way, may easily evoke associations with the attempted by the Nazis revival of some elements of ancient religious cults and their symbolism. These traits of "barbarism," "archaism," as well as tendencies to project a

---

114   DP, 211.
115   DP, 212.
116   DP, 214.
117   See: Milton Gold, "An Historian's View of Art," *Criticism* 3, no. 4 (Fall 1961), 269.

distant future ("futurism") constitute "futile attempts to combat or arrest" the approaching disintegration.[118]

When society is overwhelmed by crime, crime pretends to be "virtue." Such a "virtue" is far worse when it is collective than merely individual – when there is no conscience and no integral moral agent and there is ample opportunity for self-justification with reference to illusionary interests, false versions of history, the authority of the public order, and – how common in our times – the status of being "the lesser of two evils."[119] Given that a degree of criminality in some form is unavoidable int the sphere of human affairs, Santayana ponders over the superiority of intentional criminality over a constitutional one. He refers to Socrates' claim that "to do wrong on purpose is better than not to be capable of doing right."[120] What is at stake here is the awareness of wrongdoing, the possibility of *metanoia*, and corrigibility. *Everything, then, depends on self-knowledge and the preservation of moral imagination.* Santayana shared with Socrates the belief that, in Cassirer's words, "in order to overcome the [evil] power of myth we must find and develop the ... power of 'self-knowledge'."[121] When the ruling agents happen to be fanatics or madmen, absolutely integral in their evil, or when the moral horizon of a society is disfigured by a totalitarian ideology, or nihilism, and when, in addition, good models are missing, the prevalence of collective crime in common life may be irresistible and lasting.

When purely materialistic motivations dominate in a society, its members are easily convinced that quantitative growth and incorporating more and more people into the orbit of their influence (making others to their likeness) rests in their best interest and is likely to relieve their frustration and somehow

---

118 Gold, "An Historian's View of Art," 269. Santayana mentions explicitly Toynbee's idea of "archaism" in his letter to Peter Robert Edwin Wiereck, 27 Jul. 1948, LGS8: 82–83. As for Santayana's relation to Toynbee's work, one learns from his correspondence that he ordered and read with considerable interest the subsequent volumes of *A Study of History*. He appreciated Toynbee's historical research and reflection, including his account of the way historical events are connected to one another. He might have been inspired, among other things, by the historian's idea of the "age of trouble" followed by the rise of a "Universal Empire," which he applied to the turbulent twentieth century. He was critical of what he called Toynbee's philosophy and his interpretation of the origins of Christianity. See the following letters: Letter to John Hall Wheelock, 27 Nov. 1946, LGS7: 296; to Victor Wolfgang von Hagen, 26 Nov. 1946, LGS7: 296; to Daniel M. Cory, 17 Dec. 1946, LGS7: 305; to John McKinstry Merriam, 17 Jan. 1948, LGS8: 7; to Raymond Brewer Bidwell, 29 May 1948, LGS8: 69; to Melvin N. Sommer, 8 Oct. 1948, LGS8: 107.
119 DP, 229.
120 DP, 229.
121 Cassirer, *The Myth of the State*, 60.

make them "less crowded, less insecure, less unhappy."[122] This imperialism – literal and metaphorical – raises doubts:

> Is there in this megalomania a remnant of imitation of religious propaganda? Is it for the salvation of foreigners' souls that we wish to annex and to standardize them? Is it to prevent those who are unlike ourselves from being eternally damned that we long to exterminate them?[123]

For Toynbee, empires, as attempts to form universal states able to secure internal peace, are, in a long-run, doomed to failure due to their violent origins. An empire is fighting "a desperate losing battle against an unexorcized demon of Violence in its own bosom."[124] On the basis of his historical research into the fate of civilizations, Toynbee derives a regularity, which he turns into a principle – of a historiosophical or quasi-metaphysical nature – about the "the inefficacy of force as an instrument of salvation."[125] Santayana, unlike Toynbee, did not formulate any laws of history. Neither did he believe any such laws existed. Yet, his existential and anthropological convictions, like the ones about the fatality of *hubris* and the ominous disproportion between technological progress and moral/spiritual condition of humans, would sometimes work to similar ends. While he was tempted by the idea of an empire, the suggested above tendency to uniformization and the desire to "devour" and digest the other (in Toynbee's view being one of the master-tendencies among the manifestations of civilizational decay),[126] was what Santayana wholeheartedly abhorred as it stood in stark opposition to his pluralism, and must have represented in his eyes a way of disarming humanity against the threats of dehumanization.

Returning to the idea of managing necessity and connecting it to the most obvious manifestation of militancy, which is war, war is an example of an irresistible power of necessity, and its special case at the same time. Unlike some other forms of necessity, its fatality, limited and controlled by conscious human intervention – even if this control may be lost under some circumstances, such

---

122　DP, 208.
123　DP, 208.
124　Toynbee, *War and Civilisation*, 157.
125　Toynbee, *War and Civilization*, 146.
126　As evidenced clearly by the following words: "We must ask whether, as we look back over the ground we have traversed, we can discern any master-tendency at work, and we do in fact unmistakably descry a tendency towards standardization and uniformity: a tendency which is the correlative and opposite of the tendency towards differentiation and diversity which we have found to be the mark of the growth stage of civilization." Toynbee, *A Study of History*, 555.

as an unstoppable bilateral escalation of violence – may be triggered, administered in dosages, withheld. Next, war belongs to the harshest means of coercion. War, however, with its overwhelming quality and spectacular – in their potential efficiency exceeding any human effort – results, tends to elude common sense and inspire imagination. Santayana suggests that the sense of one's own agency, and the enemy's agency alike, during, and even more so after the war, may become vague, uncertain, and diffuse into a contrary feeling of falling victim to a conspiracy of inhuman forces. When approached reflectively, war is a theme for idealization, dramatization and poetry. "The enemy is a hero in his own eyes, and may ultimately become in ours."[127] Art may and actually often does just this. "Blind nature was working irresistibly in us both, at cross purposes with herself ... The ravages of war are immense, and have always been irreparable; yet we still exist."[128] Leaving aside the fact of a moral ambiguity that such artistic endeavors may involve, they form part of human culture and evidence of its appropriation of trauma, ruin, death, as well as a symbolic victory over politics itself. The more detached the artist or the spectator and the more distant the events, the more probable the conclusion that "[t]hese evils, in their essence, would have overtaken us in any case. Our real enemy is too large to be seen, being the universe; or too near, being within ourselves."[129]

Santayana's controversial ruminations at this point reveal what I read as the author's escape from a difficult judgment into an aesthetic contemplation of eternal themes. He nevertheless seems to be right about the healing, solace-bringing, culture-forming, reflective function of art. The hermeneutic and communicative dimension of art may indeed assist humans in overcoming the vicious circle of vengeful violence. There remains, however, a danger, of aestheticization (or: aestheticization) becoming anesthetization.[130] The direction of Santayana's reflections is likely to provoke similar questions and leave them unresolved. His ruminations here culminate in a simple assertion that spirit is capable of "purifying" everything by raising it to its ideal, disinterested realm.

---

127 DP, 216.
128 DP, 216.
129 DP, 217.
130 Without making any direct reference to Santayana at this point, whose reflections seem to be a mere declaration of disengagement and spiritual emigration, I would like to draw the reader's attention to Walter Benjamin's immensely engaging insights into the aestheticization of politics (as practiced by fascist regimes) and the response to it in the form of the politicization of art (being part of the communist practice). See: Walter Benjamin, "The Work of Art in the Age of Mechanical Reproduction" (1935), in *Illuminations*, trans. Harry Zohn, ed. and introduction by Hannah Arendt (New York: Schocken Books, 1969), 217–252.

Even death does not appear fearsome from its crystal palace. "It is easy, almost pleasant, to give up the world, if we know what the world is; and we never die too soon, if we have found something eternal to live with."[131]

I would suggest that a friendly reader, willing to account for these more or less controversial phrases, should take a step back and see that Santayana in his last book keeps switching in-between two or even three different masks – that of an insightful observer and a critic, a moralist, and a detached and disillusioned poet dwelling in his unworldly realm. The three masks are three perspectives; that of a critic and that of a moralist often converge and complete one another; the third one, that of a pure spirit looking at things with no stakes in the game of existence, being rather experimental, is incommensurable with the remaining two. Its presence may be explained only as a reminder of there being another option of looking at things, one undermining all the passions except for purely ideal, loosening all conventions, relieving the grip of fanaticism, lunacy, self-love, and megalomania. But, doesn't it, by the same token, condemn one to being inhuman in the sense of being indifferent? Alternatively, it may be read as a poetic expression of a sense of helplessness, when one thinks that the only lasting victory possible for humans struggling in "the infinite vacuity" of the world is of a spiritual kind.[132]

131 DP, 218.
132 The phrase comes from: DP, 212.

CHAPTER 5

Arts as Powers and as Dominations

> Means would be pursued as if they were ends, and ends, under the illusion that they were forces, would be expected to further some activity, itself without justification.
>
> LR, 265

∴

By art – a form of human action justified in the light of the life of reason – Santayana understands "any [conscious, intentional and teachable] operation which ... humanizes and rationalizes objects."[1] Arts transform the world by making it more friendly to human existence, more congenial to reason, and by establishing "a ground whence values may continually spring up."[2] The existence of arts opens opportunities for men to actualize their potential, develop virtues, and live a good life.[3] Yet, liberal and economic arts, all animated by some passions and interests, "are powers in danger of becoming dominations."[4] They are powers insofar as they are conducive to satisfying the real needs and achieving satisfaction and completion. They are congenial to the life of reason inasmuch as they develop in harmony with one another and with other areas of

---

1   LR, 301. In the introduction to *The Life of Reason* one reads: "Operations become arts when their purpose is conscious and their method teachable. In perfect art the whole idea is creative and exists only to be embodied while every part of the product is rational and gives delightful expression to that idea." See: LR1, 4.
2   LR, 302.
3   A general, Aristotelian, understanding of virtue as a disposition in respect to action and thought may be helpful here. Practical wisdom is an example of virtue which concerns the ability to deliberate, form opinion and choose, and, as such, is the basis of living well (which is an end in itself). See: Aristotle, *The Nicomachean Ethics*, trans. Benjamin Jowett (Oxford: Clarendon Press, 1908), 1140a25–1140b30. Political wisdom seems to be closely related to practical wisdom, or a variety of it, extended to (governing) others. Practical wisdom, though, concerns the means of attaining an end rather than the ability to set aims. Setting aims requires a specifically moral virtue/excellence, which, by the way, is achieved not without the support of practical wisdom. See: Aristotle, *The Nicomachean Ethics*, 1144a- 1145a. A key moral excellence with regard to political action, lawmaking in particular, is justice.
4   DP, 94.

human life rather than at their expense. Economic arts, for example, may be called rational in the sense that they make labour lighter and more enjoyable in its performance and effects; they thus facilitate a liberal life.[5] This ideal, in turn, brings to light some other issues, such as the freedom of choice and control humans have over what they engage in (which is part of their rational self-government), or the transparency and accountability of arts in the era of rapid technological transformation and globalization.[6] It also turns our attention towards the question of ends and ideals under the *aegis* of which arts, especially productive arts – *poietike techne* – are developed.

The complexity and non-transparency of the world, along with the unquestioned prevalence of materialistic motivations, create myriads of opportunities for turning – both involuntarily and deliberately – arts into dominations, and work into enslavement. Understanding the influence given activities and directions in development are likely to exert on humans and their environment in a longer perspective is a challenge. But even the presence of a correct foresight does not always prevent people from wrong decisions when a humane factor is missing. Likewise, rationality, unless attached to some ideal allegiance, becomes a lifeless procedure guided by any externally imposed standard or goal. To refer to Toynbee's genealogy of civilizational and cultural crisis again, when creative minority loses its spiritual prerogatives and its influence on society, positive imitation, which vitalizes culture in its period of growth, is gone and replaced by the already mentioned mimetic substitutes such as artificial resurrection of old forms or futurist utopias. Other than that, diversity and uniqueness of styles tend to be replaced by "a standardized and composite style,"[7] displaying a "mechanical combination of *motifs*," often characterized by vulgarity, sometimes by extravagance.[8]

The crisis described by Santayana consists, first, in the increasing instrumentalization of arts, and, second, in the fact that humans are exposed – in a larger degree than ever – to experiencing their own actions as unpredictable, irrational, uncontrollable trends. To refer to the categories employed in this book – *human action becomes part of necessity affecting the collective sphere*

---

5   LR, 305.
6   Santayana thinks agriculture, of all human economic arts, is the most "humble" as long as it "begins and ends close to nature." Agricultural communities understand necessity and built their wisdom, often looked down upon by cultures of other type, upon this bedrock. The forms of economic activities they engage in are less prone to escape human control and become unpredictable. See: DP, 98–99.
7   Toynbee, *A Study of History*, 431.
8   Toynbee, *A Study of History*, 466.

of helplessness. It is a paradoxical moment when arts, the economy they are part of, and progress itself, seem to be autonomous engines, just about to turn against humans in unforeseeable and unstoppable ways. Isn't it a moment of a global alienation? Humans in their effort to control nature and accumulate power engage in self-destructive activities on many levels. In this light, Santayana's idea – previously criticized by me – of subterranean material forces having control over the human world, acquires a new, critical and prophetic dimension at once. Interestingly, not only the alienation mentioned above but also – paradoxically – Santayana's articulation of this fact, fit into Toynbee's pattern of civilizational decadence. While humans may suffer from a sense of agency crisis, intellectuals often enjoy worldviews where human failures are ascribed to forces, says Toynbee, "entirely beyond their control … This was the philosophy of Lucretius,"[9] of which Santayana, in some respects at least, considered himself to be a follower.

It is worth keeping in mind that Santayana's ideas about arts, virtues, and vital liberty connect him with both Platonic and Aristotelian ideas concerning a just political order and an individual *autoteleia*. *Taken together, these ideals call for the preservation of a human scale in the management of human affairs, which solely justifies the role of common sense and wisdom in political thought and practice.* The just polis is organized in such a way that each is given the opportunity to occupy the place they are most fitted for. In this paradigm, marked by a tendency to anthropomorphize politics, everything is organized on the said human scale, being potentially intelligible and controllable. "The complementary 'wholeness' of *psyche* and *polis*, soul and state, constitutes the condition for the elimination of *stasis* [conflict] in each, and such 'wholeness' is justice, in either *the psyche* or *polis*."[10] One may also discern here the idea of "justice 'as doing one's own',"[11] and authenticity as fidelity to one's native psychic capacities and a condition of possibility of a good life. It concerns not only individuals but also collectivities in connection to the arts and virtues they have developed in the generative order. The way a given culture and a socio-political arrangement regulate and prioritize relations between: man and arts, the individual, society and economy, determines the ways of and the chances for attaining this ideal. These ancient ideals may have been crafted with different types of human communities in view, yet they contained elements of universal wisdom. Santayana's critique of the inhuman scale in modern arts, replacement of a plurality of virtues by a single, instrumental virtue of

---

9   Toynbee, *A Study of History*, 247.
10   Wallach, *The Platonic Political Art*, 254.
11   Wallach, *The Platonic Political Art*, 253.

efficiency (and adjustability), the retreat of the ideal of a harmonious order in favor of a militant order of expansion and growth, is meant to reveal the ways in which the modern world – quite contrarily to what it declares – may distract the possibility of attaining vital liberty and reduce the number of those capable of authentic flourishing.

Meanwhile, behind the human world there stands "[t]he secret economy of an animal organism," with its potentially misunderstood and insatiable appetites.[12] Ideally, both liberal and economic arts, which form the "economic articulation of society," may be a vehicle for the development of natural human creativity, which is reconcilable with their being useful practically[13] and sustainable in a harmonious and enlightened society, where "few or none of the offices of daily life would lack a spiritual [i.e., moral or ideal] sanction."[14] Santayana neither hopes for a complete and lasting realization of this ideal, nor dismisses it as a pure utopia. Rather, he sets it as a horizon against which he criticizes the "economic articulation" of his era, when, according to his diagnosis, *arts, from the perspective of the majority of society, assumed the form of dominations.*

The spirit of Santayana's analysis, in many respects, reminds of what Theodor Adorno and Max Horkheimer, in *Dialectic of Enlightenment* (1947), say about culture industry in capitalism. Both Santayana and the representatives of the Frankfurt School are interested in the impact of power relations on the status of work and fine arts, and point to the fact that human diversity, spontaneous originality, as well as objective criteria and standards of excellence are squandered thereby. Whereas Adorno and Horkheimer focus more on the "mass" character of culture, its class nature, and the new media, Santayana's remarks extend to what they call the late liberal stage.[15] Nevertheless, their criticisms are congenial in surprisingly many details.

---

12   DP, 93.

13   Santayana was by no means dismissive of the criterion of usefulness or utility. On the contrary, he thought that manufacturing useful things could itself be a source of excellence and satisfaction related to vital liberty. Useful things themselves could exhibit harmony and beauty. Analogously, certain instinctive and primitive human attitudes, such as the drive to possess and accumulate, gave rise to civilizations and by way of refinement and, one may add, sublimation, triggered "an endlessly elaborate system of instruments," which may themselves embody complex forms consisting of three layers – bodily, instrumental, and ideal. The ideal layer, "formed of images and of moral relations" and fueled by the secret psychic lives of humans, would become a nucleus of new meanings formation. See: DP, 97–98.

14   DP, 91.

15   Theodor Adorno and Max Horkheimer, "The Culture Industry: Enlightenment as Mass Deception," in *Dialectic of Enlightenment*, trans. John Cumming (New York: Continuum, 1989), 120–167.

Enterprise, being "a form of militancy without moral provocation and without enemies," writes Santayana, "is indeed less social than faction in its inspiration, so that the world is naturally less concerned with it as it arises, although society may be more affected by it in the end."[16] Nothing or nearly nothing in culture is left exempt from the market mechanisms. When the class of producers and merchants dictates the rules, making the government its hostage, work, without being an upright slavery, assumes some features of forced work. The meaning of forced work in Santayana's dictionary may evoke associations with Marx's alienated labor as long as this kind of work deprives man of the possibility to take advantage of his vital powers and of his dignity as a creator of values. At other occasions, Santayana simply speaks of monotonous, exhausting work as man's lot, which could be alleviated only by means of an unspecified, thorough reform of human economy. Hence, the irony contained in the following words: "Certain moralists, without meaning to be satirical, often say that the sovereign cure for unhappiness is work."[17]

Similar dehumanizing tendencies are particularly pervasive when business, politics, culture, and technology enter into tight alliances with one another so that none of these spheres remains the sphere of liberty but all form a system of generating profit and distributing privileges. Social relations are then permeated by parasitic forms of economic militancy, as it sometimes happens, for example, in neoliberal capitalism (understood as deregulated market capitalism),[18] where democracy assumes some features of oligarchy, some signs of which did not escape Santayana's attention. All this is made possible by the simple fact that in the human world, all artifacts, including results of a possibly disinterested activity, such as works of art, represent – accordingly to the needs they might satisfy – some measurable value in society, whereby they become "nuclei for a whole web of interests that seem all the more urgent in that they are precarious."[19]

---

16   DP, 245.
17   LR, 262.
18   Santayana uses the notion "capitalism" rarely, and when he does, it is in a pejorative sense. I decided to use the notion whenever context allows to infer that this is an appropriate term to convey some of his ideas. In short, Santayana understands capitalism as a system that makes it possible for some to live on unearned or virtual money, or "invisible wealth." See, for example, DP, 251. See also the following letters: to George Sturgis, 18 Jan. 1932, 4: 313; to John Hall Wheelock, 24 Aug. 1948, 8: 90 (this is where he calls capitalism "criminal"); to John W. Yolton, 2 May 1952, 8: 442; to Sydney Hook, 15 Apr. 1933, 5: 21. In the final of the letters listed here, Santayana declares he agrees with Marx's reluctance towards capitalism.
19   DP, 93.

One of the questions to ask is whether certain human prerogatives and rational self-government in society allows it to handle the relations between man and goods in such a way that humans, in their natural pursuit of prosperity, are not overwhelmed by the very chase and are able to keep their all-too-human, but at some point self-destructive, appetites at bay. Should such prerogatives be missing, aggressive entrepreneurs, "[h]aving power over society ... will push their corporate claims to the utmost, be turbulent in politics, and ready to impose monopolies and even governments."[20] The "evil" here is not attached to industry or wealth in any "metaphysical" sense but rather stems from disorientation and vices such as lack of moderation – "blind alleys of avarice and luxury ... greed and cupidity"[21] – to which capitalism may be conducive unless there exists some political, social and spiritual counterweight to it. An aggressive capitalism poses, in Santayana's eye, a threat for society and culture, as it *tends to undermine and even liquidate non-economic structures and values that stand on its way*. "Cooperative vices may build a Tower of Babel, until the foundations give way, and vain indulgence and vain labour collapse together."[22] These concerns engage the philosopher in a dilemma for which he seems to miss a decisive resolution, namely – whether and to what extent the government should control economy. Santayana is aware of the fact that one of the key functions of government is to facilitate prosperity. Free competition and individual inspiration are among the most powerful triggers of the development of arts. Yet, at a ripe phase of economic development a limited governmental control may be needed, if not necessary, not least for the fact that it should 1) prevent and control possible processes of the degeneration of the free market, 2) take care of the creation and preservation of the common good.[23]

A theme recurrent in Santayana's writings is criticism of industrialism – "the present plight of a mechanized world" – and the rapid technological progress with its "profound duplicity."[24] Santayana mentions a couple of arguments that might be put forth from the perspective of (an ill-conceived) patriotism against the industrial ideal, which is international, and the concomitant mechanical production and the division of labour. He then dismisses this kind of argumentation as motivated by prejudice, but proceeds to make a more compelling one on behalf of the life of reason.[25] Without adjudicating the issue, he

20 DP, 90.
21 DP, 93.
22 DP, 91.
23 See: DP, 424.
24 DP, 89.
25 LR, 116.

asks whether and how wealth produced and gained contributes to a greater happiness and excellence in people's life, while taking into account the way that mechanical production of goods and an extreme division of labour – two aspects of modern industry – may violate the "natural genius" of humans. He reminds that neither industry nor work in itself is "a self-justifying activity."[26] At the beginning of the twentieth century Santayana sees signs of a civilizational crisis in the fact that a few became very rich without "achieving any dignity or true magnificence," while the poor, some of whom are slightly better off, have not become happier or "notably wiser."[27] He also complains about an unjust distribution of gains from industrial economy, which obliterates the promise of the emancipation of large groups of humans from poverty and exhausting work. As I will show in the subsequent chapter, in-between the two great wars, in his criticism of liberalism, Santayana would express a similar opinion, though in a more radical way, namely – that the increase in wealth, by contributing only to the well-being of narrow elites and increasing the demand for luxury, failed to meet the moral criterion of its justification, especially in the light of its cost.

Santayana's criticism of industrialism may be better understood with reference to his general views on progress. Progress conceived of as an immanent quality of all life, or merely of human life, a metaphysical principle underlying history or defining the dynamics of human society, progress as a march towards an ultimate harmony of everything, a completion or an earthly salvation – all these ideas are dismissed by Santayana as human delusions and a veil covering a much more inhuman and indifferent reality.[28] In opposition to the bustling, growth-oriented optimism of the era, he says, subversively and almost provocatively, that "we never die to soon"[29] and "[e]verything in this world, considered temporally, is a progress towards death."[30] The vision of a universal progress is at odds with Santayana's idea of contingent universe, his pluralism, and rejection of teleology both in respect to psyches and larger units, such as nations or humanity. The world is not harmonious, its unity is not ideal but crudely material. If one, speculatively, envisages a "formal perfection of the universe, as completely expressing its own nature and laws," what is beneath

---

26 LR, 117.
27 LR, 118. "A barbaric civilization, built on blind impulse and ambition, should fear to awaken a deeper detestation than could ever be aroused by those more beautiful tyrannies, chivalrous or religious, against which past revolutions have been directed." LR, 119.
28 DP, 94.
29 DP, 217.
30 DP, 94.

is still "a moral chaos, in which the vital nature or law of each thing is defeated and turned into a maimed and monstrous caricature of what that thing was capable of becoming."[31] Also Santayana's pluralism defies the idea of a universal progress as long as its recognition would require assuming that there is a universal unanimity of goals and common criteria of their attainment.

This is not to say that progress is impossible. Neither does it mean that humans are not interconnected, may have no common goals, or cannot achieve them by way of a sustained cooperation and effort. On the contrary, humans are universally conditioned (materially) and able to communicate. As Santayana once said, *necessities construct society*. Insofar as common problems may be identified and then solved, progress is possible. It is, however, neither universal, nor necessary. It is not and cannot be made everlasting. Phases of progress happen in the human world when a measurable development – supported by human effort and favorable circumstances – is achieved in a specific area. There may be a personal progress too, towards some excellence. But even these local and temporary periods of controlled effort and evolution do not deserve the name of *human* progress unless they are accompanied by or conducive to moral and spiritual progress, or, in other words, the creation of virtue, beauty, increase in rationality, etc. In a most general, universally human sense, progress would stand for "bettering the conditions of existence" while approaching the life of reason, or, in other words, a "sustained advance in rationality."[32] The problem is that material progress often happens to be at odds with moral progress thus understood.

Toynbee believed that behind the great inventions of civilizational significance, there stand exceptional individuals (or creative minorities) "and at each successive advance the great majority of the members of the society are left behind. ... Our Western scientific knowledge and our technique for turning it to account is perilously esoteric."[33] In relation to the "great new social forces of Democracy and Industrialism" masses of people had been left behind, "substantially on the same intellectual and moral level on which it lay before the titanic new social forces began to emerge."[34] Participation in the global, technological competition, Santayana notes rather indifferently, has proved to be a "blind lead" for Europe and it began losing its hegemony. Besides, "this mechanical melting pot" swallows countless traditional arts and threatens local identities with extinction, forcing them sometimes to violent self-assertion. Technology

---

31 DP, 181.
32 LR, 302.
33 Toynbee, *A Study of History*, 214.
34 Toynbee, *A Study of History*, 214.

facilitates and accelerates the spreading of fads and ideologies drawing on the power of mimetism and social contagion. As a result of political factions using the tool of propaganda, "[p]rimary needs and passions are enlisted in the service of the most baseless dreams, as if by some verbal shibboleth human nature could be transformed."[35] Likewise, the representatives of the Frankfurt School note an attack on individual autonomy occurring in the mass society of the late capitalist era, which reminds of "a constant initiation rite," where one has to prove his belonging to the very power which "is belaboring him."[36]

The ambiguity involved in a rapid technological development is most evident in the case of military technology. It is dubious whether the inventions of the military industry, no matter how spectacular, deserve the name of progress, unless one argues that the presence of nuclear weapons acts as a deterrent to actual wars, contributing to global peace, which is the basic condition for human well-being. This effect, however, someone else might respond, is incidental and should be counted among the unintended consequences of certain actions. Looking at the origins of army, Santayana notes that it reminded "a ravenous and lusty horde quartered in a conquered country" – an image, which, in his view, is helpful in dispelling certain illusions about an alleged "rational device for defensive purpose" and understanding both the deeper causes for and the cost of contemporary militarism.[37] Even if, in some cases and within a limited scope, armies do indeed contribute to securing peace, and one might consider Santayana's critique of the presence of the military as irresponsible in its one-sidedness, there remains the problem of "the hateful actuality of military taxes, military service, and military arrogance."[38] Very much in the spirit of René Girard's theory of escalating violence, Santayana thinks that under the shadow of militarism, the purveyors of a new barbarism act as "panegyrists of war" and there is an unceasing "recalling, foretelling, and meditating war."[39] His opinion seems to be, then, that ultimately humans are dominated rather than empowered by the existence of modern military technology, the presence of which creates an unprecedented opportunity for a "madman," a fanatic, or simply a human error, to erase the human race from the Earth, and, thus, to "exterminate the bearers of every moral tradition."[40] To evoke Toynbee once again, he went even further and generalized the suicidal nature of militarism,

---

35   DP, 180.
36   Adorno and Horkheimer, *Dialectic of Enlightenment*, 153.
37   LR, 125.
38   LR, 125.
39   LR, 126.
40   DP, 89.

extending it to all the previously existing civilizations and – with a high probability – to the present and future ones. He thought of militarism as a decadent phase in the life of civilizations and ascribed to it the role of both a manifestation and a cause of their ultimate disintegration.

Some aspects of Santayana's critique of different aspects of modernity may be regarded as an expression of his conservative viewpoint. Still, even if the thinker was attached to some cultural forms of the past, the ground for his criticism as a whole seems to me rational and humanistic rather than sentimental or dogmatic. In any case, philosophically, the criticism and the shape of his political hermeneutics were consistent with his consciously chosen perspective, being, in his own words, "the fortunes of vital liberty in the face of all kinds of alien oppression."[41] With this horizon in view, he reached a major conclusion, to which he remained loyal throughout his writings:

> There is a sense, indeed, in which the effort to dominate matter materially is, in the Stoics' phrase, "contrary to nature"; not that it cannot be done and done brilliantly up to a certain point, but that the intrinsic constitution of man and of the world he lives in limits the profitable effects that they can have on one another.[42]

Given this principle – let me call it *the principle of limited benefit from material progress* (or: the principle of spiritual vindication) – from the point of view of living a good life, *material improvement cannot compensate for cultural and moral deprivation in society*. What is more, "[e]ven material well-being may be jeopardized by material development. Economic security is not attained, and moral simplicity is lost; thus the greatest material progress may only expose the poor to foolish ambition."[43] Armed with this conclusion, we may pass to the next section.

5.1 Mass Society, Business, and Culture

> The second half of that [19th] century ... was filled with brilliant enterprise in science and industry, producing a revolution in the equipment of human life and mind, which has continued with acceleration to the present time, and is presumably destined to make a wholly new era in

---

41   DP, 94.
42   DP, 91.
43   DP, 180.

the relation of mankind to the latent energies of matter. Medicine, most beneficently, communications and means of transit most astonishingly by radio and air, have respectively relieved and frivolously complicated human existence.[44]

With this promising civilizational achievement in the background, the turbulent political events of the twentieth century – the Russian Revolution and the two world wars – marked an era of great international alliances, like the League of Nations, about the efficiency of which in sustaining peaceful cooperation Santayana was more than skeptical, and an ever tighter marriage between politics and business. What Santayana calls "Enterprise" – the capital "E" was probably meant to emphasize not only the importance of business but also a fetish aspect attached to it – turned from a merely economic activity (which is justified insofar as all people want to prosper) to one aspiring to a worldview, if not ideology, with entrepreneurs becoming "prophets of Enterprise" and willing to transform, or rather – *to convert* – the world. This and some other ways of establishing a universal authority – such as those put forth both by the founders of the League of Nations and the leaders of the Soviet Bloc – were examples of "militancy *in excelsis*"[45] and, Santayana predicted, would turn out unsuccessful in one way or another. This being said, the thinker did not exclude that some kind of an authority of supra-national range would be needed and would emerge in future.

Instead of regular business, he observed, "we now have advertising and propaganda: arts explicitly bent on bending the public mind to party advantage. The process is like that of a lottery, catering to human weakness and popular delusions for the benefit of partial interests themselves probably hollow and deceptive."[46] Beneath there is another, more fundamental but purer and apparently milder, form of domination, one that cannot be associated with a specific political faction, namely – the domination of money themselves. In the case of a primitive exchange of goods or early, simple forms of trade with the use of money, transactions were transparent enough to be understood and controlled by parties, who usually manufactured the goods that they traded and had a clear insight into their needs, resources, and alternatives. The introduction of money, being a groundbreaking civilizational achievement, meant also the emergence of "a middle term pregnant with terrible dangers."[47] The

---

44 DP, 246.
45 DP, 246.
46 DP, 249.
47 DP, 249.

abstract dimension of money allows it to become not only a common currency, able to go beyond any locality, but also a measure of value, an "equalizer," transcending any apparently unbridgeable difference and specificity. With a silent acceptance of culture, money can replace or stand for *anything*. Money represents pure instrumentality, or, in other words, is the purest example of a tool in the human world, "a tool of endlessly diverse and extensive uses," as noted by Georg Simmel.[48]

Overseas travel gives rise to international trade and colonies. Here, locality is in fact taken advantage of by adventurous, sailing merchants, who, however, are at the same time discoverers, contributing enormously to the growth of knowledge and civilizational development. The romantic aspect and inspirational function of these voyagers and entrepreneurs is set aside by the appearance of competition, the emergence of varied institutional establishments, and the professionalization of the whole enterprise. Supply and demand are the terms in which local communities and whole societies are made subject to domination. As for the activity of money-making, at some point it becomes an impossible synthesis of means and ends, the moral power of which – determined by the synthesis of quality with quantity – comes to a full realization in the process of the development of global capitalism.

> The point is to capture the public, and then, by force of fashion and custom, to induce the public to perpetuate your business, Society is then dominated by the producer's interests, and trade proper takes a secondary and inglorious place. Capitalists and bankers are merchants sublimated and reduced to the abstract function of doing nothing but invest their money in order to increase its nominal total ... Nothing therefore has any quality in their eyes except its quantity.[49]

---

48   Georg Simmel, *The Philosophy of Money*, trans. Tom Bottomore and David Frisby, ed. David Frisby (London and New York: Routledge, 1978/2004), 210–11. The abstractness of money and the infinity of its purpose is best expressed by the following characterization by Georg Simmel. "Money is totally indifferent to the objects because it is separated from them by the fact of exchange ... Money in its perfected forms is an absolute means because, on the one hand, it is completely teleologically determined and is not influenced by any [other] determination ..., while on the other hand it is restricted to being a pure means and tool in relation to a given end ... Money is perhaps the clearest expression and demonstration of the fact that man is a 'toolmaking' animal." See: Simmel, *The Philosophy of Money*, 210–11. Furthermore, Simmel points that the abstract quality of money, its lack of internal significance and its relation to potentially unlimited possibilities lead to the neutralization and relativization of all specificity and uniqueness in the human world, including that of human personalities. See: Simmel, *The Philosophy of Money*, 212, 216.

49   DP, 251.

Global capitalism, for this is clearly what Santayana has in mind, neutralizes local differences and creates "an economic organism larger than the political one and moral one and rooted in all the nations employing their services."[50]

One can imagine Santayana's skepticism about contemporary derivative financial instruments and virtual currencies, which represent yet another level of the abstract dimension of money, and the prominence of which was made possible due to the digital technologies. These instruments, he might say, constitute nothing but the spectre of human art, utterly monopolized by the idea of an easy and quick material profit, and the possible excitement involved in taking risk. It is possible to argue that man, provided that he is rational, may still make a good use of these instruments, as some surely do. I do think John Lachs has a point in charging Santayana with underestimating the importance of material values in life. Santayana's criticism of "wordliness" and materialistic motivations, I would add, may seem exaggerated, repetitive, one-sided, and may strike as elitist. Yet, following now Santayana's way of thinking, one cannot avoid an important question – to what an extent a culture infatuated deeply with material success may still nest personalities that, while engaging their life energy in the pursuit of material power for its own sake, are capable of preserving a degree of self-limitation, critical self-reflection, and intellectual and moral autonomy allowing them to step out of the vicious circle? What chance is there for such a culture to preserve the criteria of judgment allowing its participants to appreciate excellence and originality from beyond its gain- and efficiency-oriented scope and consumerist attitude? When culture is part of industry, "[i]t is claimed," Adorno and Horkheimer note, "that standards were based in the first place on consumers' needs and for that reason were accepted with so little resistance. The result is a system of manipulation and retroactive need."[51] It is in provoking this kind of questions and introducing a broader, existential and humane context when looking at social and economic issues that Santayana's critique matters, even when one disagrees with the thinker on many points. As to the two questions asked, I think Santayana might respond that as long as there remain the human, vital genius at work and some "islands" of cultural heritage available, there are always chances for flourishing, even if, under unfavorable conditions, they be small. Santayana, often to the reader's surprise, was not utterly dismissive of, even when saddened by, what he thought to be the mediocre cultural standards of his era. One finds

---

50 DP, 251–252.
51 Adorno and Horkheimer, *Dialectic of Enlightenment*, 121.

no dogmatism in his views; he was aware of his own bias, and, every now and then, ready to admit that the humanity of every age had its highlights, vanities, and vices.

Despite his cosmopolitan sympathies, the thinker is concerned about the globalization occurring at the price of cultural diversity and for the sake of big businesses, whose interests are too detached from those of concrete societies. It is true that globalization may discount unnecessary, old superstitions and raise the general level of basic education and technical knowledge, but, at the same time, the values it creates are shallow, and the uniform mono-culture, adjusted to the needs of business, is spread encapsulated in "empty phrases that at least alienate nobody."[52] In its apparent inclusiveness, though, it tends to exclude individualistic attitudes, so that those "who suspect the fallacy, or feel some cross-inspiration, may learn to put these doubts away as temptations, and be actually ashamed of them. Thus the grossest vanity and cheapest rhetoric are likely to carry the day politically."[53] Here we are presented with a criticism of a global mass society and the indoctrination it is susceptible to. Education, when subjugated to the needs of business and technology, stops performing one of its key functions, namely – liberal or emancipatory one. To prevent this deprivation, education should always contain non-instrumental elements of liberal arts, games allowing for the free play of imagination, and "occasions for delight," with the purpose of retaining a disinterested "intellectual vitality" in view, or, in other words, with a purely liberal purpose.[54] Likewise, religion serves the people's spiritual needs best when autonomous in relation to politics and the state. Santayana thinks that the modern state, insofar as it aspires to rationality, may and should respect people's religious beliefs, but should not "base their policy on religious motives,"[55] propagate, persecute, or reform religion.

The rampant economic development, the two pillars of which are international commerce and industrialization, which in the nineteenth century contributed to the rise and growing wealth of bourgeoisie, continues to stimulate the flourishing of intellectual culture and liberal arts. At the same time, though, the cosmopolitan culture weakens older, local cultures and traditions, introducing new standards, which seem to Santayana superficial and abstract. In his social critique, Santayana points to a number of both weaknesses and benefactions – with stress on weaknesses – related to the rise of the middle class with

---

52   DP, 252.
53   DP, 252.
54   DP, 424.
55   DP, 425.

its cosmopolitan sympathies. It helps to disarm militant, religious dogmatism, it is conducive to abstract and critical forms of expression, for example in philosophy and arts, it cultivates pluralism and the recognition of and interest in otherness in many senses, it may help sustaining sophisticated forms of artistic expression, which find amateurs among the wealthy. But there are cleavages in this society. Middle class, always aspiring to the level of the upper, while it tries to represent an "emancipated mental vivacity," is in fact susceptible to all kinds of theoretical and ideological influences.[56] Thus, elements of enlightenment may become an instrument of domination in some agents' hands. Luckily, Santayana notes, the basis of the self-preservation of the middle class is to be sought in something more fundamental, namely – its commercial background and the degree of "honesty and steadiness" it requires.[57]

Santayana, as I interpret him, presents the middle class as a peculiar combination of mimetism and self-assertion. In terms of economic enterprise it is assertive, and in terms of culture, liberal arts in particular – mimetic. It thus conspires to the domination of a militant form of activity, such as enterprise, and the prevalence of materialistic values in society without contributing in any significant measure to the creation of what Santayana would call liberal, disinterested or autotelic cultural values, except for the obvious fact that it consumes them, creating a market for them, which, in turn, influences the very nature of these values.

Capitalism condemns arts to the flattering of the tastes of the public. Also science – "a spiritual good in itself"[58] – stimulated by economy, became dependent on the needs and interests of business patronage. Santayana complains about the mechanisms of mass production, which dehumanize arts and work ("production on a large scale in standardized forms; ... useful arts grow[ing] cheap and mechanical")[59] and the tastes of the average consumers of these goods. He is even more concerned with a kind of nihilism, which consists in "a sudden, though unconfessed, collapse of the theoretic and artistic convictions which, in the nineteenth century, kept the polite capitalist world in countenance. Conviction has deserted the civilized mind,"[60] and has been replaced by a kind of overarching "economic philosophy,"[61] which renders all values and theories arbitrary save for those that secure favorable conditions for enterprise.

---

56   DP, 253.
57   DP, 253.
58   DP, 260.
59   DP, 261.
60   DP, 254.
61   DP, 257.

"A man of business must not be interrupted or coerced by threats to his person," says Santayana not without irony.[62] This may be read as an allusion to the centrality of economic freedom in liberalism and its consequences, of which Santayana was moderately skeptical.

The culture in question, as mentioned, has its bright sides and is not unattractive for many of its participants. But the consumerist approach to all goods affects both these goods and, by way of *detour*, the consumers themselves. This is reflected in the condition and status of so-called "high culture," which owes its position in such a society to the fact that the wealthy can afford it and cherish it as something adding to their nobility. Yet, "it floats ornamentally at the top," and, preserved in special places – museums and libraries – becomes object of consumption and study,

> reabsorbed by specialists in each generation; and a fresh crop of criticism, histories, and biographies may continually diffuse the traditional treasure, augmented by the contribution which the latest critics supply. The best part, if not the whole, of criticism will soon be to criticize previous critics. ... What will be lacking in such a cultivated plutocracy will be only a native culture.[63]

If the reader at this point has already made up his mind and classified Santayana's view as decisively anti-modernist, they may have missed the consistency with which the thinker escapes such identifications. One learns – all of a sudden – that all these facts do not "render such a culture inferior; on the contrary, while a rooted national and moral culture would necessarily be one-sided and narrow, a loosely floating supervening culture may be universal."[64] Universality is a human good and it is not universality as such that Santayana quarrels with. Instrumental thinking, standardized uniformity or, in Adorno's and Horkheimer's words, "the ruthless unity of culture industry,"[65] and mechanistic mass production have degraded human work and arts in many senses. Consumerism and the class structure of society have contributed to the social alienation of fine arts, as indicated in the quotation above. Meanwhile, it was Santayana's life-long conviction that the condition of liberal arts is highly relevant for the well-being of humans. Let us have a look then, at Santayana's reflection on the status of liberal arts and the modern artist in Western society.

---

62 DP, 258.
63 DP, 258.
64 DP, 258.
65 Adorno and Horkheimer, *Dialectic of Enlightenment*, 123.

5.2 Liberal Arts and the Artist

Cut off from its vital social sources – traditional inspirations, the criterion of public acceptance, the combination of utility with beauty, the idea of serving "the honour of the soul," and the artist's status of a public servant – art became art for its own sake. The human genius, suffering from the freedom of emptiness, has ever since pretended "to create substance out of form."[66] The artist "then becomes an amateur; he plays with surfaces or falls into extravagances. Originality, which in living things comes unmasked, is sought for to the point of cultivating absurdity and letting it pass for genius."[67] Fine arts become "semi-private" goods, meant to be consumed by the wealthy and the connoisseurs. This marked the beginning of the dissolution of arts, "an omen of the end: for works of art now were prized as curiosities, detachable, detached."[68] It was, of course, not the end of art as such, but the end of art's original – social and public – vitality and authenticity. One may say, referring to Santayana's categories, that it meant shifting the presence of art from the generative order of society, where it played an integrating function, to the militant one, where it became instrumentalized. The art's second life was running in the close circuit, among artists, who became "superior persons," critics, collectors, "aesthetes," and, eventually, in museums.

No doubt, even after this change, the human genius was still there and could achieve something valuable.[69] But Santayana is interested in the social results of the alienation of art. Is becoming bohemian "a gain in dignity"? What is the price, paid by culture at large, of artists thinking of themselves as "lords of life"?[70] These issues, save for the fact that they are only loosely reflected on by Santayana, are a theme for a separate study. Here I will limit myself to a brief discussion and conclusions relevant to the larger context of Santayana's social and cultural critique.

In the romantic period artists consciously sought autonomy and liberation from patronage. However, this emancipatory attitude was by no means socially exclusivist. On the contrary, artists often emphasized their connection to the

---

66 DP, 259.
67 DP, 259.
68 DP, 275.
69 "The arts are like truant children who think their life will be glorious if they only run away and play for ever; no need is felt of a dominant ideal passion and theme, nor of any moral interest in the interpretation of nature. Artists have no less talent than ever; their taste, their vision, their sentiment are often interesting; they are mighty in their independence and feeble only in their works." See: Santayana, *Winds of Doctrine*, 11.
70 DP, 276.

people, assuming the role of a prophet, a revolutionary, the artist as a voice of a people under alien domination.[71] Thus, art exhibited a critical potential, which Santayana, unfortunately, overlooks or underestimates. The evidence of the artistic potential of the nineteenth-century *boheme*, who, still inspired by the romantic ideals, consciously rebelled against the philistine, middle-class values, ideals, and standards, as well as the official circuit of art, is to be found, for example, in the work of the French Impressionists. Choosing life in poverty, many of them rebelled also against economic dependence on the capricious bourgeois patronage, which before the French Revolution was in the hands of aristocracy.

Now, Santayana's critique has two layers. First, it concerns the fundamentals of art, its loss of connection with art as craft, and its loss of the spontaneity of being an expression of human vitality. Ideally, "[i]n a thoroughly humanized society everything – clothes, speech, manners, government – is a work of art, being done as to be a pleasure and a stimulus in itself." Already the cliché that an "artist is a person undertaking to produce immortal works" advances an unfortunate estrangement of fine arts from life.[72] Secondly, and more specifically, his criticism is targeted at the neo-romantic period of modernism, when the said emancipatory attitude of artists is radicalized, and the sense of connectedness with the public at large severed. The artist often creates his identity by way of opposition to the common man, to the point of considering himself to be – literally – the Nietzschean superman. The supermanhood of the artist was, quite literally, "announced" for example by an emblematic Polish modernist writer and poet, Stanisław Przybyszewski (1868–1927), in his then famous text, published in German, *Zur Psychologie des Individuums*.[73] At that time, being part of *boheme* becomes a pursued lifestyle, an aesthetic pose, as Santayana would call it, and the artist himself – often a celebrity. Meanwhile, snobbery among the bourgeois motivates them to approach and imitate *boheme*.

Let me try to develop, very briefly, the rationale of Santayana's critique of the modern artist from a social perspective. From artists' perspective, the way of distinguishing oneself from society as described above is not unattractive. If we agree – in Marx's spirit – that man's alienation from his work is a serious cultural and existential problem, the emancipated artist's status makes one

---

71 Examples of writers representing similar attitudes include: Adam Mickiewicz, Lord Byron, Sándor Petőfi.
72 Both quotations come from: George Santayana, "Marginal notes on Civilization," in *The Genteel Tradition. Nine Essays by George Santayana*, 145.
73 Stanisław Przybyszewski, *Zur Psychologie des Individuums* (Berlin: Fontane & Co, 1892).

less susceptible to alienation than a common man is. In other words, if an artist manages to live off his art, without making excessive compromises, then they indeed escape alienation mechanism, endowing their life, and, presumably, art, with the sense and dignity of authenticity. Nonetheless, some objections may be made at this point. The attractive status of the artist is a lure for many, including those less predestined to this vocation. When, simultaneously, the definition of art becomes broader, and the criteria of assessment much more liberal – facts about which Santayana complains – a paradoxical reversal of the status quo is possible. An artist is not someone who creates works of art, but rather works of art are identified by the status of their author. Thus, art is in danger of turning into fiction, or falling prey to social status. According to Santayana's harsh verdict, "[s]nobbery, the anxiety to succeed, and a sort of cowardly social instinct stand between the artist and his work. It is because he wants 'to be in things' that he fails, and deserves to fail."[74] This may even turn into a mechanism of negative selection working against those talented artists who lack a "proper" social background or self-promotion skills. The said "lords of life," then, may turn out to be not so much artists but rather "men of action, the masters of things, the directors of political events."[75]

A crucial point in Santayana's criticism seems to me to be that art has lost its role of integrating communication between the artist and the public. Even for a talented artist, there is a danger that "instead of serving the public and helping them to recognize and refine their natural feelings, he may attempt to stimulate in himself some unprecedented emotion, and may waste his cleverness in abusing mankind for not appreciating his folly."[76] In other words, art in isolation from society, becomes lifeless and loses its transforming influence over public life. Among his contemporaries, Santayana was not alone in diagnosing a crisis in art and placing it in a broader, socio-political context. An interesting example is his contemporary compatriot, Ortega y Gasset.

Artists of the day, breaking all ties with tradition, adjust themselves to the currently dominant trend.[77] The artistic results of this move are unsatisfactory. Commenting on an Iberian artists' painting exhibition, y Gasset says explicitly that contemporary art "is barely more than nothing."[78] Throughout the ages art

---

74   Santayana, *The Genteel Tradition. Nine Essays by George Santayana*, 147.
75   DP, 276.
76   DP, 277.
77   José Ortega y Gasset, "O krytyce artystycznej" [On art criticism] in *Dehumanizacja sztuki i inne eseje* [The Dehumanization of Art And Other Essays], trans. Piotr Niklewicz, ed. Stanisław Cichowicz (Warszawa: Czytelnik 1980), 263.
78   José Ortega y Gasset, "Sztuka w czasie teraźniejszym i przeszłym" [Art in the present and in the past], in *Dehumanizacja sztuki i inne eseje*, 266.

consisted in a creative evolution, drawing an unceasing inspiration from existing traditions. Forms created by artists, even when innovative, were "intelligible" because they conveyed a nucleus of continuity. But at a certain moment an experience of an utter exhaustion appeared. This was not merely an artistic exhaustion of possibilities, but rather – a facet of a larger crisis, which in politics manifested itself in the exhaustion of a default alternative: a sanctified socio-political order vs. revolution inspired by ideals.

The dissolution of these alternatives, according to y Gasset, allowed one to expect an era of a permanent crisis – no less in politics than in art. Art reflects, thinks y Gasset, the deepest, often hidden, system of convictions held by a given generation. These are not of rational origins, although they may be rationalized. Rather, they are born in the dark recesses of human vitality. In the situation of the said crisis, the only option for a genuine artist is to try to start everything anew. While Santayana sees not much hope in artistic creation *ex nihilo*, according to y Gasset artists have no other option since the past is as dead as it has never been before. Art of the past is lifeless, and if we admire its "ghostly" presence, we do it "ironically" and by virtue of reverence for the past achievements.[79] Authentic continuity seems no more an option. The discord between past and present and the concomitant cultural "disorientation" should be acknowledged by a critic, a philosopher, or a historian, and taken as a ray of hope that humans, finally, will find a way of living without dogmas.

The Spanish philosopher speaks also about the process of "dehumanization" of art, which started already in the nineteenth century and achieved its peak in the twentieth.[80] In brief, the said dehumanization involves the abandonment of themes, forms, and methods that make art familiar to the people at large. While some may understand dehumanization narrowly in terms of nonrepresentational art, it seems that the idea is broader and encompasses all art that is no more concerned with universal human experience to the point of becoming "iconoclastic" in relation to humans! Among its representatives are listed: Wagner, Mallarme, Proust, Joyce, Stravinsky. Socially, the dehumanized art introduces the distinction between those who are able to understand and appreciate it and those who don't. The new art is not for everyone, it is for a minority, an elite, whereby it may make the rest feel humiliated, frustrated,

---

79   Gasset, "Sztuka w czasie teraźniejszym i przeszłym," in *Dehumanizacja sztuki i inne eseje*, 268, 273.
80   Gasset, "Dehumanizacja sztuki," in *Dehumanizacja sztuki i inne eseje*, 278–323. This essay appears in English language under the title "The Dehumanization of Art," in *Dehumanization of Art and Other Essays on Art, Culture, and Literature* by José Ortega y Gasset (Princeton, NJ: Princeton University Press, 1968), 3–56.

hostile. This phenomenon, as y Gasset seems to suggest, compensates for, and, at the same time, reveals, the falsity of the idea of the equality of all people. A class of "artists" and people with particular sensitivity and, presumably, potential, is likely to emerge in response to the new art. Ultimately, all the spheres of social life are likely to be marked by this division between common and exceptional men. Moreover, art in its dehumanized phase is deprived of the old, transcendent and redemptive horizon. It may, nevertheless, perform a different, powerful, morally sanative, and rejuvenating role in relation to the chaos-driven Europe.

Thus, y Gasset, skeptical about the condition of the art of his times and aware of the unprecedented break with tradition, nevertheless, unlike Santayana, committed himself to a futuristic interpretation, endowed with some, though not excessive, optimism. In his theory of the dehumanization of art, partly coextensive with the said crisis of the new art, he also gave expression to his Nietzschean inspirations and modernist sympathies. Meanwhile, Santayana, even though considered by some an elitist thinker, one who sometimes spoke about the aristocracy of spirit, chose to "entrench" himself in the conviction about the superiority of tradition and continuity, and the public function of art, without making the slightest effort to understand the young art of his time. Y Gasset's openness to the spirit of his time and the way his analysis and argument are carried out makes these particular reflections of his superior to Santayana's remarks from *Dominations and Powers*, which, by the way, may be charged with dilettantism in respect to modern art. Also y Gasset's effort at making a positive nucleus out of a diagnosis of a crisis may be said to be more inspiring. One may even say that this sketchy juxtaposition with y Gasset brings to light certain weaknesses of Santayana's way of philosophizing, such as an excessive tendency to generalize and expressing opinions too heavily colored by personal sympathies. Having said this, some readers may have an impression that the insightfulness of Santayana's criticism in respect to – let me stress – not modern art in itself, where Santayana is an unreliable guide, but its dynamic dependence on socio-political and economic trends find no equal in y Gasset's reflections. At this point, Santayana's position of a detached observer, skeptical about the winds of time and doctrine, as well as his conviction that a look that has a hold on the past is more likely to catch a glimpse of the future, may seem more persuasive.

All in all, Santayana's judgment on culture in the era of capitalism, despite the fact that he acknowledges some benefits of modernization – "[w]ealth and progress in wealth with all its intellectual luxuries are visible gains"[81] – is crushing. Enterprise, he says, "will have produced loose wealth without a

---

81   DP, 252.

function, and omnivorous taste without a standard."[82] The profits from enterprise go to the wealthy few and the demand for luxury rises. Meanwhile, the depth of social inequalities in wealth and opportunity and the number of the poor raise concern. Society, he estimated, was becoming more consumption-oriented rather than wealthier.

The criticism of global, economic militancy is accompanied by that of what he calls militancy in faction, or, in other words, political militancy, the source of which are warlike nation-states. Toynbee believed that civilizations are threatened and ultimately defeated by their own, internal, barbarian militarism. At this point, at least, their paths converge. Of course, Santayana's vision lacks the rigidity of a law or a necessary regularity. Militarism, from the perspective of culture, is a blind lead, because the concentration of vitality in xenophobic and warlike feelings and endeavors – Sparta being an emblematic case – occurs at the price of "a hopeless monotony, ultimately dwindling into decay."[83] Militancy of both kinds, Santayana concludes, "is equally distracted and barren, considered rationally; but each has its passions and incidental compensations for those whom it genuinely enlists and inspires."[84]

Santayana seems to assume that man as an artisan, or an artist, may develop his creativity and contribute to the common good best when a certain balance between tradition and openness is achieved. In other words, a concrete environment, traditional enough to offer materials, methods, and criteria of judgment, but at the same time free from the fear of influence and otherness, is sought.[85] Among the challenges of modernity, then, two are important in this context: 1) finding a golden mean between originality and influence so that the former is alive and the latter a source of inspiration rather than mere mimetism; and, 2) reconciliation between art (here in the broad sense of *techne*) as the realization of one's vital potential and work as a means of survival. Santayana thinks there are signs of failure in both respects. The most abstract cultural expression of the failure is the domination of quantity over quality, standard over originality, efficiency over virtue. He sees the consequences of the "militant commercial industry" as

> unintended, profound, and morally fatal. They have turned industry from a liberal art become, for a few, a means of livelihood, into a militant

---

82 DP, 260.
83 DP, 262.
84 DP, 262.
85 Santayana points to Byzantine, Gothic, Saracenic and Renaissance styles as examples of arts that retained their originality without rejecting influence.

> process of making as much money as possible ... *The free life of neither class has any moral roots in their working life.*[86]

These ideas are accompanied by Santayana's personal impressions. As a travelling scholar, he had enough opportunity to observe the lifestyles of different classes, first in America, later in Europe. Even in their free time, he notes, people do not know how to live a good life. Working class indulges in simple pleasures that allow them to forget the mundane routines; managers "are bored to death, except when the post brings them their business letters, or alone in a corner they ... make for the third time some important calculation."[87] Likewise, the authors of *Dialectic of Enlightenment* note that "[a]musement in the late capitalism is the prolongation of work ... mechanization has such power over a man's leisure and happiness."[88] People have become like a miser "who lives like a pauper for the sake of growing rich."[89] In a couple of critical essays on liberalism, Santayana is concerned with what he sees as egoism and vanity of liberal culture, which, by the way, he considered snobbish. "We see that the man whose success is *merely personal* – the actor, the sophist, the millionaire, the aesthete – is incurably vulgar."[90] He also comments on the dubious satisfaction in rich men's lives, although he admits this is just an opinion of an observer, someone who has never shared in their experience. "I hear no laughter among the rich which is not forced and nervous. I find no sense of security amongst them, no happy freedom, no mastery over anything."[91]

5.3   A Digression on Secularization

Let me conclude this chapter with a reflection on secularization, which constitutes yet another context of Santayana's cultural criticism and a recurrent theme in his writings. In Santayana's view, the long-range results of the Reformation consisted in secularizing "society without emancipating it."[92] This diagnosis may be associated with the views of Max Weber on the negative influence of asceticism, efficiency-oriented rationalization, bureaucratization of social life

---

86   DP, 263. My emphasis.
87   DP, 264.
88   Adorno and Horkheimer, *Dialectic of Enlightenment*, 137.
89   DP, 264.
90   SiELS, 177. My emphasis.
91   SiELS, 185.
92   DP, 264.

and materialistic motivations on the autonomy of the individual, often evoked with reference to the famous "iron cage" idea.

> The Puritan wanted to work in a calling; we are forced to do so. For when asceticism was carried out of monastic cells into everyday life, and began to dominate worldly morality, it did its part in building the tremendous cosmos of the modern economic order. This order is now bound to the technical and economic conditions of machine production which today determine the lives of all the individuals who are born into this mechanism, not only those directly concerned with economic acquisition, with irresistible force. ... Today the spirit of religious asceticism – whether finally, who knows? – has escaped from the cage. But victorious capitalism, since it rests on mechanical foundations, needs its support no longer.[93]

Santayana, in his turn, thinks that man was freed from the bondage of metaphysical illusions and rituals only to be subjected to a mundane and overpowering service to society and prosperity, one of the pillars of which was, to refer to Weber's words, "passionate preaching of hard, continuous, bodily or mental labour."[94] The worship of labour, by the way, for Santayana meant mistaking means with ends, and, more specifically, forgetting that safety and wealth are not absolute goods but their value is relative "to the further values they may help to secure."[95]

Santayana's comments on secularization may also be read with reference to Charles Taylor's understanding of secularity and the role played by the Reformation. Taylor lists three meanings of secularity. The first one consists in the separation of the public sphere from religion. As a result, social life functions predominantly in accordance to norms and rules that do not refer to God or any religious belief. Another, common understanding of this notion focuses on the fact that people abandon religious practice and faith. Society may be secular in this sense independently of whether religious references are present in the public sphere or not. Finally, one may speak of secularity in terms of a general, moral and intellectual orientation in a society, as well as "conditions of understanding" or, in other words, a hermeneutic context in which

---

93   Max Weber, *The Protestant Work Ethic and The Spirit of Capitalism*, trans. Talcott Parsons, introduction Anthony Giddens (London, New York: Routledge, 1930/2005), 124.
94   Weber, *The Protestant Work Ethic*, 105.
95   LR, 115. Likewise, "[w]hether civilization [itself] is a blessing depends ... on its ulterior uses." LR, 116.

one positions themselves towards faith and spirituality. In a secular society, people, both believers and non-believers, function in a pluralistic milieu and consider religious faith "as one option among others, and frequently not the easiest to embrace."[96] This is accompanied by the emergence of novel (in relation to the non-secular epoch) models of the highest fulfillment for human life. In practice, phenomena corresponding to the three above mentioned meanings of secularity overlap, but under some circumstances they may occur autonomously, fulfilling one of the definitions of secularity. Taylor, for the purpose of his analysis of the paths of secularity in the West, focuses on the third one, which he considers essential for the modern experience, or the life of the modern mind.

Taylor's third meaning is relevant for our context insofar as Santayana, in his loose remarks, is interested in the influence of secularization on society, culture and the horizon of human imagination. What he means by the *unfinished emancipation* is that the disenchantment of the world ultimately facilitated the process in which the logic of Enterprise gained prevalence over social life and human imagination. Interestingly, Taylor notes that in the older, organic type of societies, with their "enchanted" worldviews, a sort of inner equilibrium could be sustained thanks to the complementarity of the functions performed (and the incommensurable models of life fulfillment realized) by different social classes and groups, as well as cultural mechanisms of releasing tensions by way of intervals of "anti-structure," Carnival being an example. Along with the collapse of the traditional, hierarchical social structure, the ability to neutralize social tensions evaporated. The rise of new, more egalitarian models of social organization involved, on the one hand, growing individualization, or, even, atomization, and, on the other, the rising temptation to impose a rigid, homogenous socio-political order, one preventing the emergence of any "anti-structure." Without traditional mechanisms of social self-regulation, individuals and societies became more susceptible to imposed, arbitrary dominations, the discussed by Santayana domination of business culture being one example. The rise of a new domination is feasible due to the fact that "[r]eligions do not disappear when they are discredited; it is requisite that they should be replaced."[97] Some attempts to dissolve religious mythologies result in the emergence of an idolatry, where "idols" are substitutes of the ideal values earlier conveyed by a religion. Santayana also remarks on the results of the said dissolution of the pre-modern social organization,

---

96 Charles Taylor, *A Secular Age* (Cambridge, Massachusetts, and London, England: The Belknap Press of Harvard University Press, 2007), 2–3.
97 LR, 242.

with its inner diversity, cohesion, and the safeguards it provided. Instead of a variety of models of human completion that one would expect secularization to invite, a rather uniform horizon was formed in response to the requirements of business and other powerful leveling trends of modernity. This being said, let me stress that Santayana's critique of modernity is not accompanied by any suggestion of a possibility, a need, or, let alone, a call for an intentional regress to older forms.

An alternative scenario of secularization might consist in, as hinted by Santayana vaguely in diverse writings, accepting the fact of a slow weakening and/or changing faith while retaining religion in its imaginative and spiritual dimension, perhaps preserving also something of its formal, ritualistic side. Religion thus transformed would continue to be the source of a sense of belonging to a moral and intellectual tradition, rich in symbolically conveyed, existential truths, as well as an aesthetic inspiration. Santayana seems to have assumed this might be a kind of *emancipation without secularization*. Time and experience encapsulated in a tradition, especially when the tradition is not uncritically embraced, might be conducive to an intellectual and moral integrity, constituting at least partial resistance to new forms of mental and material enslavement.

One even finds in Santayana's writings a speculation on an alternative vision of the history of Christianity, where the development of a skeptical humanism – instead of the Reformation – leads to a slow transformation of the Western world. The victorious humanism might have assimilated Christianity "as a form of paganism, as an ornament and poetic expression of human life," and, following the path of reason, it might "have led to general enlightenment without dividing Christendom, [and] kindling ... national passions."[98] This vision, by the way, might be viewed as congenial with his imaginative, multinational state of the future, uniting diverse cultures in a peaceful mosaic.

I suggest that Santayana's speculations about the status of arts, secularization, and emancipation be viewed in the light of his primary concern about the fate of the individual and vital liberty in the power-domination paradigm. Who is to be empowered and to what ends? Ideally, individuals in their self-government, with a good life and harmonious coexistence with others in view. In less favorable circumstances, individuals should be empowered in their self-government, drawing on the available cultural and moral resources, *against* government, political factions, and other units acting as agents of enslavement.

---

98   LR, 238–239.

CHAPTER 6

The Fragility of Liberalism

> Unless we can shake off the hubristic illusions of liberalism, the spiralling decline in our civilization is unlikely to be arrested, and may well end in the collapse of liberal society itself.
>
> JOHN GRAY, *Post-liberalism*, 31

∴

Santayana's criticism of liberalism is directed both at liberal theory and practice, and may be divided – with respect to its main thematic focus – into the critique of its main ideas, socio-economic and political practice, and culture. In reality, the three areas are tightly interconnected so the division cannot but be highly artificial. I nevertheless employ it here to curb Santayana's loose and scattered reflections, and add clarity and structure to the substance of this chapter.

6.1   Ideas

Definitions of liberalism abound. Despite the historical heterogeneity of its sources, liberalism is said to convey, nevertheless, a single and

> definite conception, distinctly modern in character, of man and society. … It is *individualist,* in that it asserts the moral primacy of the person against the claims of any social collectivity; *egalitarian* inasmuch as it confers on all men the same moral status and denies the relevance to legal or political order of differences in moral worth among human beings; *universalist,* affirming the moral unity of the human species and according a secondary importance to specific historic associations and cultural forms; and *meliorist* in its affirmation of the corrigibility and improvability of all social institutions and political arrangements. It is

this conception of man and society which gives liberalism a definite identity which transcends its vast internal variety and complexity.[1]

If one would like to use the above characterization as a measure of Santayana's liberal inclinations, the result will be all but unequivocal. One might say, for example, that his affinity with these four criteria weakens in proportion to the position in the sequence in which they are listed above, starting with a fairly strong in respect to the first and the second. Insofar as meliorism translates itself into a belief in progress, Santayana would object. The thinker certainly enjoyed a set of ideas congenial to the spirit of liberalism. He promoted a moderate individualism, cultural and religious freedom, pluralism of opinion. Tolerance was one of the chief virtues he extolled. He sometimes called the state, as classical liberals did, "a permanent necessary evil,"[2] and thought that a well-organized society should provide opportunities to escape the burden of excessive socialization to whomever desired it. As early as in *The Life of Reason* he articulated the primacy of the individual over the family, the society, and the state. A highly developed society, he noted, favors individualism in one form or another as long as the quality of any social order is measured against "its effects on conscious individuals."[3] While man is, undoubtedly, a natural and moral unit, society should not be hypostasized into something beyond its functions. As for the family, even though Santayana was aware of the threats involved in its dissolution, he nevertheless noted that "in a barbarous age [it] remains sacrosanct and traditional" condemning many individuals to unhappiness. When "barbarism recedes" the integrity and power of the family weaken in favour of its individual members' wellbeing and autonomy.[4]

Measuring Santayana's affinity to liberalism, though, is not my main intention in this chapter. Rather, agreeing with Gray, who sees in Santayana, next to Burke and Oakeshott, an incisive critic, whose ideas "liberal thought neglects at its peril,"[5] I aim to take a closer look at his criticism of liberalism, which is

---

1 LIB, X.
2 LIB, 81.
3 LR, 112.
4 LR, 112–113. In what follows Santayana asks about the scope of liberties and their influence on the possibility of rational life. He speculates about the emancipation of women and its possible adverse results for women themselves, in case it ended in a complete dissolution of the family. All in all, Santayana notices the bright sides of emancipation and individualism, one of them being the idea of marriage as a fruit of love. Yet, he complains about an overall, unfortunate moral fragmentation working against personal happiness in Western society, namely – "a morality compacted of three inharmonious parts, with incompatible ideals, each in its way legitimate: I mean the ideals of passion, of convention, and of reason." LR, p. 114.
5 LIB, 83.

inseparable from his assessment of the dominant phenomena and trends of the era, connected to democracy, industrialization, and mass society. The era, by the way, was marked, in Santayana's view, by a profound moral and intellectual confusion, inherited from the nineteenth century. While it was, theoretically, still attached to the ideals and great narratives of the Enlightenment, reflected in the capital "L" Liberalism, practically, it operated in the spirit of "Darwin, Bismarck and Nietzsche."[6] This confusion or hypocrisy is reflected in what the thinker called the ironies of liberalism.[7]

Liberalism, notices Santayana, is founded on an ancient and orthodox conviction about there being one, discoverable system of political organization, which is superior to all others. Its skeleton "consists in limiting the prescriptions of the law to a few points, for the most part negative, leaving it to the initiative and conscience of individuals to order their life and conversation as they like, provided only they do not interfere with the same freedom of others."[8] A concomitant, tacit theory of human nature assumes that it is practically indeterminate and infinitely flexible, which encourages one to ignore people's historical heritage and cultural identity, and ascribe to a human individual a merely abstract identity of a subject of law, one among many equals. Neither does the universe offer any stable foundations for formulating a positive truth about the human condition.[9] The liberal perspective, then, wishfully assumes – not for its own inconvenience – the possibility of a human *tabula rasa* and a social *carte blanche*. Circumventing the natural human diversity, a 19th century liberal hoped that the future humanity would unite under the banner of a common type of virtue and a common idea of happiness. Finally, he assumed it to be possible to harmonize two human interests: in material comfort, and in moral liberty. He thought that "in politics, discussion would explain and conciliate all differences, and compromise would render all actions complementary."[10] Materially secured, culturally and morally free, educated to tolerance,

---

6 Santayana, *Winds of Doctrine*, 8.
7 Santayana observed the ironies of liberalism, as noted by Moreno, in that the shortcomings of liberalism make it drift in two opposite directions, both of which are a departure from its primary idea: 1) anti-statism and anarchism, 2) socialism, sometimes allied with nationalism. See: Moreno, *Santayana the Philosopher*, 96.
8 SEiLS, 174.
9 Santayana does not contradict these assumptions with any set of essential "truths" about humans, but he is less radical about the said indeterminacy of human nature. Perhaps humans at large cannot be said to be thus-and-so in general, or even at any given moment, but tradition, experience, as well as sane and disciplined observation provide enough material to risk a richer account of the dynamics of human existence, one that might serve as a prelude to a political philosophy without falling into naïve simplifications.
10 DP, 319.

people were expected to coexist peacefully. "[A]ll grievances being righted and everyone quite free, we hoped in the nineteenth century to remain for ever in unchallengeable enjoyment of our private property, our private religions, and our private morals."[11]

By no means antipathetic to some forms of universalism, Santayana doubts in the universal applicability of liberal values and quarrels with the liberal progressivism insofar as both elude the existing historical and cultural diversity among peoples. There are many, possibly incommensurable, goods to be sought and attained not only by individuals but also by whole peoples. If the primary function of government is securing the true good of a given people, "the criterion by which to judge what is the true good of a people or of an individual lies *within* that individual or that people."[12] Santayana inclines towards (a very modern indeed) view that universal and "ultimate [human] aims are not discerned, for the excellent reason that they do not exist."[13] The awareness of this fact should not altogether debilitate the ability to set ideal aims, but rather remind of the need to reconcile them with the existing circumstances. Likewise, rationality in politics, postulated by the thinker, is a contextual rationality and not an absolute one; from an abstract, absolute perspective, "no human undertaking could be anything but an irrational and unnecessary commitment."[14] Hence, rather than striving to materialize its own theoretical vision, rational politics focuses on reforming the existing institutions so that they serve better the empowerment and harmonization of the diverse human efforts and aspirations.

The liberal view of a universal improvement of the human world assumed the immanence of progress ("continued change for the better")[15] in the human world and its continuous orientation – towards increasing liberty. In its universalist aspiration, it wished to see everybody "on the same compulsory voyage."[16] The path of progress was dogmatically assumed, complains Santayana, to lead through "vast numbers, material complexity, moral uniformity, and economic interdependence."[17] "It is not that Santayana," remarks Gray, "in a spirit of misanthropic perversity, denies that human arrangements are ever improvable."[18]

---

11 DP, 448.
12 DP, 421. My emphasis.
13 DP, 427.
14 DP, 432.
15 SiELS, 179.
16 SiELS, 181.
17 SiELS, 180.
18 PLIB, 21.

The thinker admits the possibility of progress understood as advancement in a given area of human activity and within a given period of time. Appreciative of the achievements of the Enlightenment as he was, he nevertheless rejected some of its elements such as the cult of human progress. Another shortcoming of the idea of progress noted by Santayana is that it assumes there to be relatively fixed criteria of measuring improvement, whereas in reality ideals, aims, and the standards of improvement are temporary, some of them only local, and change under the influence of historical and cultural factors.[19] What is more, it was assumed that ultimately "the people's interests should be identical for all" and material progress would be accompanied by a universal moral transformation.[20] Santayana thought it naïve to rely on a future unanimity of humans, who – after gaining the promised freedom – would all wish to be tolerant and polite. By making such an assumption, liberalism proved that its anthropology was "hopelessly pre-Nietzschean; it was Victorian."[21] It underestimated natural human variety, the impact of history, necessity, and contingency on the vicissitudes of human efforts, as well as the impact of the militant and competitive aspect of human will on politics and culture.

Some features of liberalism as a doctrine, then, make it a morally "transcendental" and dogmatically teleological worldview rather than an empirical and pluralist one, as one might expect it to be. The presence of these idealist tendencies within the liberal worldview not only weakened its practicability but also, possibly, marked a tendency to either diminish the actual reality of evil and injustice as only temporary, or justify their presence in the name of a better future.

At this point, prior to any further discussion of Santayana's criticism, let me remind briefly, following John Gray, the classical ways of justifying the liberal commitment. First, there is the doctrine of natural rights, as formulated, among others, by John Locke, which ascribes to human beings rights that are "pre-conventional, morally prior to any … contractual arrangement," and which manifest themselves in the human ability to judge, i.e., make "valid and weighty claims in justice against each other, society and government."[22] The main weakness of this thesis rests in that it is tenable only at the background of a universal, natural law of divine origin. It is in this sense that Santayana considers the idea of natural rights to be overly ambitious metaphysically. Having said this, a minimalist and empirical version of a natural law, manifest in "the

---

19   PLIB, 23.
20   DP, 390.
21   SiELS, 183.
22   LIB, 45–46.

natural necessities of human social life," and implying the existence of certain moral limits valid for most human societies, as proposed by David Hume, may still be defensible.[23] A naturalistic and humanistic version of such constraints is traceable also in Santayana's philosophy and may even be said, tentatively, to set limits to his relativism.

Another classical justification of liberal rights is the transcendental one, originating with Kant. Human beings do not act morally by virtue of their nature or a natural law. They do not act morally out of necessity or a natural inclination in the first place. The condition of possibility of morality (the existence of which is derived by Kant from the fact of human moral conceptions) is the existence of a free individual, endowed with an *autonomous* will, which is understood as the ability to act according to principles, the exclusive source of which is *a priori* reasoning. This will in itself is unconditionally good. The status of a free person, being the only source of a universal moral law, and capable of acting in accordance with it, endows human beings with an intrinsic dignity. The bearers of this dignity are to be treated, without exceptions, as ends in themselves and never as a means to some other end. It follows that the state (of ends) is one that provides conditions for practicing moral autonomy by humans, or, in other words, excludes obstacles (different forms of coercion) that might debilitate human capacity to follow the rules of their own reason. Liberal order, then, is a space of freedom, where rational agents act morally, or, in other words, fulfill moral duties in relation to oneself and other persons. Morality, for Kant, has its source in freedom, in the strict, transcendental sense of this notion. This vision, as has been pointed out by critics, lacks "universality as an image of moral life," and is too dependent on the specific Kantian conception of a transcendental human self.[24] Schopenhauer, with whom Santayana would agree at this point, criticized it for the failure to provide an empirical motivation for moral acts. Santayana, in whose view morality has natural sources and is propagated, to a large degree, through culture and thanks to human mimetism, is at a far remove from the Kantian standpoint. Santayana's opinion on Kant notwithstanding, the importance of Kant as a modern exponent of the idea of freedom as autonomy and self-rule is undisputable. Santayana seems to have underestimated the fact that the Kantian understanding of freedom legitimizes critical philosophy insofar as it (critical philosophy) exposes ways in which society and the state corrupt individual autonomy and instrumentalize persons.

---

23 LIB, 49.
24 LIB, 51.

If I were to juxtapose the above described position with that of Santayana, rephrasing what has already been told in this book in terms of the Kantian notion of "dignity," I would suggest that according to Santayana, the source of the dignity of human life may be sought in its: 1) *autotelia*, 2) creativity, 3) the faculty of understanding and contemplation. Each life is lived for its own sake and while attaining its own specific goods – alone or with others – produces, transforms and cherishes *forms* – arts, symbols, virtues, objects, customs, etc. It is through forms that human life sublimates its impulses and expresses itself. The creative dimension is accompanied by the contemplative one, which crowns vital flourishing and prompts the recognition of the intrinsic value of other vital forms. Advancing vital liberty, then, becomes the ultimate, or, to use the Kantian language, "apodictic" justification for the existence of human government. In connection to that, one may distinguish two types of inalienable freedom ascribed by Santayana to each and every human being – that of an autonomous judge ("[e]ssentially and inwardly, each man is autonomous, the only seat and absolute final judge of all judgments"),[25] and the imaginative freedom of a poet or a free spirit.[26] All this allows one to understand better Santayana's insistence on the protection of diversity as an expression of freedom and the source of variety of traditions, schools, criteria of excellence, and hence – forms. Santayana should find liberalism a worthy option at least insofar as the liberal rule: 1) is conducive to the preservation of a peaceful human diversity; 2) is reasonably protective of individual lives in pursuit of their varied forms of completion; 3) recognizes and rewards mastery and eminence as sources of standards and criteria in society and culture.

Another version of the relation between freedom and autonomy is to be found in Spinoza, whom Santayana held in great reverence. The two notions here are closely related but not identical. The first refers rather to human actions, while the second – to the mental processes of forming convictions, judging, and decision-making. It thus stands for a self-rule or a capacity to self-rule. In Spinoza's system, where people, as natural beings, are causally determined, it is understanding, rational deliberation, and deciding in accordance with one's own beliefs and commitments that form the content of the idea of autonomy. "Spinoza identified autonomy with rational behaviour," notes Matthew J. Kisner.[27] What is more, autonomy requires that one has "adequate ideas," or, in other words, knowledge.[28] Autonomy matters because it

---

25   DP, 368.
26   … a free spirit for whom "heteronomy is suicide." LR1, 169.
27   Matthew J. Kisner, *Spinoza on Human Freedom: Reason, Autonomy and the Good Life* (Cambridge, Ma: Cambridge University Press, 2013), 61.
28   Kisner, *Spinoza on Human Freedom*, 59.

"is integral to our flourishing and happiness."[29] One may search here for an affinity with Santayana's ideas of rational self-government, sanity, the freedom of mental life and its importance in the completion of human life in general. Kerr-Lawson argues persuasively that Spinoza and Santayana shared the idea of human freedom as spontaneity and defended some sort of compatibility between necessity and freedom. Although these similarities, due to the differences between their general philosophical outlooks, may be restricted in depth, they still work to similar ends and are telling in respect to such issues as happiness or the moral dimension of politics.[30]

Finally, there is the utilitarian justification of liberalism, which weds the protection of liberty with the promotion of welfare. Criticism of utilitarianism has a long history. To mention a single example of this multifaceted debate, from the perspective of Kantian philosophy, the assumption of happiness as a criterion in moral judgment undermines the whole idea of human dignity as embedded in the autonomy of reason. John S. Mill's idea of liberty as a condition for happiness and his notion of harm done to others as a factor limiting individual liberty pose problems too. In practice "harm may be prevented, and the general welfare promoted, by liberty-restricting policies that impose grossly unequal and inequitable burdens on different social groups."[31] According to K. Aksiuto, "the protection of individual autonomy against political tyranny and mass conformity" and, more specifically, the perfectionist ideal of human individuality defended by J.S. Mill in *On Liberty*, seems to be at odds with the broader utilitarian background of his ethics.[32] The author reminds that utilitarianism, as a utopian and rationalistic project, may evoke fears related to the dangers of social engineering. Aldous Huxley's anti-utopia, *Brave New World*, is a literary illustration of a social order where people are subject to a totalitarian control, including genetic engineering, and yet, unaware of the huge manipulation, are kept in a state of subjective happiness or at least self-complacency.[33] Indeed, the very formula of politics of maximizing happiness may provoke in a thoughtful layman a sense of being treated like a child, of one's autonomy, liberty, and privacy being under threat.

---

29   Kisner, *Spinoza on Human Freedom*, 72.
30   Among such differences one may list Spinoza's deterministic vision of the universe. Besides, neither liberty nor rationality in Santayana's understanding rely on knowledge in the strong Spinozian sense. For a detailed, comparative discussion of Santayana's and Spinoza's conceptions of freedom see: Kerr-Lawson, "Freedom and Free Will."
31   LIB, 54.
32   Kamil Aksiuto, *Szczęście i wolność: utylitarystyczny liberalizm Johna Stuarta Milla* (Warszawa: Wydawnictwo Studiów Politycznych PAN, 2016), 26.
33   Aksiuto, *Szczęście i wolność*, 53–54.

Santayana, in his rare and brief remarks on utilitarianism, wrote that a moralist philosopher who thinks himself capable of defining happiness and pleasure, and designing a proper "benevolent legislation," would have to possess a thorough knowledge of human nature in all its variety, which is something hardly achievable. Santayana, nevertheless, expresses sympathy towards the moral aspect of the utilitarian endeavor. It wished "to transform institutions to fit human nature better and to educate human nature by those new institutions so that it might better realise its latent capacities. These are matters which a man may modify by his acts and they are therefore the proper concern of the moralist."[34] Mill's effort expressed a nobly revolutionary and deeply humane protest "against the world and its oppressions; it was the moral side of utilitarianism, of the rebellion against irrational morality."[35] The weakness of utilitarianism, in Santayana's view, was that it proposed an almost utopian, positive project, aimed at an illusory happiness, instead of focusing more on concrete, empirical suffering, "misery and pain," in which case it would express more truly the real stakes of the endeavor. "[I]t would have been wiser and truer to their real inspiration, to have laid all emphasis on evils to be abated, leaving the good to shape itself in freedom."[36] Besides, in these reservations there resonates an intuition that setting happiness as an upright positive goal of politics may be burdened with the shadow of *nemesis*. It is true that "happiness is the only sanction of life; where happiness fails, existence remains a mad and lamentable experiment."[37] However, happiness may be a resultant or even a side-effect of reforms but not the formally established aim. Interestingly, one may read in J.S. Mill autobiography that at a mature stage of his life he understood that happiness is achievable if and only if not set up as an indirect aim. "The only chance is to treat, not happiness, but some end external to it, as the purpose of life," he wrote.[38] John Gray, in his turn, sheds light on an important paradox in Mill's theory, namely – if increasing happiness is the goal, "liberty would dwindle in value as knowledge of the most effective means to happiness increased."[39] This insight, by the way, illuminates at once the problematic relation between

---

34 George Santayana, *Some Turns of Thought in Modern Philosophy* (Cambridge: Cambridge University Press, 1933), 56.
35 Santayana, *Some Turns of Thought*, 57.
36 Santayana, *Some Turns of Thought*, 57.
37 LR, 63.
38 John Stuart Mill, *Autobiography* (Oxford: Oxford University Press, 2018), 82. See also: Aksiuto, *Szczęście i wolność*, 56.
39 John Gray, *Seven Types of Atheism* (Penguin Books, 2018), 91.

liberty and knowledge, to which Santayana was sensitive while speculating about a possible beneficence of being governed by a knowledgeable and honestly representative yet authoritarian government. Other than that, in Santayana's writings one comes across an idea that it is precisely the ineradicable and universal human *ignorance* that, in some contexts at least, provides an argument in favour of both the democratic principle of self-rule and the liberal negative freedom.

6.2 The Fate of the Liberal Ideals under the Liberal Rule

Ideally, politics is but a means of approaching the life of reason, defined as "the art of satisfying our compatible inclinations in the midst of our inevitable circumstances."[40] This idea along with the epistemic humility and the moderate individualism of Santayana may be said to make him akin to a modern, largely disillusioned, and pragmatically-oriented kind of liberal outlook, just as Hobbes's individualism makes its author, although the nature of their individualisms differ. Interestingly, both shed light on a sort of primordial basis for egalitarianism, but they locate it elsewhere. Santayana sees *necessity* and the human condition as the only plane of natural equality, and equality of opportunity as a sufficient dimension of social equality; for Hobbes it is the *freedom* of people in the state of nature that makes them equal. In neither case is equality understood as equality in powers or achievement. Rather, it is a kind of equality in existential, pre-social situatedness.

Negative freedom in Santayana's thought, for better or for worse, is not framed in terms of an apodictic priority. Nevertheless, there are reasons to believe that Santayana would roughly agree with the view of the function and historical embeddedness of basic liberties

> as framing the necessary conditions of autonomous agency. A free man is one who possesses the rights and privileges needed for him to think and act autonomously – to rule himself and be ruled by another. The content of the basic liberties need not be fixed or immutable, but will embody the conditions necessary in a given historical circumstance for the growth and exercise of powers of autonomous thought and action.[41]

---

40   DP, 159.
41   LIB, 60–61.

Keeping this sense of contextuality in mind, Santayana points to what he thinks to be tensions or discrepancies between the aspirations that negative freedom accompanies or invites in practice, on the one hand, and the liberal-democratic, humanitarian, and egalitarian ideals, on the other. There reappears in his reflections on liberalism the idea – conveyed in the quotation below – that the failure to raise the many to a certain economic and cultural level, at which they might be able to start taking advantage of the legal freedom at their disposal, exposes them to some forms of enslavement, of which the economic one is the most obvious.

> Equality and, later, democracy have been nominal battle-cries of liberalism; but ... [r]eal equality is incompatible with that private wealth and that moral liberty which were at bottom the aspiration of this school. Moral liberty invites diversity, and presupposes it. Why should we be incited to differ if we all in fact and by nature agreed? And we do agree in fact and by nature in wishing to be comfortable and free; while we profoundly differ by nature and in fact as to what we are able to do, or wish to do, with our comfort and freedom. ... The age of liberalism, the second half of the nineteenth century, succeeded in describing this natural diversity of life ... but it failed sadly in universalizing comfort, and spreading through all nations an individual moral liberty ... The people had been freed politically and nominally by being given the vote, and enslaved economically.[42]

Leaving aside the fact that Santayana, throughout his *oeuvre*, exhibits a somewhat confusing tendency to use the notions of diversity and equality as antonyms, the above passage introduces one to a spectrum of ways in which liberty under the liberal rule has become – for many – fictitious. This fact and its consequences form one of the targets of Santayana's criticism.

A certain superficiality characterizes the liberal outlook and practice and manifests itself in neglecting some fundamental issues, such as the satisfaction of basic material necessities, the diffusion of wealth, the need for defining and attending to matters of public concern, and people's craving for some relatively stable identity.

> The rightness of liberalism is exactly proportional to the diversity of human nature, to its vague hold on its ideals. Where this vagueness and

---

42   DP, 319.

play of variation stop, and they stop not far below the surface, the sphere of public organization should begin. It is in the subsoil of uniformity, of tradition, of dire necessity that human welfare is rooted. ... the flowers of culture that do not draw their sap from that soil are only paper flowers.[43]

Given this and other similar passages, Santayana would agree with John Gray's assertion that "an authoritarian type of government may sometimes do better from a liberal standpoint than a democratic regime," provided that it does not violate basic civil liberties.[44] Rather than betting on the self-reliance of (unprepared) individuals, governments might do better, Santayana thinks, assuming that humans are "by nature fundamentally helpless and automatic."[45] Liberty as conceived of by liberals, in practice may be conducive to deep injustice unless some mechanisms controlling the distribution of the costs of necessity are introduced. In other words, negative conception of freedom need be somehow associated with the *opportunity* for self-realization. Witnessing the rise of populism and predicting its future waves, Santayana connects this phenomenon to the social frustration caused by governmental inertia and neglectfulness.

In-between the two world wars it seemed clear to Santayana that liberalism provided effective freedom only to the well-off, betraying its initial ideals. Although he had never declared socialist sympathies, from a couple of brief essays from the collection *Soliloquies in England* one may infer that the contrast between the humanitarian ideals of liberalism and the social and cultural degradation of a substantial part of population stroke him as inhuman and a bad omen for the future of the liberal order. Legal freedom to compete for the same goods when powers are unequal creates a space where a new social organization, one based on predatory and acquisitive passions, takes roots. In consequence, it may provoke an unexpected wave of socio-political radicalization:

> Now the mass, hopelessly out of the running in the race for wealth, falls out and drifts into squalor. ... [One] becomes a denizen of those slimy quarters, under the shadow of railway bridges, breweries and gas-works ...; but perhaps God does not see all this, because a pall hangs over it perpetually of impenetrable smoke. The liberal system, which sought to raise the individual, has degraded masses; and this on so vast a scale and to so pitiable a degree, that the other element in liberalism, philanthropic

---

43   SiElS, 177–178.
44   LIB, 74.
45   DP, 436.

zeal, has come again to the fore. Liberty go hang, say the new radicals; let us save the people.[46]

Now, if one wonders whether Santayana is motivated here by empathy towards his fellow creatures, a concern about injustice, or a regret about the dissolving, old system, the answer probably is – all of them. Regardless of his personal motivations, his insights into what I call, metaphorically, a *nemesis* mechanism revealing itself under the liberal rule not only were valid back then, but, I believe, retain something of their validity up to this day.

There are many, more or less explicit, indications in the passages quoted in this and the following chapter that allow to infer that where Santayana would probably part ways with classical liberals (and libertarians) is the issue of the scope of an acceptable state intervention. I suppose Santayana would object against certain justifications of laissez-faire policy, such as Hayek's idea of free markets performing a function of an epistemic revelatory instrument in respect to so-called tacit knowledge, leading to increasing an "evolutionary rationality." Santayana would probably object against the implied therein subjugation of the humane and rational element in society and culture to the (self-regulating) rules of economic life and its alleged rationality.[47] He might assess Hayek's doctrine as dehumanizing society by exposing it to the rules of natural selection, and deconstructing its coherence by way of promoting a kind of individualism based on economic power. In other words, Santayana was aware of the fact that a laissez-faire policy might, paradoxically, become another "road to serfdom."

At this point, I think it merits evoking what Santayana's contemporary, Russian political thinkers, such as Boris Vysheslavtsev or Sergey Hessen, whose perspective was enriched with the experience of the Russian Revolution, wrote about liberalism more or less at the same time. The former thought that both the liberal and the communist order, the ideological foundations of which were focused on a certain conception of human emancipation, turn out to be different facets of industrial civilization, in which the "the logic of freedom" was bound to compete with and ultimately be defeated by "the logic of efficiency." This occurred under the conditions of "economism" – a paradigm granting to economic sphere absolute priority over the remaining spheres of human existence.[48] It was represented both by capitalism, whenever it adopted a laissez-

---

46 SiELS, 186.
47 I refer here to the ideas of Friedrich A. Hayek contained in his: *Individualism and Economic Order* (Chicago and London: University of Chicago Press, 1980).
48 Sławomir Mazurek, introduction to *Państwo prawa i socjalizm* [Legal State and Socialism], by Sergey Hessen, trans. Sławomir Mazurek (Warszawa: Wydawnictwo IFiS PAN, 2003),

faire policy with its faith in the ideal of a free market, and the Soviet totalitarianism, where state-owned economy was literally obsessed with efficiency, as evidenced richly by the propaganda of the time.[49] Both Vysheslavtsev and Hessen thought that "economism," embedded in the industrial civilization, led to the impoverishment and exploitation of large numbers of people. The category of exploitation, though, acquired in their writings a non-Marxist, ethical meaning, and stood for the instrumentalization of human persons – a phenomenon which could be restricted only by means of the state law. That "the state should guarantee the right to a dignified existence," became the main idea behind Hessen's vision of "New Liberalism," a transformed kind of a liberalism of the future, one saturated with elements of socialism and intimately connected to a democratic system of government.[50] Interestingly, many believe today that communism lost credit and succumbed not to a laissez-faire capitalism but to a vision of liberalism enriched with substantial pro-social elements.

As for Santayana's opinion about the phenomenon of abandoning a laissez-faire policy for state interventionism, it seems to be unequivocal. He clearly counts it as one of the ironies of liberalism. The movement towards welfare state seemed a natural, if not inevitable, reaction to the actual amount of injustice and suffering. Principally, as already mentioned, Santayana does not exclude that a paternal state may be beneficent and respond more efficiently to certain social needs than a minimal government does. In some types of societies it may also be conducive to the desired unanimity. Yet, these changes, save for the fact that they exhibited certain weaknesses of the liberal rule, did not occur in a void and were not innocent themselves. They occurred in mass societies, where social reform was accompanied by a fierce competition of "propagandas," each ensuing its own, often authoritarian or totalitarian schemes of leadership. Political capitals were growing on manipulated popular conscience. These "propagandas" "appeal to different weaknesses of human nature; they are alike, however, in being equally illiberal."[51] Santayana, then, to stress it once again, sees the evolution of the liberal order in terms of a

---

xiii,xiv,xv. See also: Sławomir Mazurek, "Wydajność i wolność (kryzys kultury industrialnej w diagnozie Borysa Wyszesławcewa)" [Efficiency and freedom (the crisis of industrial culture in Boris Vysheslavtsev's diagnosis)], in *Filantrop czyli Nieprzyjaciel i inne szkice o rosyjskim renesansie religijno-filozoficznym* (Warszawa: IFiS PAN, 2004), 24–40.

49 In an article "Why I am not a Marxist," Santayana asks the following question concerning the Soviet communists: "Would they equalize wealth because they despise it, or because they value nothing else?" George Santayana, "Why I am not a Marxist," *Modern Monthly* ix, no. 2 (April 1953), 77–79.
50 Hessen, *Państwo prawa i socjalizm*, 39.
51 SiELS, 187.

paradoxical reversal. He sees the "earnest liberals" forced to support the radical ideals of revolutionary groups, which announce the slogan of freeing the people. "But freeing the people from what?" he asks and answers in a somewhat sophistical manner: "From the consequences of freedom."[52]

The interventionist state, rising in response to the consequences of the liberal state turning a blind eye to the realities or primary necessities "interwoven before man was man into the very texture of things,"[53] carried the potentiality of its own, multi-faceted *nemesis* within. In a mass democracy, powerful interests groups, including corporate interests, arise, become politicized and benefit from the state-controlled redistribution of wealth more than individuals, or the public do, obtaining legal and economic privileges. John Gray's analysis of these phenomena may serve as a post-scriptum to Santayana's premonitions. The growing states "tend overwhelmingly to service private interests rather than protect or promote the public interest,"[54] and, consequently, deepen social injustices rather than repair them. This tendency, which began around the First World War, notes Gray, has ended up in "a political war of redistribution."[55] Not only does the modern state fails to fulfill its role of protecting the public interest, but, by becoming "a corporatist Behemoth," it has also lost its basic "Leviathan's" function of protecting a peaceful civil association.[56] Thus, not only liberal but also democratic and socialist, ideal functions of the state are paralyzed at their roots, while neither the common nor the individual good is properly protected. In a long run, the state may become – while remaining *technically* democratic – a theater of gaining legitimacy by oligarchies, an "instrument of predation,"[57] nourishing parasitic interest groups and draining the rest of society. This is where Santayana's distinction between authentic and technical or instrumental democracy, which I will discuss in more detail in the following chapter, appears useful.

The instrumentalization of the democratic state was reflected, as Santayana shows, in wars of propagandas. One of its aspects was revealing the illusoriness of the weight of the individual choice in politics – the basic democratic right to vote. Wherever there is a well-established partisan system, or the system is corrupt and manipulated by factions in a state of war, the choice tends to be – for better or for worse – illusory. Rather unfortunately, Santayana tends

---

52 SiELS, 189.
53 BR, 114.
54 PLIB, 11.
55 PLIB, 12.
56 PLIB, 13.
57 PLIB, 12.

to weave these remarks into his general reflections, such as the one about man being dependent through and through in ways we have already discussed at length. From this perspective, already the fact that one cannot decide about one's potentialities and one's birth certificate makes the remaining choice at least partly illusory. If we add to it the inescapable human ignorance, any serious choice resembles a lottery. As an argument against choice, Santayana here is unconvincing. The fact that options are limited is not enough to make the right to choose, wherever there is choice, invalid or unworthy. If, in turn, Santayana suggests that people are eluding themselves or are deluded by others about limitless possibilities that lay open before them, while much – too much indeed – has been decided behind their back, then he sounds right.

It is typical of Santayana to support his critical diagnoses with reference to psychological insights. Negative freedom is insufficient to "reconcile" individuals living in a capitalist, competitive environment, where they find themselves exposed to an almost Hobbesian condition of "a perpetual and restless desire of power after power that ceaseth only in death."[58] "Independence is cheerless," says Santayana, pointing to yet another source of potential frustration in society, "when universal freedom and chaos oblige you to decide the most important questions afresh and by accident."[59] If free choice is to be a means of effective self-government, it should be deliberate and "express an innate moral character in the people, and a dispassionate perception of the circumstances."[60] Liberalism bets on individual self-interpretation and self-reliance without attending to the fact that good judgment is an existential and intellectual challenge. In practice, access to knowledge and education in social skills *divides society into those who are successful and those who are tolerated*. Liberal kindness, then, is far from saving all, and tolerated people, remarks Santayana insightfully, "are never conciliated."[61]

Universal sympathy, impartiality, toleration – dear also to Santayana – have been "the best inspiration of liberalism."[62] Yet, certain facts concerning liberal societies turned out uncongenial to these disinterested ideals. Many a kind and tolerant individuals are left at the mercy of rather brutal rules of social promotion. Meanwhile, the democratic sphere of free speech was taken over by rival ideologies:

---

58   Thomas Hobbes, *Leviathan*, ed. and introduction J. C. A. Gaskin (Oxford and New York: Oxford University Press, 1996), pt. 1, ch.11, par. 2, 66.
59   DP, 180.
60   DP, 355.
61   DP, 436.
62   BR, 110–111.

> By giving a free rein to such propagandas, and by disgusting the people with too much optimism, toleration and neutrality, liberalism has introduced a new reign of unqualified ill-will. Hatred and willfulness are everywhere; nations and classes are called to life on purpose to embody them. These propagandas have taken shape in the blue sky of liberalism ... but they are engines of war ... Each will try to establish its universal ascendancy by force in contempt of personal freedom, or the voice of majorities.[63]

Whereas Tocqueville warned about the tyranny of majority as a result of certain developments within democracy, Santayana, who sometimes expressed a similar concern, now points out that liberalism has open way to *a tyranny of an aggressive minority*. "Minorities everywhere have their way; and majorities, grown familiar with projects that at first shocked them ... follow like sheep." The power of minority was likely to rely on a sectarian zeal among its own members and the herd instinct, docility, and "apathy ... of the million."[64] A perfect example of a scheme of domination of a minority over masses manifested itself in the October (Bolshevik) Revolution of 1917. Santayana also noticed a chaos in the political life itself. Indeed, before WWI both liberal and social-democratic parties became saturated with nationalism and racism and ready to betray its ideals. In 1913 Santayana wrote:

> It had seemed that an age that was levelling and connecting all nations, an age whose real achievements were of international application, was destined to establish the solidarity of mankind as a sort of axiom. The idea of solidarity is indeed often invoked in speeches, and there is an extreme socialistic party that – when a wave of national passion does not carry it the other way – believes in international brotherhood. But even here, black men and yellow men are generally excluded; and in higher circles, where history, literature, and political ambition dominate men's minds, nationalism has become of late an omnivorous all-permeating passion.[65]

Meanwhile, communist influences penetrated the body politic in Europe, leading, for example to the establishment of the Hungarian Soviet Republic in 1919. *Whatever the resolution of those struggles for domination might be, Santayana*

---

63 SiELS, 187–8.
64 Both quotations: SiELS, 188.
65 Santayana, *Winds of Doctrine,* 5.

predicted, the new orders would be vengefully illiberal. In "Alternatives to Liberalism," an essay written in 1934, the philosopher distinguishes between liberalism as a policy and "a method of government," and liberalism as an idealistic philosophy, which in itself could be preserved in people's minds under varied political arrangements. He thinks that establishing the former may, ironically, result in the expulsion of the latter.[66]

Thus, public disillusionment and frustration could be taken advantage of by a new kind of leader, one "posing as a Titan" and willing to establish a new kind of order by means of an all-embracing control of life, or, in other words, a totalitarian order. As noted by Herman J. Saatkamp, Santayana viewed the rise of the famous dictators of the era – Lenin, Mussolini, and Hitler – "as a natural result of the sway of public opinion and the pressing need for order."[67] "I am afraid a city so founded, if it could stand, would be an iron City of Dis," comments Santayana. "These heroes would have entrenched themselves in hell … and would have reason to pine for the liberal chaos from which their Satanic system had saved them."[68] The hellish new order may be compared to what John Gray calls a "genocidal modernism," giving rise to "a Hobbesian anomie."[69]

Referring to the specific categories of Santayana's philosophy, "vital liberty differentiates" and requires differentiation, just as "beauty, culture, genius, or virtue" do. When dissociated from vital liberty, empty freedom either "leaves all in the same anonymous crowd,"[70] leading to the condition of *undifferentiation*, to use René Girard's notion, or invites factionism and particularism. In case the liberal vision of universal unanimity and toleration ever came true, speculates Santayana, what would be the fate of human variety, so precious to him? Toleration, for which Santayana happened to be a spokesman at many occasions, might then accompany

> the euthanasia of differences. Everybody would be free to be what he liked, and no one would care to be anything but what pleased everybody. Concessions and tolerance and equality would thus have really led to peace, and to peace of the most radical kind, the peace of moral extinction. Between two nothings there is eternal peace; but between

---

66 BR, 109.
67 Herman J. Saatkamp, Jr, introduction to BR, xxvi.
68 BR, 115.
69 LIB, 85.
70 Both quotations come from DP, 358. My emphasis.

two somethings if they come within range of each other, there is always danger of war.[71]

Diversity and conflict tend to coexist. Some kind of response to it is contained in Santayana's speculations about a multi-national empire, where violent forms of conflict are kept at bay by the state. Elsewhere, however, one finds Santayana reflecting on how equality understood as uniformity and/or *undifferentiation*, can be conducive to fierce rivalry and violence. I will return to this topic in the chapter devoted to Santayana's views on communism. For now let me only say that, in the spirit of René Girard, it is precisely the multitude of "nothings" here that is engaged in an endless struggle, motivated either by the human desire to become different (a "something") or, in case of the scarcity of resources, by the will to survive and prevail.

Paradoxically, the liberal and democratic rule, according to Santayana, leaves not enough space for true diversity. Theoretically, liberalism secures legal protection to every individual and, by respecting the distinction between private and public sphere, prevents a pervasive politicization of life. All are expected to cooperate only in the legal sphere, all the remaining ones consisting of matters of free choice. In practice, however, the liberal system – Santayana refers particularly to the English and American examples – leaves a much narrower margin in the sphere of culture and morality than one would expect it to do. The organization of economic life, liberal education, and the dominant hierarchy of values make the sphere of freedom, Santayana thinks, illusory and even "derisive." "If you sanctify private property, you impose a corresponding set of virtues, distinctions, ambitions, and rancours. It is a material social bondage that enslaves the mind ... *freedom of mind depends on freedom to rearrange material conditions.*"[72] Moreover, under a democratic rule, one is still expected to acquiesce to the reign of majority and conform to the standards of an average man. Thus, the diversity and pluralism that are meant to be secured by the legal "hard core" of the liberal state are, in a sense, stifled.

When the protection of private property becomes *the* utmost legal concern, and business enterprise – the most respected form of life activity, all the rest starts to seem almost illusory. In this caricature of a reversed Platonic order of being, the large sphere of "the free life beyond," the sphere of individuality and difference, "rather confused and vaporous," becomes an easy target of propaganda, to which modern, atomized society is susceptible. Meanwhile, the state

---

71   DP, 449.
72   DP, 353. My emphasis.

cannot be consistent in its liberal commitment as it finds itself forced to take control– in its subjects' interest – over some areas, such as education and the military. But then, control becomes only a matter of degree. After all,

> the same solicitude and the same constructive impulse would consistently justify the state in controlling industry, ... arts, and religion. ... Totally to control life in the governed ... has always been the aim of theocracies, and was the ideal proposed on rational moral grounds by Plato.[73]

This is understandable due to the fact that "[p]erhaps without official coercion it would be impossible to form a definite type of citizen in our vast, amorphous populations, and to create a respect for a definite set of virtues and satisfactions."[74] Mass media become the main channels of influence on public imagination, and it surprises Santayana how efficient propaganda turns out to be in relatively well-educated societies. He is concerned with the emerging "absolute subjection of the individual, in soul and body, to the instincts of the majority – the most cruel and unprogressive of masters."[75]

The Scylla of an excessive state intervention and indoctrination has an alternative in the Charybdis of the factionalism or particularism of civil society. In both cases negative freedom reveals something of its elitist, fragile, and demanding nature. A "[v]irginal liberty," Santayana writes not without irony, "is good only to be surrendered at the time to a right influence."[76] Reduction of the state to the minimum leads to the emergence of countless public, semi-private and private associations, churches, religious orders, and clubs; "otherwise that state would hardly be civilized and nothing of importance would ever be done in it."[77] Alexis de Tocqueville, who feared the tyranny of majority and the centralization of power in the state's hands, praised the American ability to associate and considered it an effective tool of a genuine self-government and a counter-weight for state initiative. Not that he wasn't aware of the possibility of an "absorption" of individualities by the public life, but he considered it an unavoidable cost. Social atomization posed a more serious danger than the soft pressure exerted on individuals by civil society. Santayana, in turn, writing two centuries later, spares no criticism towards what he thinks to be liberal illusions about individual autonomy and pluralism of opinion. The pervasiveness of the

---

73   BR, 111.
74   BR, 113.
75   Santayana, *Winds of Doctrine*, 5.
76   SiELS, 174–175.
77   SiELS, 175.

aforementioned associations and organizations threatens intellectual autonomy and "jeopardize[s] the perfect liberty which individuals are supposed to enjoy."[78] He resorts to exaggeration when saying that "no paternal government has ever exerted so pervasive and indiscreet an influence" on individuals as these organizations are capable of doing. Man "finds his life supervised," the grim account continues, "his opportunities pre-empted, his conscience intimidated, and his pocket drained. ... At every turn he must choose between being incorporated or being ostracized."[79] Likewise, the authors of *Dialectic of Enlightenment* describe the excessive pressure of civil associations in terms of a powerful and oppressive system of social control in a liberal and capitalist society. "Everybody is guaranteed formal freedom," they write, but anyone "who wants to avoid ruin must see that he is not found wanting when weighed in the scales of this apparatus."[80]

The above ideas may be associated with Santayana's broader speculations on secularity and ideological neutrality of the state. A dogmatic autocracy would have to deal with a mass of humans, not all of whom "can possibly aspire to the same virtues, or recognize the same hierarchy of excellences ... there will not only be ineradicable vices; there will also be ineradicable virtues and aspirations contrary to the prevalent public ways."[81] An obvious alternative is a secular society and a neutral state. This ideal, however, also requires a certain *paideia*. Children should be brought up in a relatively neutral and tolerant environment, and choose their ideal allegiances only as adults, conscious of their vocation and choices. To an extent this happens in the case of Protestant churches. However, unless an authority and discipline existing at home renders it otherwise, there is a tendency for these religious affiliations to become superficial and even "marginal." "This yields us, then, a moralizing society, but not a moral one."[82]

A problematic aspect of a secular society is that it tends to leave certain human needs unsatisfied. Rival powers, ready to fill the void, are likely to emerge. Some of these agents will be able to establish themselves firmly enough, penetrate society, and influence it in ways quite contrary to the expectations and hopes attached to such a society. In other words, secularity itself does not warrant bringing humans closer to the life of reason. The government "may disregard the thing officially, but *the private body will become in fact a*

---

78 SiELS, 175.
79 SiELS, 175.
80 Adorno and Horkheimer, *Dialectic of Enlightenment*, 149–150.
81 DP, 450.
82 DP, 450.

second government, a part of that officious social order which really dominates mankind."[83] Among prominent sources of moral and intellectual authority in the twentieth century Santayana enumerates private institutions of higher education and sports. Their influence on people's allegiances and choices becomes the measure of their political significance even if they do not evoke explicitly any political ideal or option. Today, in the era of internet and the disappearing boundary between the private and the public, the agents of influence are diffused, yet considerably influential, some of them unpredictable and unaccountable. Any government, then, and a democratic one in particular, to preserve its authority, is forced to take these powers into account, negotiate with them, and even imitate their methods and compete with them. While Santayana's inexplicit postulate of protecting culture from excessive politicization remains, as I believe, valid, it may be the case that, on a deeper level, it is not so much politics that is the source of the politicization of modern life, but – this life itself.

Santayana, then, views liberalism as, on the one hand, dogmatic and, on the other, shortsighted and naïve in its ungrounded optimism about the future evolution of human society. The liberal rule proved incapable of protecting society and the state from the whole range of ailments related not only (and, perhaps, not predominantly) to the inner ironies of liberalism but also to larger socio-economic, political, and cultural factors, in confrontation with which the criticized by Santayana artificiality and fragility of liberalism were fully exposed. The thinker seems to view liberalism as a noble but lofty dream, forgetful of its own origins, a skyrocket shot in the air and exploding in a spectacular array of colours, leaving a lasting afterimage in the witness's mind. When a political doctrine is too idealistic and impatient with the inherent diversity and recalcitrance of nature, "there can only be a brilliant flare and a quick collapse."[84]

6.3 Culture

There is, I believe, a deep insight for consideration in the following reflections on the decline of liberalism, coming from Santayana's last work. Liberal culture, he argues, since its birth in the nineteenth century, has been an "over-ripe fruit" of a declining civilization, and is marked by a largely unconscious, decadent thread. Its reformatory zeal, then, has always been somewhat misplaced,

---

83   DP, 451. My emphasis.
84   DP, 355.

even though it was based on a correct premonition that many conventions, superstitions, and arrangements had outlived their function. Liberals seem to Santayana strangely ignorant both of the depth of their own historical dependence and the possible, upcoming decline of their culture. Thus, forgetfulness and shortsightedness go hand in hand. Had liberalism no ancient and Christian heritage on which it could draw, had it been a foundational system, "it would left human genius in the most depressed and forlorn condition."[85] Liberalism happened to be the heir of many generations of thinkers representing diverse strands of reflection in the West, from Hume, Spinoza, Kant, Locke and Voltaire, to J.S. Mill. The liberal doctrine could have arisen "only in the post-traditional society of Europe,"[86] notes Gray. It wouldn't have arisen were it not for the bulk of ideas conveying the special position of the human individual (made in God's likeness), and the teleological (and/or eschatological) conception of time. But the ground had been paved already by the Sophists and the Stoics, who introduced the idea of the equality of all humans and the cosmopolitan ideal into Western civilization.

There is, however, yet another kind of inheritance that liberals tend to turn a blind eye to, reminds Santayana. The culture inherited had been built on

> the discipline and the sacrifices they deplore, ... the wealth they possess was amassed by appropriating lands and conducting enterprises in the high-handed manner which they denounce, and ... the fine arts and refined luxuries they revel in arise in the service of superstitions that they deride and despotisms that they abhor.[87]

Liberalism, then, is "a mere loosening of an older structure."[88] Having relieved the power of the convictions and restrictions inherent in those older traditions, in the twentieth century the liberals are reluctant to see the possibility that their own achievement is likely to "dissolve ... in some strange barbarism."[89]

---

85   SiELS, 175.
86   LIB, 82. Elsewhere the same author writes: "Locke's thought is indebted to Christianity at every point, and his liberalism is a clear and direct descendant from monotheism." See: Gray, *Seven Types of Atheism*, 90.
87   DP, 438.
88   SiELS, 176. And yet, the liberal reformers had not been bold enough, as Santayana points out elsewhere, to question the adequacy of the Christian vision of the constitution of the world and man's vocation in it. Doing so might be tantamount to choosing the path of "the Renaissance and the Revolution – that is, the re-establishment of Christian nations upon pagan basis." See: DP, 164.
89   DP, 438.

Culture becomes a source of beneficent empowerment particularly when it is able to synthesize two apparently contradictory influences: an ingrained tradition and an openness, readiness to adopt alien elements and criticize one's own without rejecting them altogether. Such, as one knows from other Santayana's writings, was the case of Great Britain up to a certain point. Looking at the example of England in his last work, Santayana notices that behind an apparent harmony between continuity and change there seems to be "a triumph of progress under the mask of conservatism."[90] He thus conveys a thought similar to the one about the reigning spirit of Darwin and Nietzsche, mentioned at the beginning of this chapter. Activism, the dominance of the present moment in human life, and the preference for "struggle over subjection"[91] stand in contrast to the liberal spirit of detachment "from all sorts of accidental tyrannies. ... that sweet, scholarly, tenderly moral, critically superior attitude of mind."[92] Thus, those who have integrated liberal ideals in their souls may find themselves torn in-between the requirement of a carefree politeness and a rather precarious environment dominated by the rules of natural selection. They may have achieved a self-discipline allowing them to accept limitations and even become "reconciled to a decent poverty and a special form of economic drudgery."[93] Would they not wish, however, that all other people share the cost of necessity and progress in a more or less the same manner as they do?

The indirect answer suggested by Santayana at this point is unlikely to satisfy all. The fact that liberalism, with all its benevolence and sophistication, should have arisen amidst inequalities, may not be a paradox but a manifestation of a certain regularity. It may be the case that accepting inequalities and the fact of the existence of privileged groups in society, we "save civilization by abandoning liberalism."[94] In other words, egalitarianism could be but a very late product of a ripe civilization, the rise of which was conditioned by very different social relations. These reflections concern a divergence between liberal culture and social practice, but they also convey a more general idea about the cost of civilization, which in the case of Western civilization amounts to its illiberal past. Other than that, alluding to the liberal optimism, Santayana suggests that the scope of charity and beneficence cannot but be limited, or, in other words, must have a specific target. This principle becomes most evident

---

90 DP, 437.
91 DP, 437.
92 SiELS, 176.
93 DP, 437.
94 DP, 437.

when a society is oriented at a single good, which fact, almost automatically, intensifies pressure, and engenders exclusion. The hectic life and the necessities of competition in the late liberal era, for example, produce and favor a specific human type, someone interested only in concrete results, who keeps to his "special hunting grounds," and whose independence "turns and turns in a narrow circuit."[95]

The blessing and the curse of indebtedness to history concern any human society and undermine the imagined power of social contracts, reforms, and new beginnings. The coercion of which any government is a source is related to the necessity this government inherits and manages. This assertion is not meant to defy the possibility of reform or justify cruel and unnecessary coercion, which liberalism, Santayana admits, rightly tries to prevent or minimize. "[T]he rational criticism and reform of it undertaken by liberals may correct some of its evils, but cannot replace its efficient causes and foundations."[96] These reflections reveal certain traits of Santayana's political views – prudence, skepticism, and an acute awareness of the fallibility of grand designs, owed to their "political myopia."[97]

In a couple of sketches, entitled "Liberalism and culture" and "The irony of liberalism," one comes across a pessimist vision of the future of liberalism. Around 1915 it was already clear that the liberal order was in a deep crisis, or, in other words, it was failing the test of history. "If there were signs of growing illiberalism in the last decades of the nineteenth century, the First World War broke the liberal order into pieces and initiated an era of wars and tyrannies."[98] Already prior to that, notes Gray, a clash between liberalism and certain democratic mechanisms, such as competition for votes, revealed its corrupting power in respect to the former.[99] "The days of liberalism are numbered," writes Santayana in an essay, in which he argues for the strictest connection between liberalism and culture, and which I consider to be a *tour-de-force* of his criticism.[100]

"Culture requires liberalism for its foundation, and liberalism requires culture for its crown. It is culture that integrates in imagination the activities which liberalism so dangerously disperses in practice."[101] For culture to evolve at least

---

95   DP, 437.
96   DP, 354.
97   DP, 437.
98   LIB, 36.
99   LIB, 33.
100 SiELS, 177.
101 SiELS, 176.

a small degree of mental liberality in the form of curiosity, sympathy, openness and toleration to the new and the different is needed. Then, as already discussed, culture, understood accumulatively and collectively, was necessary for liberalism to be born at all. Broadly understood and individually integrated culture is necessary for liberalism, with its benevolent,[102] disinterested, and universalist aspect, to survive. Finally, as a well of forms and venues for self-realization, culture endows the ideal of individual freedom from interference with additional meaning and value. In general, these prerogatives and assets had been handed down, as Santayana thinks, from older traditions and could survive for some time. Yet, liberal culture, cut off from its roots and under the pressure of massive socio-economic changes, found itself too displaced and fragile to protect its spirit of "polite humanity" against some more primitive, predatory forces, heralds of "brute humanity."

Culture as an individual value was a child of the Renaissance. It emancipated the mind, making it capable of judging, appreciating alien "qualities and values of things," and "distinguishing the better from the worse. This conscientiousness, after all, is the only form of morality that a liberal society can insist upon."[103] These words reveal Santayana's appreciation of the liberal culture, which he considers to be rational, individualistic, and emancipated, or, in other words, an approximation of what a variety of the life of reason might be. "Culture [thus understood] is a triumph of the individual over society. It is his way of profiting intellectually by a world he has not helped to make."[104] Needless to say, this is an enormously demanding and extremely fallible ideal.

Except for such obvious factors as nationalism, imperialism, war, and totalitarianism, Santayana points to certain elements of capitalist and consumerist culture and mentality as conspiring against the liberal culture and the viability of the very ideal of individual liberty under the rule of law. A disinterested, universalist benevolence was among the original motivations of liberalism. But, as discussed in the previous chapter, an incessant pursuit of

---

102 Santayana sometimes uses the term "humanitarian" in reference to both liberal and democratic ideals in an ironic and even pejorative sense and does so in two contexts. First, he presents humanitarian "slogans" as a demagogic way of attracting voters. Second, he thinks humanitarian attitude is oriented predominantly towards fulfilling the most pressing, current material needs of the governed, while neglecting those human interests that are less explicit and require setting far-sighted goals. He thus seems to oppose a "humanitarian morality" to a humanistic one. By doing so, however, he may be contradicting his own criticism of liberal idealism and its neglect of actual injustice and suffering. See: DP, 398.
103 SiELS, 177.
104 SiElS, 176.

wealth and the centrality of work tend to instrumentalize human life and thus, "kill liberty in the individual."[105] The dehumanizing "horrors of competition" literally "discredited" liberalism.[106] Santayana notices the crisis of individual agency – without naming it so *expressis verbis* – in modern society, and, to use Richard Sennett's classical term, a certain "corrosion of character." *Thus, society betrayed the integral and polite individual on whom liberalism, more or less consciously, had bet.*

Concentration on change, efficiency, and constant improvement preempted the meaning and experience of time. On the one hand, it overshadowed the value of being in the present as well as the idea of eternity, and, hence, squandered the human ability to contemplate, draining culture of an important aspect of spiritual life. On the other hand, an apparently contrary tendency, a typically modern tendency to focus only on the fleeting and the momentary emerged, impeding the ability to learn from experience and, hence, to predict wisely. Moreover, the idea of progress went hand in hand with what the Frankfurt School named "instrumental thinking," or what Charles Taylor calls "procedural mentality," and which consists in an inability to conceive of things as ends in themselves. From the viewpoint of Santayana's philosophy, the main normative assumption of which is that each human life is an end in itself, the hegemony of instrumental thinking is a serious threat for the individual and human culture alike. This "schizophrenia," by the way, this stretching in-between a complete immersion in the present, or, simply hedonism, and living under the shadow of futurity, may evoke a distant association with Daniel Bell's analysis of the cultural contradictions of the late capitalism. The (historical) ethos of capitalism, based on protestant work ethics and the principle of delayed gratification is contradicted by the pressure towards and the desire for an immediate satisfaction of wants, typical of a consumerist culture.

Moving beyond the context of liberalism to the broader context of modernity, there is yet another, negative side of the concentration on a continuous movement forward and the concomitant falling into disfavor of what has been relatively constant and traditional. It may be part of the deconstruction of certain protective mechanisms engendered by human societies, which renders them (human societies) more susceptible to totalitarian influences. To evoke an insightful remark of Hannah Arendt about totalitarianism and the deconstruction of legality that is part of it, "[i]n the interpretation of totalitarianism all laws have become laws of movement." When leaders in such a system speak

---

105   SiELS, 178.
106   SEiLS, 177.

of laws of nature or history, "neither nature nor history is any longer the stabilizing source of authority for the actions of mortal men; they are movements in themselves."[107]

"It is not politics that can bring true liberty to the soul," one reads, "that must be achieved, if at all, by philosophy; but liberalism may bring large opportunities for achievement in a man's outward life."[108] From the viewpoint of society as a whole, this promise cannot be fulfilled when opportunities or chances at the start are unequal, to which fact Santayana is sensitive. This may bring one to a conclusion that Hayek – in this context – was right when claiming that "the equation of liberty with the power to act" is "inimical to the liberal ideal of equal freedom because power cannot by its nature be distributed equally."[109] That is why, on the one hand, Santayana's ideal of vital liberty is not followed by a postulate of equality other than the equality of chances, and, on the other hand, he repeatedly notes in his criticism of liberalism that merely negative freedom gives rise to deep inequalities resulting from the competition of powers. As sanely noticed by Gray, implicit in John Locke's idea that private property conditions individual independence is a claim that "a civil society demands the *widespread diffusion of personal property.*"[110] This, Santayana asserted, did not occur. Plutocracy arose and, with the support of the (nominally) collective and common goods such as science and culture, perpetuated its kind. The very existence of elites in society did not bother Santayana. On the contrary, he thought them potentially beneficent for society. What bothered him was that, while existing by the price of the degradation of others, they "wounded" liberalism by withdrawing from the very "benevolent and intellectual leadership which they had supposed themselves fitted for."[111] A class or a caste living for its own sake and at the expense of all others did not fit into his ideal of a harmonious society.

Even though Santayana understood that under certain circumstances state-interventionism might embark on an authoritarian or totalitarian path, for the reasons mentioned above, he did not embrace the libertarian perspective of a decisive anti-interventionism and anti-statism. One may say that he was aware of the Scylla of non-interventionism and the Charybdis of unjust interventionism. Both the logic of Enterprise and that of a "barbarous form of statism,"[112]

---

107 Hannah Arendt, *The Origins of Totalitarianism* (New York: Harcourt Brace Jovanovich, 1973), 463.
108 SiELS, 184.
109 LIB, 58.
110 LIB, 13. My emphasis.
111 DP, 319.
112 LIB, 36.

thriving, for example, under governance by an aggressive minority faction, posed a danger of a total control of life.

Personally, I find Gray right when he says, first, that no serious and practically successful alternative to liberalism appeared in the Western political practice in the twentieth century, and, second, that there is no escape from addressing the problem of inherited (and growing) economic injustices and that some way of the redistribution of capital should be considered.[113] As for Santayana, it seems clear to me that while he excelled in revealing the shortcomings of liberal order, he did not see much hope for correcting liberalism within the scope of its influence. The twenty first century, with its crisis of liberal democratic regimes – even if the prophecies of their ultimate collapse be premature – makes one want to reconsider the ideas of Santayana.

Having said all this, one should keep in mind that Santayana's personal sympathies used to fluctuate and drift in different directions. While certain key liberal values remained dear to him, he was never a fully committed liberal, for some not a liberal at all. In Gray's reading, part of Santayana's message is that the survival of liberal legacy requires "a comprehensive disenchantment with liberal theory."[114] This idea makes sense in the light of a crucial distinction proposed by Santayana, and shared by Gray, namely – between liberalism as a doctrine, too entangled in its internal aporias and contradictions, and liberal practice, the aim of which is finding a *modus vivendi* – a way of peaceful coexistence among diverse individuals and peoples. Indeed, both Santayana and Gray treat diversity as an "ultimate fact," and the former, additionally, as a human good.[115]

Much as I am convinced that liberalism defended goods that Santayana himself valued highly, and, one may add, Santayana's chosen lifestyle of a vagabond savant fitted into the liberal, universalistic, and individualistic spirit, he might have been too disillusioned to lay a wager on the lasting endurance of the liberal order. He might also lack the spirit of activism to struggle for the preservation of liberalism. If he did, he did it indirectly, by virtue of his life-long participation in culture, his somewhat seditious humanism, and his

---

113   LIB, 89.
114   PLIB, 31.
115   LIB, 56. Gray comments here on the promising contemporary contractarian conceptions of John Rawls and James Buchanan, both of whom rely on individualist ethics and minimal moral postulates that comply with "the moral diversity of modernity as an ultimate fact." In later works he would be much more critical about the Kantian foundations and the "artificiality" of Rawls's theory. See: *Enlightenment's Wake* (London and New York: Routledge, 1995/2007).

contribution to human intellectual history. Santayana did not predict any sort of an end of (political) history, although he did consider the history of liberalism to be back then "virtually closed."[116] One should not be misled by the bitter tone of Santayana's criticism; his predictions were not apocalyptic. He expected subsequent waves of change, possibly a major crisis of the Western world, or its absorption by powers from beyond its civilizational scope, either of which, in turn, might pave way for some other, perhaps more harmonious, maybe even spiritually-oriented, arrangement in an unspecified future.

116   DP, 447.

CHAPTER 7

Reflections on Self-Government, Democracy, and Justice

7.1 A Few Remarks on Government by Politicians

In correspondence to the twofold understanding of politics, one may speak of government as an art and government as found. As for the former, the art of government consists in

> studying the nature of things, and of man in the midst of them, so as to devise an equilibrium in which man may attain, as far as possible, to his natural perfection … the sacrifices imposed by good government are balanced by many immediate benefits, which the people, or large portions of them, will not fail to appreciate.[1]

The latter may be compared to "a natural fatality" and is merely "a lesser evil than anarchy."[2] In modern times, it is formed by professional politicians, usually members of a ruling party, interested in self-preservation. As for its composition, three layers or three identities may be distinguished. First, government is "a material formation with an origin, life, and tendency of its own."[3] It is natural, historical, fallible, and in a democracy it should be constantly renewed. The materiality of government condemns it to the inconstancy and unpredictability of the flux of existence, which is aggravated by the fact of it being a "compound unit." Formally, government consists of men in the office. Yet, from a naturalist's perspective, governmental dynamics is an alien supplement to the lives of the persons who compose it. The union between these persons, established by virtue of common duties and, sometimes, shared ideals, may prove lasting and strong under certain circumstances, but in principle is porous and susceptible to internal and external turbulences. Its fragility rests in that 1) it is composed of independent minds, which fact, from the viewpoint of Santayana's naturalism, puts the government's integrity at risk, and, 2) the

---

1 DP, 419–420.
2 DP, 419.
3 DP, 268.

medium of their cooperation is rather social than ideal, and, hence, instable and dependent on changing interests.

Party membership constitutes a kind of faction unity. In times of extraordinary mobilization the union between its members may seem unequivocal, but it then resembles the unity of the mob and is short-lived. Finally, another, morally ambivalent and materially dangerous, source of unity emerges, one which may be described as giving rise to some forms of democratic decay, or, simply, turning the government into a parasite, namely -

> *a corporate instinct of self-preservation.* Office gives everyone concerned a new set of private interests, passions, and necessities, quite irrelevant to the public good, but most influential over public affairs. Quite apart from obsession with party policy, which after all is something verbally noble, a government is wedded to itself, to its own material inertia and effort at equilibrium. Its own life is its first concern … *What will not a government do in order not to fall, or in order so to fall as to be able to rise again?*[4]

The extent to which this more or less parasitic organism represents or misrepresents the interest of its constituency and of other subjects is contingent on many factors. But in any case, it establishes a system of dominations in society – an engine, which, justified partly by tradition and partly by the representation of its subjects' current interests, may become the tool of pushing forward the ruling agents' own, egoistic interests.

7.2 Perfection versus Freedom

In *Dialogues in Limbo* one finds two dialogues devoted to self-government. In it, the living Stranger, being a *port-parole* of Santayana, dialogues with Socrates (who, I suggest, may be regarded as Santayana's *alter ego*) now dwelling among the dead, in a "realm of sanity." The topic of their discussion is an "obscure oracle," coming from the crazy realm of the living, which has reached Socrates, and which says that the "right government rests on the will of the governed."[5] What the ghost, or the soul, of Socrates is concerned about is whether right government stands for a good one and what is the relation between the will of the governed and their *true* interests. The Stranger tries to excuse himself from

---

[4] DP, 270. My emphasis.
[5] George Santayana, *Dialogues in Limbo* (Ann Arbor: University of Michigan Press, 1957), 90. Subsequently this source is cited as DL.

giving an adequate and accurate answer by saying that he has lost faith in the power of words and ideas to convey the truth about material reality: "events in the long run will falsify any policy and render obsolete any conviction."[6] They may, at best, constitute a nebulous rendering of current trends in culture and politics. Moreover, no political strategy has hitherto managed to alleviate the tragedy of human self-government being "the tragedy of those who do as they wish, but do not get what they want."[7] Clearly, government based on self-government by definition is likely to expose humans to the effects of this predicament.

To avoid ambiguity, the Stranger and Socrates agree that self-government, in this case, does not mean government of self, which is an individual virtue and an art, but rather a situation where each individual is governed by all others, which, ironically, as Socrates notes, may result in undermining individual autonomy rather than empowering it. The Stranger admits this may be the case, but it usually happens in a non-violent way, by way of imitation and inertia. Memory as well as personal and political perspectives of an average contemporary man – whom in *Dominations and Powers* Santayana named "the momentary man"[8] – are short. He is in love with change, novelty, and competition, yet misses good judgment and consistency. Both interlocutors agree that humans, in the long-run, may benefit from conscious, deliberate action, based on knowledge and continuity, or, in other words, action that is an art. When action consists in governing others, it is even more pressing that it becomes an art. This does not occur in contemporary democracies, asserts the Stranger, where government resembles "a fatality" rather than an art. Politics has become an untransparent sphere of faction, competition for votes, defending narrow and temporary interests. As a result, many a citizen turn away, disillusioned, from a politics that has lost all its splendor and bears odium instead. But even if the problem of corruption were solved, politics would still suffer from shortsightedness and temporariness. Added to it the lack of proper *paideia* in the lives of the citizens, and the concomitant poor individual self-government, politics becomes *a measure of dealing with a (constant) crisis*. Hence, "[y]ours rulers are physicians summoned in your extremity," says Socrates.[9] Politics becomes an improvised action under pressure. Elsewhere Santayana's "momentary man" asks an emblematic question: "Why be dominated by the past or the future, when both are now only imagined?" By deriding "imagination as attention

---

6   DL, 91.
7   DL, 93. This may be read as an allusion to the theme of Plato's *Gorgias*.
8   DP, 350.
9   DL, 97.

wasted in absent things, they are abandoning the function of imagination in directing the present," which hinders the ability to govern oneself and others.[10]

What nevertheless may be said in defense of democracy is that the basis of all occurrences in the human world is material and it is instinct and imitation – functions of natural automatism – more than reason that *de facto* determine the shape of this world, which may suggest that the role of reason and individual virtue in government should not be overestimated. Besides, in the light of the fact that a complete knowledge necessary for what might pass for a fully rational and competent government is unattainable, and the results of our decisions are always to an extent unpredicted and unwanted, humans may prefer to risk and decide about certain matters themselves. Nature and accident might well prepare a better future for them than schemes designed by abstract sages. Socrates thinks, as Santayana notices elsewhere, that "it is knowledge, not accidental desires or opinions, that makes conduct rational and right. What Socrates seems to have forgotten to say is that the knowledge requisite to make action rational in this sense lies entirely beyond the reach of mankind."[11] Given this margin of ignorance, one should admit that habit, intuition, and luck often co-determine major decisions in politics. Despite certain shortcomings of democracy, says the Stranger, "life among us is in many ways safer, freer, more comfortable, and more entertaining than it was in your model cities, with their divine founders and law-givers."[12]

Socrates looks down at the idea of government based on the spontaneous will of the many and reminds that the task of reason, which is the main human prerogative, is to institute its own rule, the rule of *perfection*, amidst the blind moves of nature. The Stranger, though, contradicts the idea of perfection with that of *freedom*. It is congenial both to the spontaneous animality in man and the spiritual ideal of freedom, from the perspective of which society is merely an accident, and, if "it is to be justified morally, it must be justified at the bar of individual conscience."[13] Democracy, then, is legitimized as an expression of the inalienable right to self-rule held by autonomous individuals, who form this or that collective body.

Having, thus, placed perfection and freedom in opposition to one another, both interlocutors agree at least upon one point, namely – that Socrates' initial reservation about the identity of the "right" and "good" government is justified.

---

10 DP, 445.
11 DP, 301.
12 DL, 98. Unfortunately, the thinker tends to underestimate the advantages of democracy. This sentence is one of very few upright praises of democracy in his writings.
13 DL, 99.

"Legitimacy in a government depends on the origin of its authority: excellence depends on its fruits."[14] The first is mostly legal and relies on procedures, the latter depends on virtue and art applied to action directed towards some more or less ideal goals. They both agree that a right government may happen to be a bad one. But even having admitted this, the Stranger hesitates over betraying the democratic ideal, which he considers to be tantamount to betraying human life itself, life as represented by an individual will craving for freedom. It is at this point that a possible synthesis of life with perfection as manifesting itself in art and virtue is suggested by Socrates, who thinks, expressing Santayana's own perspective, that life without ideal goals and some instruction as to what is worth pursuing and how it can be attained, is mere chaos. Needless to say, Santayana's idea of vital liberty attained through the life of reason may be read as an attempt at this kind of synthesis.

At some point, however, the conservative radicality of Socrates, who says that "[t]he living cannot live well unless the dead govern them,"[15] is countered by the Stranger, who once again stands up for the freedom and spontaneity of the living. No less radical than Socrates, he comments on the dogmatic rule of the sages: "no tyranny is worse than that of a belated or fanatical conscience, oppressing a world it does not understand in the name of another world which is non-existent."[16] We witness here two powerful assertions, two truths being played one against the other and forming an unresolvable opposition. Where the paths of the Stranger and Socrates converge again is in the idea that ultimately the form of government is less important than its ability to represent and forward the true interests of the governed, called by Santayana, also in other texts, "moral representation." An individual or a group of leaders are morally representative when they possess the ability and the willingness "to bring about the existence, welfare, or safety" of others.[17] Except for knowledge and experience, virtues of "cooperation, unselfishness and sacrifice" are prerequisite, especially in a democracy, for a morally representative government, one willing to understand and reconcile the interests (including future ones) of diverse groups in a society.[18] The Stranger's prejudice against monarchy is based on the fear of a possible abuse of power when concentrated in one person's or a very narrow group's hands. Yet, he admits that in case the king proves that his rule is beneficent and just, he earns legitimacy among the

---

14   DL, 100.
15   DL, 101.
16   DL, 102–103.
17   DP, 374.
18   DP, 374.

governed. Both interlocutors seem to agree that a good government is a legitimate one. Or, reformulating the words of the "oracle" overheard by Socrates, a good government is the right one. There remains, however, the unresolved issue of the intrinsic dignity of human freedom and the fact of compulsion being "degrading in itself."[19] The thesis about the dignity of freedom, Socrates replies, is meaningful when one is capable of using this freedom to one's advantage, which requires a sufficient knowledge of self and the world. Without the support of knowledge, autonomy oftentimes becomes the driving force behind a tragedy. The first dialogue ends with Socrates' contention that "there is no right government except good government,"[20] or, in other words, legitimacy may be obtained only through honest and efficient representation of interests.

The second dialogue, which is a continuation of the first, begins with the Stranger's reflection upon the relation between human condition and autonomy. Brevity of life, insufficiency of individual experience to grow wise, ignorance – all these conspire to make man a poor judge. But it is doubtful that this fact alone be a sufficient evidence for the superiority of an external authority. Neither is it justified to assume that the lessons of past experiences always provide adequate measures for dealing with currents issues. But even if they did, this fact alone would not suffice to deprive man of the right to find his own way and experiment with it. Even if man fails and acknowledges the failure, it does not follow that "it was wrong to have made the experiment."[21]

The matter becomes more complicated, though, when it comes to issues concerning democratic practice. Relying on the vote of majority, as it happens to be at a given moment, and on an accidental compromise, may, under certain circumstances, expose community to the perils of profound ignorance, a momentary collective delusion, shortsightedness, or sophistical manipulation. The principle of the citizen's sovereignty itself is not fulfilled perfectly in a democracy because there are always some, who, for different reasons, remain unrepresented. The question of Socrates is whether (and, if so, then with what rationale) a community can afford rejecting the opportunity of relying on the knowledge, skill, and competence of the most eminent citizens. Then, he asks about the limits of democracy and its *spiritus movens* – egalitarianism. One of them has already been exposed – it is the limit of representation reflected, for example, in an irrational tyranny of majority. Then, there are limits both to equality and unanimity. Third, the scope of purely democratic/popular decision is obviously limited and usually does not extend to matters of highest

---

19 DL, 104.
20 DL, 106.
21 DL, 112.

importance and those requiring expertise, such as the military, health, international relations. When it comes to cultural and moral matters, including religious beliefs and ideal allegiances, in a modern democracy, asserts the Stranger, things are neither determined by popular vote nor by tradition, but rather are shaped by fashions and reigning ideologies. Even language is hardly resistant to this kind of formation. Such worship of artificial ideas, as both agree, deserves the name of *idolatry*, and, one may add, can hardly be considered a perfect expression of human autonomy.

Yet another doubt voiced by Socrates refers to the boundary between convention and nature or convention and truth. He asks, ironically, whether family relations, such as parenthood or sisterhood, are also established by children's consent expressed in voting, and whether majority decides "what shall have been the history of your country."[22] He thus alludes to possible dangers related to the degeneration of democracy in the direction of an Orwellian reign of an ideological terror. This, by the way, is also an intended irony on the part of Santayana addressed at Plato's utopia with its idea of the state taking responsibility for children's upbringing. The Stranger seems to be convinced by the absurdity of a limitless democracy as revealed in Socrates' questions and admits the need for criticism. However, before leaving, he is advised by Socrates not to take Socrates' own arguments for granted but rather weigh them carefully against counter-considerations and form his own judgment, "for it would be of little profit to have been saved from one error if, under my blind guidance, you fell into another."[23]

These fine, although brief and mostly deconstructive, dialogues, full of irony and ambivalence, may themselves be regarded as representative of the spirit of deliberative democracy and the fact that democracy requires an internal and external criticism. Santayana is playing here pairs of concepts and ideas – such as freedom and perfection, individual autonomy and the rule of majority, nature and convention, speech and deeds – against one another. By illuminating the limits and paradoxes of democracy, he exposes, at the same time, the weakness of any theory aspiring to the status of a supreme and universally valid precept for the organization of human government.[24] The problem of the best and, at the same time, practicable, political regime cannot be resolved on the level of deliberation at least for two reasons – because of the mutability of

---

22 DL, 123.
23 DL, 123.
24 Elsewhere Santayana wrote: "[N]ature brings to light a great variety of beauties … There is room, there is peace, there is opportunity, here for one type of life and there for another type. And so political ideals have their innings, none of them perfectly realized." DP, 355.

existence and the shortcomings of human language. A material embodiment of the most coherent theory is likely to reveal tensions and contradictions. What is possible, however, is an ongoing attempt to establish reasonable criteria against which one may criticize the past and the existing political practice while trying to predict future forms of its derangement. This kind of activity is congenial to the idea of government as negotiating, balancing, regulating, and adjusting.

Having said this, one should not fail to note that some of Socrates' arguments, which seem to win over those of the Stranger, are both of *illiberal* and *undemocratic*. It is clearly the case with the idea that has been expressed by Santayana at a few occasions and today may be described as somewhat paternalistic, namely – that moral representation consists in representing the *true* interests of the subjects rather than advocating the interests that the subjects themselves recognize as theirs. The very same view, though, has been challenged by the thinker, quite effectively, with reference to the dignity (and beauty) of individual freedom, improbability of attaining a complete knowledge in complex matters concerning human affairs, and the very contingency and unpredictability of existence, which undermines any authority. While there remains some ambiguity as to the resolution of this dilemma, Santayana's overall outlook leans towards discipline, self-constraint and reliance on some verified authority.

7.3 The Ironies of Democracy

Santayana held a view that, irrespective of its form, "[a]ll just government pursues the general good; … One arrangement will be better fitted to one place and time, and another to another."[25] By the same token he undermined the sacrosanct status of democracy as a future destiny of mankind. Both in *The Life of Reason* and *Dominations and Powers* one comes across a number of brief subchapters and scattered passages where Santayana voices his, usually skeptical or overtly critical, insights into the ironies of democracy. His intention, I'd suggest, is not to discredit democracy, but rather to show the ways in which it may fail or actually does fail both from the perspective of Santayana's criterion of approaching the life of reason and by betraying its own ideals of self-government, equality, and freedom.

---

25 LR, 142.

As established in the dialogues, universal suffrage itself is not a guarantee of just and representative government. It should be stressed, though, that the early Santayana is far from glorifying authoritarian regimes on account of an alleged excellence of their leaders. On the contrary, as evidenced in the following passage, he emphasizes the fact that authoritarian leadership, even if promising at the beginning, tends to degenerate in the direction of its violent, if not upright "criminal" origins:

> *Democratic theory seems to be right, however, about the actual failure of theocracies, monarchies, and oligarchies to secure the general good.* The true eminence which natural leaders may have possessed at the beginning usually declines into a conventional and baseless authority. The guiding powers which came to save and express humanity fatten in office and end by reversing their function. The government reverts to the primeval robber; the church stands in the way of all wisdom. Under such circumstances it is a happy thing if the people possess enough initiative to assert themselves and, after clearing the ground in a more or less summary fashion, allow some new organization, more representative of actual interests, to replace the old encumbrances and tyrannies.[26]

A natural, meritocratic aristocracy might be a better option, but, as one learns from Plato's idea of the evolution of political regimes, it too tends to unfold in a descending order of eminence. Thus, Santayana sees in democracy, especially a representative one, where power is delegated, *latent but potent anti-democratic, oligarchic tendencies*, by virtue of which a powerful minority emerges and takes over leadership. Besides, within society, there exists an unsatisfied desire for distinction and recognition, which usually leads to the formation of both informal and formal associations and organizations, where the said needs may be satisfied. The emergence of such "havens" may also be explained with reference to presumed residues of *tribalism*. These, according to Santayana, are natural tendencies, able to lay dormant for a long time and then reemerge right in the womb of democracy. They constitute at once a germ of desirable diversity but also of social and political ills.[27]

It is worth attention that Santayana distinguishes between a natural, spontaneous democracy, encountered in some historical communities, such as those of the Swiss cantons or the early North American colonists, and an

---

26   LR, 142. My emphasis.
27   The need for distinction is particularly powerful on ethnic and religious ground. See: DP: 360–362.

"artificial," political democracy, which stands for a form of political arrangement where people have a more or less direct share in governing. The latter type of democracy is technical and instrumental, it is a means to an end. The former type is close to the ideal of social equality and the "most democratic of governments – no government at all."[28] It is a natural democracy, brotherly and centered around the ideals of liberty and egalitarianism alike. Although it may seem to be "idyllic," it usually is established as a means of facing natural necessity, and the authority of its self-government is "rooted in persons" more than in land, resources, or the state.[29] Thus, Santayana adds, it is hardly compatible with traditional institutions such as the family or the law of property inheritance.[30] Rampant individualism may destabilize this kind of democracy too, although individualism is not altogether excluded and may, in some degree, be accommodated by a natural democracy, as it was in the case of the American pioneers, who "claim[ed] no privileges but insist[ed] on independence."[31] In such a democracy, if it elected its representatives, "the men chosen for representatives were naturally representative men, because almost anyone would have been representative."[32] Thus, it avoided the evils of professionalization in politics, with which contemporary, "artificial" democracies are confronted. Referring, then, to a later phase of American history, Santayana points to Abraham's Lincoln's Gettysburg speech and its phrase "of the people, by the people, for the people." The phrase was perfectly justified inasmuch as Lincoln addressed

> self-made men like himself, and it was natural to assume that they knew their own interests and if left alone would spontaneously secure them ... The natural success of each enterprising honest individual would open fresh opportunities to the enterprise of others; and the freedom of each would make the happiness of all.[33]

Yet, this sort of founding experience and circumstances, where democracy finds its relatively genuine and spontaneous expression, and where even the idea of vacant freedom is not a vain delusion, have been rare in history and perhaps not to be repeated.

---

28   LR, 140.
29   DP, 392.
30   DP, 345–346.
31   DP, 348.
32   DP, 385.
33   DP, 426.

In the twentieth century, with parliamentary democracies operative in large societies, some of them increasingly antagonized internally, not only the ideals of liberty and equality seem to stand in a deeper contradiction to one another than in the earlier forms of democracy, but also those of self-government and genuine representation have become opaque. Santayana is sensitive to the challenge posed by the convergence of the democratic ideal of self-government and the phenomenon of mass society. *He sees the modern democracy as being in a state of a chronic crisis.* The ancient analogy between an individual human being and the state, between individual and collective self-government, loses most of its heuristic function in the modern world. The ideas of an organic unity between man and his community and the self-mastery of a human person are at a far remove from the artificial unity of large societies, attained by legal and institutional measures, and their unanimity, which, in a degree that it exists, is based on crowd contagion, dissimulation, or is lost altogether among atomized individuals or hostile groups.

In Santayana's view people benefit from self-government best when they may simultaneously rely on "the prior existence and tacit acceptance of traditions, laws, and institutions which already govern them and which supply models, subject to opportune variations," for political action.[34] Meanwhile, he warns, unanimity is dwelling predominantly "in the realm of metaphor and rhetorical illusion."[35] He observes social and cultural disintegration, which undermines the quality and efficiency of self-government by the people. At the same time, while the dynamics of political life itself changes and governing has become "complex beyond imagination,"[36] the role of experts and the professionalization in politics increases. "How far can the government of the people, in these circumstances, remain the people's own government?"[37] And what is the position of a sovereign individual therein?

These problems of contemporary democracies, even though to some extent historically specific, may be still viewed in reference to certain universal tendencies as described by ancient thinkers. A deputy may be a better interpreter of the people's interest than an average individual, and may assure a greater possibility of satisfying them under the existing circumstances. Yet, the said superiority in knowledge and competence, when coupled with party allegiance or private aspirations, may contribute to government turning into "an oligarchy or a bureaucracy."[38] Besides, no real life government is a government by

---

[34] DP, 408.
[35] DP, 408.
[36] DP, 397.
[37] DP, 397.
[38] DP, 409.

all people and for all people, because that would require a perfect unanimity. Rather, it always is a domination, where the dominant power represents part of the people – "the stronger part, in ability, material force, wealth, or numbers … [ruling] the weaker part."[39] The specificity of contemporary democracies, such as the growing role of experts, the ever tighter connection between politics and business, the availability of powerful, technological tools of manipulating public opinion, means an increased risk of domination by an alienated group or body. Thus, Santayana demystifies the idea, and the rhetoric, of people's self-government.

The problematic legitimacy and the façade nature of elected representation, especially in the light of the lack of civil society institutions, (which, by the way, Santayana did not trust much either), undercuts also individual sovereignty. It is left for the individual to "take part in the election of one or another deputy selected by rival party machines; who when elected shall decide everything for him, or leave everything undecided, according to the instincts and interests of that party machine."[40] Voting plays an important psychological function but "[i]f [contemporary] Parliaments were judged by the theory of morally representative government – that they represent the Will of the People, which in turn expresses their true interests – there is no condemnation of their modern form that would be too sweeping."[41] Interestingly, Santayana, probably inspired by the ancient Greek democracy and Aristotle, thinks that election by lot (sortition) would be a better democratic method than election by ballot, as the former expresses faith in equality and diminishes the opportunity for dishonesty and manipulation. He refers to the example of choosing juries by lot in the Anglo-Saxon countries, seeing in this institution an authentic manifestation of the spirit of democracy.

The deputies in contemporary parliaments, who seem to occupy a very safe position, stand in contrast to some historical, heroic figures of tribunes, such as the Roman Gracchi, who were murdered for being earnest and idealistic representatives of the people. The contemporary representatives usually are party adherents, whose initiative does not go beyond their party policy. They may be sensitive to the public judgment and react to the criticism of their voters by changing their demagoguery. Here one touches upon a serious problem in democracy, analyzed already by Plato, namely the devaluation of speech. Except for the fact of demagoguery, speeches delivered by the deputies, Santayana notes, not only have lost importance, but are literally "wasted" as

---

39   DP, 409.
40   DP, 387.
41   DP, 385.

long as acceptance of proposals depends mainly on previous party resolution. The fate of politicians in democracy, many of whom, as Santayana presents them, are opportunistic conformist, depends not so much on their knowledge, competence, or virtue, but rather on the caprices of the public and history, which means that they are controlled by some irrational forces. Sadly and paradoxically, this degree of unpredictability, which might be evil from the viewpoint of an ideal of rational government, in the conditions of mass democracy seems to carry a promise of a relief and a deliverance from any thinkable human cruelty and folly.

However, evoking again Santayana's methodical ambiguity and readiness to see the relativity of his own critique, the verdict passed by him on contemporary politicians turns out, in the end, not so crushing. "The domination of politicians – which is what representative government means in practice – although the most ignoble of governments, is not necessarily the worst."[42] On what grounds is Santayana, after expressing so many critical opinions, almost ready to justify politicians' being thus-and-so? According to my reading – on pragmatic and commonsensical grounds of a lesser evil. Politicians, as ordinary people, "are really too much in the same plight as the people they profess to represent."[43] How much more can there be done in a world so complex, where there are no more conditions for what was originally supposed to amount to a genuine democracy? Would not a dictatorship by a fanatic or a sect of dubious authority be a worse alternative both for the people and, finally, for the leaders themselves? Politicians in contemporary democracies are not incapable of recognizing the evils and errors of concrete policies, and, sometimes, of politics at large. Neither are they incapable of changing party affiliation, alarming the public, rebelling, or embarking on a different career.[44] At this point, however, a recourse to culture as well as personal *paideia* and virtue is made again, inexplicitly. Santayana's broader view on political virtue and current politics is expressed in the following words: *"Political conscience and political wisdom are not bred by political life; they are rather prejudiced and cheapened by it."*[45] In other words, regardless of the efficacy of institutions and procedures, the quality of government never ceases to depend on education, culture at large, and the merits of individuals engaged in its operation. That is why one way of enhancing it is through

---

42   DP, 388.
43   DP, 388.
44   DP, 388.
45   DP, 389. My emphasis.

securing a share of excellence among its members, which, in a democracy, is more likely to be achieved when there is separation of powers.

Evoking Montesquieu and the authors of the American Constitution, Santayana emphasizes that a relatively autonomous, executive institution, a kind of a far-sighted and "self-perpetuating body," able to provide for a traditional continuity representative of the given people's interests, may constitute a counterbalance for the elected legislative. Examples of such institutions in the modern world were the House of Lords in England, the Senate and the President in the United States of America.[46] Santayana has doubts as to whether and for how long these bodies will be autonomous and capable of performing the said function effectively. Nevertheless, an effective separation of powers in general is the source of mechanisms protecting the governed from the incompetence and the abuses of power by the government. Some kind of an independent and continuing tribunal is needed "to defend us against our defenders."[47]

In a partisan system, a collective body – a political party – is expected to be capable of honest moral representation. Meanwhile, it is tacitly accepted that there are always some unrepresented people in democracy – a minority of those who did not vote, voted for a rival party, or voted for the elected party but feel their interests are being betrayed. In any case, "[a] party is not the whole people, and if a representative is bound to express only the will of his party he is not a fair representative of a truly self-governing people."[48] But even if a party were to represent morally all the people, it would naturally aspire to be the only party in the government. A situation of this kind seems to occur in mature democracies with two dominant political parties that do not differ fundamentally and form a bipartisan consensus. As a result, whichever party wins majority in the parliament, it is likely to draw on the former government's achievement rather than destroy it, and continue some of its policies. This continuity secures evolution in some areas, which is of beneficence for the governed, provided that they are unanimous in fundamentals. There is no certainty as to whether the truly important, long-term interests of the given people are being represented, but this insecurity is inscribed into the operation of any representative government.

A serious dilemma pertaining to representative democracy is whether the elected representatives should rather act according to the public momentary caprices, in an effort to please their voters, or care about what they regard to be

---

46   DP, 381.
47   DP, 423.
48   DP, 383.

the voters' true interests, even by the price of criticism and temporary loss of popularity. Ideally, the latter option fulfills the highest standards of representation and this is the approach Santayana sides with, albeit not without some reservations. In some cases the dilemma may assume an extreme form for a ruler or a representative: "either to die as a traitor for resisting the apparent will of his people, or to lead that people to their moral ruin."[49] An ideal moral representation, however, which requires some unity among the governed, may be but a futile mirage in immanently conflicted societies or in "a decadent age, where rival conditions clash and every sort of morality and immorality finds publicly respected advocates."[50] Here, more than elsewhere, *governing as managing necessity, managing conflicting diversity and minimizing sacrifices is a formula more expedient than that of an ideal moral representation.*

Among the vices of partisan democracy (whether it be a single party or many), Santayana is sensitive to the problem of "ideologies,"[51] sectarianism, militant factionism, and corruption. In the mid-twentieth century, in the West, Santayana sees some hope for the revival of an honest representation of interests and "the genuine value of collective demands made by an economic power" in the activity of labour parties.[52] Representing trade unions, they attempt to reform the deeply pathological system of sharing profits from industrial production. He even envisages a possible new order, probably far from faultless itself, based on different property arrangements.

Santayana's optimism is waning as he looks deeper into the sources and faces of the degradation of the working class and the social estrangement not only of the poor but also of the wealthy, and, presumably, political leaders themselves. He fears that the organization of work and cultural deprivation of masses of people might make the attempted reform wanton, as long as the wealthy miss virtue and the poor's relation to work and life in general requires a deep social transformation rather than merely higher wages and a vague benefit of having access to the goods of a "decadent aristocratic culture."[53] Leaving aside the impression of some paternalism in Santayana's tone, it is important to note that – as indicated in the previous chapter – he shares the view of at least a couple of cultural and social critics of his era, who quarreled with the elites not performing their social function and pointed to the fatal consequences of

---

49   DP, 384.
50   DP, 384.
51   Conscious of the ambiguity of this term, the author places it in inverted commas, as for example in DP, 378.
52   DP, 390.
53   DP, 379.

this failure.[54] While Santayana often points to the importance of social hierarchy and privilege – a view commonly banned from the contemporary political discussion – he also seems to think that having a privileged social position comes at a price, or, in other words, it means having a duty in respect to society.

The above is part of a broader problem related to the very possibility of rational self-government by the uneducated and unskilled many, "whose work makes them masters of nothing except the day's or the week's wages."[55] Santayana thinks that without some social integrity, self-consciousness and basic political competence of the working class, rational self-government is hardly possible. He sees this sort of deprivation "happening in Europe under our eyes."[56] Hence, people are condemned to be governed by professional politicians, some of them demagogues, *who constitute a class in itself*, one focused on the preservation of power. As for the people,

> [f]or labour really to become a school for political competence and also for personal virtue, it must be spontaneous, on a human scale in the object and in the strain of it, and capable of becoming in part a liberal art; for as an art, it trains the workman to respect the nature of things and to prosper by cooperation with it. And what better lesson would there be for the practice of government?[57]

A peculiar form of mass democracy, which exhibits a distinct sort of anomaly of political representation, is communism, called by the philosopher "revolutionary democracy." Here power is supposed to rest in the hands of the vast numbers of uprooted proletarians. The case of the Soviet Union, where the regime quickly degenerates into a dictatorship and an "all-pervasive" authoritarianism (i.e., totalitarianism), confirms Santayana's disbelief in the

---

54 An interesting example of this kind of critique is contained in a book by a Polish sociologist, Florian Znaniecki, *Upadek cywilizacji zachodniej* [*The Decline of Western Civilization*] (1921). In it Znaniecki presents his theory of two types of aristocracy: the authentic, *spiritual one*, the members of which owe their status to their own intellectual and artistic talents and achievement, and *parasitic one*, which possesses prestige by way of inheritance, social connections, exploitation of the powers of the former type. When social institutions perpetuate and reinforce the status and influence of the parasitic aristocracy, the spiritual one becomes stifled and unable to play its vitalizing, creative function in respect to culture and society as a whole. Neither is it capable of refreshing itself by "recruiting" new members from society. See: Florian Znaniecki, *Upadek cywilizacji zachodniej* (Warszawa: Wydawnictwa Uniwersytetu Warszawskiego, 2013).
55 DP, 380.
56 DP, 380.
57 DP, 380.

possibility of a successful self-government by uneducated masses. Let me note that in some of his comments at this point he seems to be falling into the trap of his tendency to hasty generalizations unsupported by specific knowledge, as when he ascribes to the Russian people a historical attachment to autocracy so deep that the power of it makes them adjust themselves willingly to the Soviet totalitarianism and even enjoy its fruits. Besides, while his general intuitions about the totalitarian tendencies inherent both in communism and the global, industrial capitalism have some merit, I doubt they justify going as far as to equate the future social and humane effects of both systems, which he seems to be doing, albeit vaguely, in a somewhat light-hearted manner.[58]

Santayana considers also the possibility of a kind of socialism based on the political participation of the workers through cooperation of labour unions with the legislative. Government, seeking to fulfill the workers' demands, limits the power of private and corporate proprietors, discouraging some of them effectively from further investments and taking slowly over the control of businesses while trying to develop welfare state. Changes in economy would be followed by a change in the social hierarchy of values. The inability of the state to generate wealth may be presumed to impact negatively its power to provide social services, yet, the experiment need not end with an economic disaster if the government be competent and rational. To that end, it would not be a body elected by popular vote but rather by way of "promotion" or "co-option among the members of each branch" as it happens at universities or in the military. Perhaps a polity able to sustain the ideals of "spiritual liberty and social justice before the public eye" might emerge from this experiment.[59] Santayana neither cares to analyze the dangers related to this sort of "state capitalism" nor seems intent on persuading the reader that this vague vision, depicted in a few brush-strokes, had good chances for realization in his era or ours. Rather, his intention is to suggest that, first, the ideal of social justice might require a differently organized economy, second, that in future some kind of reorganization may be unavoidable. Then, if it were ever to emerge, it would require remarkable sacrifice on the part of the people, such as reconsidering their – deeply impacted by the actual civilizational development – attitudes towards prosperity, progress, measures of well-being, and, on a deeper level, towards the meaning and value of human life. Perhaps, one may add, only an experience of a deep and large-scale crisis, an unexpected intrusion of necessity,

---

58   See: DP, 348.
59   DP, 382.

might bring about or enforce the said reconsideration and change, which, by the way, is not an unthinkable scenario.

One may be inspired by these reflections of Santayana to ask whether economism, as a dominant (neoliberal) paradigm, is not incompatible with any ideal of social justice. One may also think of a contemporary discussion about the turn from growth-oriented economy towards an organic one, focused on a responsible, sustainable development. In a couple of private letters, Santayana, speculating vaguely about the world a hundred or two hundred years later, predicted further global demographic growth, expansion of global business and economic development of Asia and Africa. He thought that a cosmopolitan governance of some scope and level would probably by then exist.[60] Passing from a realistic prediction to a project, he speculated that it might extend over a number of nations, "moral societies" or "small societies, all different and perfect each in its way."[61] In other words, what one comes across here is yet another vision of government as *managing of necessity and preserving diversity*. The government would control, with reference to science, the realm of material necessity, with the aim of preventing "all avoidable distress and unjust distribution of burdens."[62] *The real problem to face or the real question to ask would then be "not one how to enlarge businesses but how to lead a rational life."*[63] In fact, Santayana noted, national governments as they existed in his era would do well to start asking this question immediately, without waiting for it to enforce itself. These speculations of Santayana may be worth

---

60   Santayana speaks of a possibility – in an explicit reference to Toynbee's "Universal State" – of creating a voluntary union of the USA and the British Commonwealth of Nations, "supervening over a crowd of [willing] small nations." He also foretells the shrinking of the global significance of Europe. See: Letter to John McKinstry Merriam, 17 Jan. 1948, LGS8: 7.

61   Letter to John Hall Wheelock, 5 Sept. 1948, LGS8: 95–96. See also: letter to John W. Yolton, 27 Apr. 1952, LGS8: 440–441. In it Santayana speaks of a number of "moral societies" possessing own territories and united under a government responsible for the organization of a "Scientific Universal Economy" and the military. The subject is further developed in a letter to John W. Yolton, 2 May 1952, LGS8: 441-442-443. In fact, in this letter one finds the most detailed of the existing accounts, all very brief and sketchy, of Santayana's imagined empire. Here Santayana explains that the control of universal government would extend only over matters that can be studied and regulated scientifically, such as health, hygiene, the military, safety of persons and property, industry and trade. It would also set limits on wages and profits, preventing "strikes, monopolies, labour-camps or capitalists." It would guard external safety and prevent internal violence. A free movement of individuals in-between the "moral communities" is assumed.

62   Letter to John W. Yolton, 2 May 1952, LGS8: 442.

63   Letter to John McKinstry Merriam, 17 Jan. 1948, LGS8: 7. My emphasis.

reconsidering in the context of alternative visions of future, global socio-economic organization.

7.4 The Aristocratic Ideal and a Democratic Society

A traditional, constitutional democracy, if it aims at vital liberty at all, is interested in preserving social differentiation, while it must resort continuously to public opinion in order to minimize tensions resulting from inequalities and "control the easily deranged mechanism of administration and lawgiving."[64] It is also interested in preserving a degree of unanimity indispensable in a just democracy. Unanimity, occurring naturally in spontaneous democracies, is a rare and unstable phenomenon in contemporary, instrumental democracies, which, nevertheless must count on it and tend to produce a semblance of it in the form of compromise and conformity. It is frequent even among conservative liberals, as Santayana notes ironically, who turn out to be ready to conform to some "suicidal measures carried out by the demagogues."[65] But rational compromise in politics, concerning either the choice of means or ends, is needed as long as it expresses respect for circumstances and bending under *force majeure*. Rational compromise, though, has limits beyond which it turns into a lack of integrity or mere resignation in the face of fatality. Excessive compromise in politics is a mistake since the course of things is not determined by any fixed "Fate" but rather is constantly being molded by changing circumstances, in which rational action has its share. Practiced notoriously, compromise brings disintegration and hopelessness.[66]

The democratic pursuit of unanimity, which brings about conformity or uniformity, is something Santayana the naturalist quarrels with on the grounds that it 1) underestimates the value of variety and excellence in society; 2) relies on the power of mimetic instinct, which is not a reliable foundation for a lasting and rational political order;[67] 3) blind to its own relativity, absolutizes the value of agreement and cooperation "which belongs legitimately only to special ages and special groups of men."[68] Let me quote an important passage in its entirety:

---

64 DP, 350.
65 DP, 351.
66 DP, 415.
67 For more on Santayana's naturalistic approach to mimesis see: DP, 409–410.
68 DP, 351–352.

> This persuasion that human morality, and human morality of one particular type, has an absolute authority, and measures the value, even to themselves, of all possible beings, is the cosmic assumption beneath the democratic demand for unanimity. It is politically less important than the assumption of a single good for all men in one society at one time; but speculatively it is even less judicious, because it swells the demand for moral identity not only beyond the limits of a sect or a nation, but beyond the limits of the human species, and of the whole world open to human inspection.[69]

In Santayana's critical assessment of democracy there resonates – as mentioned already in the discussion of *Dialogues in Limbo* – an association, made in the vein of Plato and Aristotle, of political democracy with a past crisis of eminence and the resultant rebellion of the governed, leading to a chain of changes in political arrangement, one of the phases of which is democratic. Meanwhile, the possibility of a representative and just government, irrespective of its form, is related to virtue and depends on

> the existence or non-existence of available practical eminence. The democratic theory is clearly wrong if it imagines that eminence is not naturally representative. Eminence is synthetic and it represents what is synthesizes. An eminence not representative would not constitute excellence, but merely extravagance or notoriety.[70]

Furthermore, democracy, as a kind of administration, inherits rather than creates a society and the state. It inherits "a prodigious self-created engine" along with "many vestiges of older and less democratic institutions."[71] There is a suggestion implicit here that democracy itself could never have produced by itself this "engine" with all its institutional diversity, which tends to last unless a radical rebellion and reorganization occurs. Democracy, then, rather than creating, deconstructs and reforms. The question is what happens when the older forms wear out, expire or atrophy.

Democracy may couple with differently structured societies. Thus, Santayana distinguishes between aristocratic and social democracy. The latter, looking up to an egalitarian ideal, abolishes class privileges and appeals to brotherhood and solidarity instead of assuming ambition, competition, and

---

69 DP, 352.
70 LR, 142.
71 LR, 141.

passion as driving forces behind the advancement of society. Now, the early Santayana of *The Life of Reason*, believes that such a democracy is likely to result in levelling all (which involves pulling some down) to a mediocre level and a rather mundane existence. Neither achievement nor personal autonomy is safe in such an environment – "[s]ocial democracy at high pressure would leave no room for liberty. The only freeman in it would be one whose ideal was to be an average man."[72] If consistent to its standards, a social democracy is in peril of sliding towards "an utterly barbarous state" of "workmen and peasants," in which "[e]very liberal tradition would perish."[73] Santayana's rationale at this point is grounded in his naturalism. Society consists of individuals representing diverse potentials and talents, and it may thrive as a whole only when these natural endowments may be noticed, developed and attached to some socially-significant, symbolic position. Furthermore, civilizational and cultural achievement is related to the existence of social diversity, creative minorities, and, psychologically, to the power of ambition. Were the democratic postulate of equality to be realized in its radical form, all these social powers would be threatened, not for the lack of talent or impulse, not even because of a presumed democratic reluctance towards excellence, but because of the lack of a *proper, formative, social experience*, which might be conducive to the actualization of people's natural and unequal potentials. All in all, Santayana believes a visibly structured society, a society in which privilege and authority are, in some form, preserved, is a better source of the kind of experience that plays a crucial role in culture-formation and human achievement. At the turn of the century, as if echoing Toynbee's views, he writes:

> [I]t is experience they cannot gather, for in gathering it they would be constituting those higher organs that make up an aristocratic society. Civilization has hitherto consisted in diffusion and dilution of habits arising in privileged centres. ... The vital genius thus bursting forth and speaking with authority gained a certain ascendency in the world; it mitigated barbarism without removing it ... To abolish aristocracy, in the sense of social privilege and sanctified authority, would be to cut off the source from which all culture has hitherto flowed.[74]

---

72 LR, 146.
73 LR, 144.
74 LR, 144.

In an ironic and provocative way, Santayana remarks that social democracy may be defended by denying that "civilization is a good."[75] Perhaps one should not exclude authoritatively the possibility that one day returning to simpler and more natural forms of life becomes a necessity. Santayana himself doubts that this option will come true in a predictable future as nothing in his era signals "that a reaction against material progress should set in ..., since as yet the tide of commercialism and population continues everywhere to rise."[76] Be it as it may, in the era of Santayana, a more probable option, one that actually materialized itself a couple of decades after he wrote these words, was a situation when a "radical democracy" (read: communism), without intending to abandon the path of material progress and growth, falls victim to a perpetual economic crisis.

As a critic of social democracy, Santayana grew increasingly aware of the fact that elements of welfare state were more of a necessity than a matter of choice in the face of the economic and cultural impoverishment of masses of people, as evidenced by many quotations from his later writings evoked by me in the chapter on liberalism. For some time he even seemed to welcome the rise of communism. But he remained concerned with the disappearance of cultural elites capable of and willing to provide patterns of excellence for the rest of society. In the absence of good models, he feared, society would turn into a crowd and there is "no tyranny so hateful as a vulgar and anonymous tyranny."[77]

Returning to *The Life of Reason*, the thinker also considers a "timocracy" – an idea inspired by Plato's *Politeia*, largely modified by Santayana himself, who removes the militaristic and power-oriented aspect of it and translates it into a kind of liberal meritocracy and possibly, but not necessarily, a form of democracy. It is meant as a response to the crisis of eminence in social democracy. In such an (ideal) state, governed by competent men of merit, who owe privileged positions solely to their eminence and virtue,[78] ambition, broadly understood,

---

75 LR, 144.
76 LR, 145.
77 LR, 145.
78 The ancient understanding of virtue (*arete*) may be evoked here: "Ancient Greek virtue, *arete*, denoted a habitual capacity to achieve success in the performance of a specific practice or set of practices. It could refer to specific actions of an individual or animal as well as to the character of an individual or animal 'as a whole.' The agent's exhibition of an *arete* fulfilled skillfully an esteemed function of the animal or person. But when *arete* referred to human beings, it also connoted excellence and superiority. Insofar as it denoted achievement, it connoted success, and insofar as it denoted success, it connoted a social and intellectual judgment of merit and ethical or moral worth." Furthermore, the following description of the practicality of virtue fits Santayana's requirement of

would be restored as *spiritus movens* behind social and civilizational advancement. Meanwhile, the governing and/or privileged minority would create models of attitudes motivated not only by a desire for personal reward and recognition but also a non-selfish ideal of contributing to the good of the whole society, the lack of which has often been a major corrupting factor in politics. The merit-oriented allocation of high positions would be safeguarded by the rule of law and equality of opportunity. Other than that, society would "display a great diversity of institutions and superposed classes, a stimulating variety in ways of living; it would be favorable to art and science and to noble idiosyncrasies ... Like social democracy, finally, it would be just and open to every man."[79]

Reading Santayana today, one may interpret him as trying to ennoble selfishness by connecting the opportunity for satisfying private ambitions with more idealistic, inclusive, community-oriented incentives. Selfishness, in his view, just like desire for distinction, is an irremovable factor in human endeavor, in particular within the scope of Western civilization. Rather than trying to eradicate it, which is impossible, or worship it, which is "barbarian," it is wiser to take advantage of it, and educate it through social institutions and good models radiating from the elites, the members of which have themselves deserved their position.

This kind of "timocracy," unlike "social democracy," preoccupied primarily with equality, would likely create an environment conducive to "the art of liberal living," where wealth could be "nobly enjoyed." Humans seek well-being and pleasure, and

> life of pleasure requires an aristocratic setting to make it interesting or really conceivable. Intellectual and artistic greatness ... sorely needs sympathy and a propitious environment. Genius, like goodness (which can stand alone), would arise in a democratic society as frequently as elsewhere; but it might not be so well fed or so well assimilated.[80]

Santayana does not claim, then, that an egalitarian society is less capable of breeding genius. He is ready to admit that this genius, if born, would be, in a

---

competence: "T[t]e performative character of arete allowed it to be critically examined in terms of the practical benefits and reliability of *technai*. Insofar as *arete* was understood to be a kind of excellence or goodness that was exhibited in identifiable actions and modes of behavior, the expert performance of a *techne* could offer the occasion for the expression of *arete*." See: Wallach, *The Platonic Political Art*, 129–130.

79 LR, 147.
80 LR, 148.

sense, more authentic and intimate, as it would not be "caught" by conventional forms as easily as it would be in an aristocratic and aesthetically more refined society. The problem is that talents might easily passed unnoticed, without permeating into the stream of liberal arts and, thus, without becoming public. In short, they might never see daylight. These reflections lead Santayana to the assertion to which he was to remain loyal, namely – "how justly flattering and profound, and at the same time how ominous, was Montesquieu's saying that *the principle of democracy is virtue.*"[81]

In all these ruminations there resonates a concern about culture and the condition of society that fails to draw on and diffuse the potential and skill of its most eminent members as well as fear of a forced and all-pervasive uniformity being a shadow side of modern democracy. Looking at how diversity may be preserved within a democratic state the Constitution of which has been inspired by an honest motivation to guarantee the equality of citizens, Santayana refers to the example of the American "melting pot." The history of the colonization of North America and immigration arriving in subsequent waves throughout centuries contributed to the establishment of a relative linguistic and cultural unity. American people are uniform at the level of duty – business, work ethos, pursuit of prosperity, everyday manners. This uniformity was formed by contagion – the newly arrived found themselves in a specific and strongly influential environment, to which they adjusted themselves.

However, the uniformity and unanimity in question are not very deep. Ethnic and cultural background continue to play a separating role in personal lives, in customs and traditions, even in liberal arts. And this, Santayana thinks, may be viewed as a chance for preserving a culture-stimulating diversity. A forced integrity at those other levels, he thinks, would produce boredom and sterility. Society in a large, multi-national country, like the USA, might be fruitfully united in some dimensions of life and naturally divided at some other levels. In business and politics, uniformity and even fraternity might prevail; in science and other areas, where expertise is most important, a professional hierarchy or a hierarchy of authority is needed; in the sphere of personal matters, liberal arts and spiritual life, human relations should be based on a spontaneous attraction and coming together – while natural variety is most welcome here, understanding beyond natural boundaries is possible too.[82] These considerations may be read in alignment with the later Santayana's speculations about a future universal state.

---

81   LR, 148. My emphasis.
82   See: DP, 358–359.

7.5 Justice as Harmonizing Diversity and Justice as Charity

In this section I interpret Santayana's conception of justice in terms of harmony and charity, which, as I claim, may be regarded as two facets of love. Respectively, two common human incentives are evoked as empirical motivations behind the pursuit of justice: to idealize the other and to feel compassion for them. The first may be associated with the Platonic understanding of (the *logos* of) justice as harmonizing what empirically remains in a relation of tension or contradiction, namely – "virtue and the political art."[83] By way of virtue, a just state conciliates *logos* with *praxis*. In Santayana's thought this relation might be reformulated in terms of the relation of the actual political practice to the standards of the life of reason. Reason, being a function of human nature, "represents or rather constitutes a single formal interest, the interest in harmony."[84] Harmony is sought when one recognizes that different goods and ideals are justified by virtue of their being goods and ideals held by some autotelic living beings, which does not mean that justice exhausts itself in the pursuit of harmony. Politically, then, justice manifests itself as a sustained pursuit of a harmonious organization of human diversity. The specific forms it assumes are to a large degree context-dependent. Under certain circumstances harmony may acquire a weak sense of an equilibrium or a *modus vivendi* – an organizing principle applied to a multitude of diverse, sometimes incompatible, forms of life.

Perhaps somewhat surprisingly, a useful, contemporary reference may be found in John Rawls's liberal-democratic model, which I will remind now briefly and return to at the end of this section. Justice here is based on two principles governing the distribution of rights, liberties, socio-economic advantages and duties: 1) equal right to the basic liberties for all citizens; 2) social and economic inequalities are distributed/organized in such a way that they work to the advantage of everyone and are "attached to positions and offices open to all." The first principle is fundamental; the second is built upon the premises of the first. "All social values … are to be distributed equally unless an unequal distribution of any … is to everyone's advantage."[85] Importantly for our discussion, an implicit definition of injustice follows: it consists in "inequalities that are not to the benefit of all."[86] Rawls distinguishes between

---

83 Wallach, *The Platonic Political Art*, 215.
84 LR, 73.
85 John Rawls, *A Theory of Justice* (Cambridge, Mass., London, England: Harvard University Press 1971/2005), 62.
86 All the quotes in this praragraph: Rawls, *A Theory of Justice*, 62.

socially controllable social goods, such as "rights and liberties, powers and opportunities, income and wealth" and those that tend to escape social control, mainly natural endowments, including health, intelligence, and others. He then imagines an ideal arrangement, where the primary and controllable goods are equally distributed.

Santayana agrees as to the fundamentality of the first principle, without absolutizing it though, but he also accepts – within reasonable limits – the fact of a natural state of inequality, as part of the generative order, where inherited results of competition between lives of unequal natural endowments are crystallized into a more or less stable social structure, or, in other words, a structure of necessity distribution. The inheritance in question counts, on the one hand, as circumstances, and, on the other, as subject to rational reform. From Santayana's perspective no society is a gathering of abstract persons that may be reorganized according to a set of abstract rules, but a people of a concrete historical and cultural background. However, as the reader already knows, Santayana does not altogether reject the possibility of universalism at some level. With reason and imagination being functions of human nature, locality and idiosyncrasy may be – to some extent – transcended, and the inherited "burden" reformed. No less importantly, there is the universally shared condition of finitude with all its implications. Besides, Santayana's socio-political hermeneutics, structured into orders as it is, accommodates diversity and uniformity in a non-exclusive way. In envisaging a multinational state of the future, Santayana pointed to *the need of establishing a controllable uniformity at some level in order to preserve a peaceful diversity on another.*

Let me now make a digression and refer to James Seaton's claim that the way Santayana frames his idea of the generative order is compatible with F.A. Hayek's conception of the "spontaneous order" of the market. More specifically, Seaton admits that Santayana personally "would have been unsympathetic" to Hayek's idea, but at once suggests that from the perspective of the implications of Santayana's philosophy, things seem otherwise.[87] I disagree with Seaton here. The economic order is, according to Santayana, "innocently" generative only at its primitive stage of the exchange of goods or at the very early stages of the development of commerce. A complex market system, as it is, for example, under the conditions of global capitalism, represents an artificial and militant realm, which, unless controlled by legal and political measures, is more than likely to form an oppressive environment, hostile to human variety and personal liberty, both easily stifled by the all-pervasive standards

---

87   James Seaton, "Santayana on Fascism and English Liberty," *Limbo*, no. 29 (2009), 97–98.

of economic efficiency. This is not to say that Santayana was essentially against free market. Rather, he was against the absolutization of the free market system, distrusted it and saw the need for reasonable efforts at curbing it. In order to prevent the self-reproduction of a cruel and unnecessarily oppressive system of dominations in the contemporary world, he recognizes the need for the equality of chances and, in my interpretation of his political thinking, ascribes to a just and rational government a function of reorganizing the inherited status quo by way of slow and moderate reform. The goal is not a society of equals but one where the existing inequalities serve to articulate natural differences between humans in a way beneficent both to society as a whole (for example by contributing to its cultural richness) and its individual members. In such a society, organizing units – classes, professional guilds, and others – would coexist enabling individuals to shape their social person, engage in the arts that correspond to their abilities and occupy positions according to merit. This idea reflects, as classified by John Rawls, *a principle of beneficent difference*, being a form of harmony and an embodiment of justice. Social status in this model would, ideally, be earned rather than inherited, which, in turn, calls for an equality of opportunity to be attended to by a just government.

Despite his general reluctance towards what he calls social democracy and the fact that in his private letters he sometimes expresses sympathies towards the bygone, nineteenth-century liberalism, Santayana is not insensitive to the fact, emphasized by Rawls, that purely formal equality of opportunities may be insufficient and lead to such inequalities that both degrade individuals and are detrimental for society. Without getting into details, and mainly by way of the criticism of the existing liberal arrangements, he seems to suggest that there may be no other way for liberal governments to fulfill their promise of universal improvement than to cater for a fairer equality of opportunities. Doing so, he displays an awareness of the deficiency of – to use Rawls' language – the system of natural liberty, which assumes a system of free market and merely formal equality of opportunity. Thus, I would suggest, tentatively, that, in specific historical circumstances, Santayana might be more sympathetic towards what Rawls calls the principle of liberal equality, which seeks to regulate socio-economic institutions so as to decrease the influence of contingencies on opportunity.

The following passage, which I quote in its entirety, conveys an overall spirit of Santayana's vision of a good (morally representative, rational, and just) governance:

> The objects intimately important to each human being are inevitably various, and the active pursuit of them is let loose by the opportunity that

circumstances seem to offer for this or that satisfaction. To secure such satisfaction for everybody cannot be the express aim of any government or of any social institution, since such an aim would be infinitely complex and variable. Neither good government, therefore, nor high morality but the play of vital liberty is the immediate multiform source of human happiness; and the best government and the best society, from this point of view, would be those whose pressure never makes itself felt. This does not mean that a man, to be free, must revert to the jungle; for in the jungle he would suffer the unmitigated pressure of all the untamed forces of nature … A good government, by economic arts, turns the forces of nature, as far as possible, from enemies into servants and the pressure of society into friendly cooperation and an opportune stimulus to each man's latent powers. It is in these ways that government can be government "for the people" and society a benefit to its members.[88]

Santayana contrasts the above ideal of harmonizing various interests and accommodating incommensurable goods with the strain of dogmatism within liberalism that assumes that the future humanity would become unanimous in its aspirations, which has not hitherto happened only because of the backwardness that is still prevailing in the world.

Speculating about different socio-political regimes, Santayana discusses a model of *natural aristocracy*, which appears to be the one preferred by him. A natural aristocratic arrangement embodying the principle of beneficent difference should fulfill the "everyone's advantage" postulate. As Rawls summarizes it, with a direct reference to Santayana, "[t]he aristocratic ideal is applied to a system that is open, at least from a legal point of view, and the better situation of those favored by it is regarded as just only when less would be had by those below, if less were given to those above."[89] This, by the way, seems to prevent injustice as defined by Rawls. One may say, then, that according to the early Santayana of *The Life of Reason*, from the perspective of just government in an ideal *politeia* the existence of natural aristocracy is legitimate exclusively on the condition that the said aristocracy recognizes its duties and bestows benefits on society as a whole. It may perform a function of a creative minority, a source of cultural inventions and mimetic patterns in Toynbee's sense, and, possibly, hold offices in a representative government. In order that the people may cherish the goods received from aristocracy, in turn, they must be provided

---

88 DP, 429–430.
89 Rawls, *A Theory of Justice*, 74.

with safety, education and leisure. If these conditions be met, craving for uniformity, says Santayana, seems almost perverse. A diversified social structure, including hierarchic forms of diversity, is a good unless it degrades people.

The said ideal of natural aristocracy, Santayana emphasizes, by no means implies the existence of natural slavery, as presented by Aristotle and easily justified by a metaphysical idealism that sanctifies facticity claiming that "what is is right."[90] In fact, these two ideas are not only not complementary but rather at odds with one another. The first suggests at least the possibility of elevation open to all, the second justifies unjust and cruel degradation serving the existing social relations of power. Indian castes are an example of a social structure not based on ability or merit but rather "on the chances of some early war, reinforced by custom and perpetuated by inheritance ... Thus stifled ability in the lower orders, and apathy or pampered incapacity in the higher, unite to deprive society of its natural leaders."[91]

Now, to the reader's surprise, if not frustration, in a manner expressive of his provocativeness and ambivalence, Santayana then proceeds to soften his judgment on the stifling role of fossilized social differences and announces that the source of human apathy should also be sought in the fact that "most men seem to miss their vocation," or, worse, "most men have no vocation."[92] Thus, a tradition and a social hierarchy may play a crucial formative function and provide the foundations on which individual potential may be linked to some definite forms, social roles, etc. An absolute rebellion against what has been established is therefore a misunderstanding. At the same time, the thinker assures that to acknowledge an initial natural inequality of chances is not tantamount to ignoring the phenomenon of injustice. "Injustice in this world is not something comparative; the wrong is deep, clear, and absolute in each private fate."[93] Injustice in the human world may be irremovable but it should not be made deeper and more acute by social relations. "Every privilege that imposes suffering involves a wrong ... suffering has an added sting when it enables others to be exempt from care and to live like gods in irresponsible ease; [then] the inequality ... becomes ... a bitter wrong."[94] These words may incline one to search for yet another principle of justice, one that might compensate for the insufficiency of the principles of harmonious diversity and beneficent difference. The other principle, according to my interpretation,

---

90   LR, 137.
91   LR, 133.
92   LR, 133.
93   LR, 136.
94   LR, 136.

may be found in Santayana's idea of *justice as charity*, at which I will take a closer look later.

In a world where injustice – for example in the guise of "justice" as understood by Thrasymachus – strengthens the oligarchies that democracy tends to engender and allows them rob individuals of their vital powers, literally wasting their lives in most undignified ways, and thus contributing to the emergence of "brute humanity," a more radical, socialist kind of state intervention might be needed and justified as a transitory stage. By way of digression, while Rawls emphasizes that the conception of the two principles of justice excludes trading basic liberties and rights for greater gains on the level of other goods, Santayana, especially in his private correspondence, and somewhat unfortunately for his moralist's image, is less convinced about the absolute status of the first principle and more ready to accept some divergences in this respect, especially when they stem from the generative order. This might explain his verbal support, even if only tentative and very short-lived, for certain radically illiberal solutions, like communism or Mussolini's fascism, to the social problems of his time. Meanwhile, the said solutions should be classified as belonging to the repertoire of the "brute" (rather than the "polite") humanity, of the ascent of which Santayana warned on a number of occasions.[95] However that might be, in some of his texts he treated the "Titans" of the first half of the twentieth century in terms of a historical *nemesis*. And this is in accordance with the implications of his political thought, where injustice rests in "mutilating other lives or thwarting their natural potentialities" when it could have been avoided. To bring about a broader context, in the conclusion of the chapter on the aristocratic ideal, Santayana writes:

> the ideal of society can never involve the infliction of injury on anybody for any purpose ... The ideal state and the ideal universe should be a family where all are not equal, but where all are happy. So that an aristocratic or theistic system in order to deserve respect must discard its sinister apologies for evil and clearly propose such an order of existences, one superposed upon the other, as should involve no suffering on any of its levels ... The privileges the system bestows on some must involve no outrage on the rest, and must not be paid for mutilating other lives or thwarting their natural potentialities.[96]

---

[95] Santayana, by the way, was by no means the only thinker of the time to speculate about the need for a charismatic leader, to mention only Oswald Spengler and Max Weber. As for his unfortunate words of support towards Mussolini, other scholars have already addressed the issue in detail. See: Seaton, "Santayana on Fascism and English Liberty."

[96] LR, 139.

Last but not least, Santayana's reflections on just and rational government embrace the possibility of a good authoritarian regime (but not a totalitarian one, which is decisively rejected as an embodiment of an irrational and extreme militancy). The offices in such a regime would be peopled by – roughly speaking – scientists and experts, representing a wide variety of fields, thoughtful and well trained in the art of governing, "persons able to discern the possibility or impossibility of human ambitions,"[97] motivated by a disinterested will to harmonize interests existing in the society. Such a government would avoid explicitly ideological, religious,[98] and partisan motivations that could threaten its impartiality. Meanwhile, "bound to defend and encourage the expression of vital freedom," it should protect intellectual and religious freedom.[99] It would "circumvent the defeats or hardships that nature imposes" and regulate social, economic, and cultural activities in such a way that they do not violate or restrict other agent's liberty. In short, it would represent "the rational art of minimizing the inevitable conflicts of primal irrational Wills against one another and against the forces of nature."[100] This description of the basic functions of government in terms of preventing, limiting, regulating, and minimizing crises (conflict, loss, waste) caused by unavoidable natural and social antagonizing factors, as sketched by the thinker in the final part of *Dominations and Powers*, allows us to evoke, once again, the idea of *managing necessity* as a reductive interpretive tool helpful in unwrapping Santayana's political thinking. To repeat, "harmonizing" in certain circumstances simply means organizing conditions for a peaceful coexistence of an irreducible human variety and whenever there is conflict – for its efficient solution.

Let me note that Santayana's "authoritarian" stands here for as much or as little as representing the authority of the will and interests of the governed in the face of the authority of things/facts. This idea, by the way, contains a universalistic incentive. As long as government is unbiased, scientific, and

---

97   DP, 434.
98   In the introduction to *The Life of Reason*, Santayana notes that the mythical dimension of Christianity, though it may represents some truths about human life, does so by the price of "misrepresenting its history and conditions," and, by confusing "poetic fictions" and ideals with real powers, it misrepresents the conditions of human action and "make[s] a rational estimate of things impossible." While one needs to keep in mind that this is but one aspect of Santayana's more complex, evolving, and often much more sympathetic view of Christianity, he remained faithful to the idea that any dogmatic prejudice inhibits government's chances for rational action based on an honest representation of circumstances. See: Santayana, introduction to LR1, 7.
99   DP, 433.
100 DP, 434.

inclined towards harmonizing diversity, "the very nature of rational economy could perfectly well extend its authority to other nations or even over the whole world."[101] Santayana realized that the chances for its realization in the twentieth century seemed bleak, yet, in the light of the undeniable and irresistible processes of globalization and interconnectedness as well as the emergence of pressing global problems requiring global responses, turning a blind eye to a future possibility of some sort of global governance would be unreasonable.

> [A] diversity of civilized peoples, each with its vital inspiration and traditional regimen, flourishing perhaps on the same universal basis of a rational economic order, would seem to me highly desirable. Mankind walks on one material planet under one material firmament; these conditions it is to their common advantage to respect. But, that toll once paid to necessity, why should not vital liberty in each heart devise the private or social or ideal order by which it would live?[102]

While harmonizing diversity, expressive of pluralism and tolerance, may be said to constitute a positive, rationally, aesthetically, and "erotically" motivated dimension of justice, one also finds in Santayana another principle of justice, one embodying the incentive to recognize injustice and minimize suffering, namely – charity. Actually, both principles may be said to converge in a simple *act of understanding* the other and "to understand is more than forgive, it is almost to adopt."[103] By understanding alien interests and empathizing with the suffering other, one assumes the attitude of humility and expands one's moral imagination. This, obviously, involves compassion. Schopenhauer, a thinker believed to have influenced some of Santayana's views,[104] saw altruism and compassion as constituting the empirical basis for moral life.[105] The connection made by Santayana between charity and justice may be an example of a direct influence by Schopenhauer's idea of "the moral drive out of which flow both the virtue of justice and the virtue of philanthropy."[106] One might also

---

101   DP, 435.
102   DP, 402.
103   LR, 71.
104   For a discussion of similarities between Santayana and Schopenhauer see chapter 5 in Michael Brodrick, *The Ethics of Detachment in Santayana's Philosophy* (New York: Palgrave Macmillan, 2015), 84–106.
105   See: Arthur Schopenhauer, *On the Basis of Morality*, par. 14–17. See also: Ursula Wolf, "How Schopenhauer's ethics of compassion can contribute to today's ethical debate," *Enrahonarn. Quaderns de Filosofia* 55 (2015): 41–49.
106   Wolf, „How Schopenhauer's ethics of compassion," 47.

think of this connection in terms of Richard Rorty's conception of justice as "expanding and contracting loyalties,"[107] in the light of which universal compassion is but an example of the most extreme expansion of loyalty (preceded by an expansion of imagination), namely – loyalty to mankind, or, perhaps, all suffering creatures. Other than that, even though an ideal government is not motivated religiously in an explicit or direct way, the example of charity makes religious heritage relevant in matters of politics.

Santayana's claim in *The Life of Reason* is rather bold – "[j]ustice and charity are identical"[108] and compatible with reason. Ideally, justice, charity, and reason form a harmonious triad insofar as their alliance serves genuine representation of human interests. When a conception of justice is utterly divorced from charity and conceived of in theoretical and abstract terms only, there appear a few problems, one of them being the risk of committing *the aristocrat's fallacy*. The said fallacy is a sense of moral omniscience and superiority translated into readiness to impose a given set of norms on others, regardless of specific circumstances, beliefs and interests of those others. This, needless to say, is often an issue when political and explicitly religious motives intertwine. What is more, behind the aristocrat's fallacy there may stand an egoistic motivation – the judge's interest in his own moral perfection – in which case, to refer to Schopenhauer again, a given judgment or decision loses any moral value.[109]

Adopting any definitive moral ideal should be accompanied by the recognition of its relativity, which is not tantamount to abandoning it as long as there are arguments for adopting it. The element of charity warrants that a given ideal is as universally representative as possible – it is adopted only after all relevant interests and claims have been considered, none being prejudged and denied as unworthy. Obviously, in a world of conflicting interests, some disputes must be settled by making mutual concessions, some claims must be sacrificed so that some other might be satisfied, but, first, "the parties to the suit must in justice be all heard, and heard *sympathetically*."[110] This is "a narrow path of charity and valour," a middle way between fanaticism and nihilism.[111]

---

107   Richard Rorty, "Justice as larger loyalty," in *Philosophy as Cultural Politics, Philosophical Papers*, vol. 4 (Cambridge: CUP: 2007), 42.
108   LR, 271.
109   See: Schopenhauer, *On the Basis of Morality*, par. 15. According to Michael Brodrick, Santayana offers a sort of prelude to an ethics of detachment. If my reading of Brodrick is correct, this kinds of ethics actually excludes pursuit of moral perfection, or moral perfection is something one should detach from. Ethics of detachment, though, "would not have us detach from those in need." Brodrick, *The Ethics of Detachment*, 4.
110   LR, 271. My emphasis.
111   LR, 270.

We are talking here about an intended and explicit attitude of the recognition of and an impartial sympathy for other moral agents.

The alliance of justice and charity belongs to a type of morality called by Santayana, in the vein of Bergson's distinction in *The Two Sources of Morality and Religion*, a first-hand or a primary morality. "The masters of life," individuals able to see through convention and recognize afresh true human interests, are fit to readjust norms so that they serve better human well-being and happiness. On the opposite pole, there is a second-hand morality, peopled by the "retailers of moral truth," inspired by prejudice, fear of change, and enmity to whatever seems alien to them.[112] All in all, there is an insightful and powerful remark made by Santayana and shedding light on his political thought as a whole, namely – *justice without charity "remains only an organized wrong."*[113] If justice is to be representative of what is the best in humans, it must involve charity. Regardless of the presence of Platonic inspirations in Santayana's work and the fact that he shared with Plato the rejection of Thrasymachus' understanding of justice, he evokes *Republic* as a model of polity organized in a wrong way. The ideal assumed by Plato is a harmoniously organized political organism, where harmony – as a manifestation of justice – refers to the very organs/parts of this state. In other words, an abstract future whole is at stake. Venturing an unsympathetic interpretation of Plato, one might say that the criterion of justice employed by him is reason seeking an aesthetic kind of perfection as embodied in a self-perpetuating political order. The ultimate aim is "arbitrary, and, in fact, perverse" for it is neither concerned with happiness of the subjects nor with the development of the variety of human potential.[114] As an alternative to this and other conceptions of justice that evoke a transcendent ideal or pure reason, Santayana refers to the idea of justice as charity. From the perspective of Santayana's readers, by the way, there is yet another reason why this idea is important. One may say that it compensates for what some describe as an apparent coldness and lack of personalism in Santayana's philosophy, which sometimes resembles an aesthetically-oriented humanism. Leaving aside the fact that Santayana's own idea of justice seems to be heterogenous, in *The Life of Reason* he defends the association with charity as fulfilling better the criterion of universality without violating pluralism. Let me quote a key passage in its entirety:

---

112   LR, 271.
113   LR, 272. My emphasis.
114   LR, 272.

There is accordingly a justice deeper and milder than that of pagan states, a universal justice called charity, a kind of all-penetrating courtesy, by which the limits of personal or corporate interests are transgressed in imagination. Value is attributed to rival forms of life; something of the intensity and narrowness inherent in the private will is surrendered to admiration and solicitude for what is most alien and hostile to one's self ... *Charity is nothing but a radical and imaginative justice* ... His own [the Christian's or the Buddhist's] salvation does not seem to either complete unless every other creature also is redeemed and forgiven.[115]

The disinterestedness and imaginativeness through which charity as justice speaks have their obvious limits imposed by finitude, history, and culture.[116] What is most important, *charity excludes moral absolutism, which tends to produce ruthless and irresponsible judgments.* Santayana was aware that religion in politics is a double-bind edge. It shapes human personalities both into the direction of fanaticism and that of charity. The latter, which, as I'd suggest, in the secular context of justice may be translated into *a pluralism supported by an effective empathy*, or: *a pluralistic and effectively emphatic imagination*, may be a safeguard against the inhuman sacrifices required by the former, militant and dogmatic attitude.[117]

From the perspective of Christian tradition, where charity received one of its formulas, charity completes a model of human relations and, as Santayana claims, may be incorporated into a model of justice. Traditionally, charity involves relieving the body and only then assisting in redeeming the soul. Acts of charity never impose themselves, they are not militant. Christ did not venture to "save them [ignorant people and children] in the regimental and prescriptive fashion adopted by the Church."[118] A just state, then, provides for mechanisms preventing the imposture of the dogmatic views of some of its subjects, no matter whether they constitute a minority or a majority, on the remaining citizens.[119]

---

115 LR, 272. My emphasis.
116 In practice, charity "extends to physical and discoverable creatures, whose destiny is interwoven dynamically with our own. Absolute and irresponsible fancy can be the basis of no duty ... A compromise made with non-existent or irrelevant interests is a wrong to the real interests on which that sacrifice is imposed gratuitously." LR, 273.
117 Finally, justice as charity is said to extend not only to moral agents but "every other creature," which might, debatably, suggest its potential applicability to non-human creatures.
118 LR, 274.
119 What is important, Santayana, to his credit, is aware of the distinction between both law and morality, and morality and religion. Law is neither the source nor the upper limit of

When reflecting upon Santayana's ideas about the intimate connection between justice and charity, an association with Paul Ricoeur's essay "Love and Justice" comes to mind. The notion of love here is broader than Santayana's "charity," but charity is definitely a vital part of it.[120] Ricoeur starts with a brief analysis of the apparently unbridgeable differences between the discourse of love, as exemplified by a few biblical sources, and that of justice. The former is poetic and speaks in analogies and metaphors. It is characterized by a logic of superabundance as opposed to the logic of equivalence, which is typical of the formalized discourse of justice. Thus, at the level of language, the two modes seem incongruent. There is, however, a shared field of application, and, hence, a promise of at least partial reconciliation between them, namely – both pertain to the realm of human action.

And indeed, in the famous commandment "you shall love your neighbour as yourself" as well as in the Sermon on the Plain (or: on the Mount), where Jesus recommends loving one's enemies, love appears in an ethical context and in an imperative form. In the latter case, love exemplifies irrational superabundance, something very distant from the principle of equivalence. Yet, it comes from a supra-ethical realm of the *economy of the gift*, where one gives because one has (already) been given by God, insofar as one participates in the realm of creation and salvation. Unlike in the utilitarian context, where – to simplify the issue – one offers so as to receive, here offering does not expect reward. We are presented here, to refer to René Girard's vocabulary, with a transcendent model of non-reciprocal action. Were it not for the possibility of this kind of benevolent imitation, the famous golden rule: "as you wish that men would do to you, do so to them" (Luke, 6:31), might be understood in terms of the logic of revenge. The supra-ethical principle of loving one's enemies seems to correct the (ethical) golden rule, whereby it protects the golden rule from becoming purely utilitarian and protects people from the effects of the abuse of the golden rule's meaning. It also establishes a broader horizon for the meaning of justice, which, since Aristotle, has been identified, reductively, with equivalence and distribution, whereby justice seemed to regulate the realm of competition rather than establish conditions for a true cooperation. Imbued thus

---

morality. In an ideal, rational state law would rather serve securing the minimum conditions for the practice of morality.

120 In point of fact, Ricoeur challenges the well-known distinction between *eros* and *agape*; he sees no bases for it in the Bible. He focuses on a few biblical sources of love discourse: 1 Corinthians 13, Song of Songs, and Sermon on the Plain in Luke, 6:20–49. See: Paul Ricoeur, "Love and Justice," in *Paul Ricoeur: The Hermeneutics of Action*, ed. Richard Kearney (London, Thousand Oaks, New Delhi: Sage Publications, 1996), 23–39.

with the spirit of superabundance (love), the ideal aim of justice aspires to mutual recognition, solidarity and magnanimity in human relations. Other than that, in this dialectical relation, love, which is extra-moral, becomes part of practical ethics under the *aegis* of justice. In other words, justice becomes a formal vehicle for the substance of love. In conclusion, Ricoeur says:

> It is only in the moral judgment made in some particular situation that this unstable equilibrium can be assured and protected. Thus we may affirm in good faith … that the enterprise of expressing this equilibrium in everyday life, on the individual, judicial, social and political planes, is perfectly practicable. I would even say that the tenacious incorporation, step by step, of a supplementary degree of compassion and generosity in all of our codes – including our penal codes and our codes of social justice, constitutes a perfectly reasonable task, however difficult and interminable it may be.[121]

These reflections bring Ricoeur, and ourselves, back to John Rawls' theory of justice as fairness. They also bring us back, quite obviously, to Santayana's insistence that charity and justice share much of their essence. Santayana's and Ricoeur's arguments, different as they are and drawing on some other subtleties of *agape*, both offer substantial support for the alliance of justice and love. Coming back to Rawls, he aims at a situation where the socially controllable goods are as equally distributed as possible. This should be achieved not by a forced and artificial allocation of goods, but by adopting a principle according to which those endowed with "undeserved" (uncontrollable) assets can get richer on condition that it is to the benefit of all, and, in particular, the worst-off citizens. Thus, a social unity based on a conscious, benevolent, and responsible cooperation is achieved. Ricoeur interprets the second principle of justice by Rawls as inexplicitly connected to the commandment of love insofar as the principle aims at *preventing harm*, in which it differs, for example, from the utilitarian maxim, which silently assumes sacrificing some minority. Also Rawls' idea of *reflective equilibrium*, which stands for a coherence between one's most abstract ideals, theoretical convictions, and specific judgments, a coherence assuming the possibility of revision on any of these levels of reflection, or, in Rorty's words, "fabricating a new practical identity,"[122] may be viewed as an expression of this connection. It is so, I believe, first, because

---

121 Ricoeur, "Love and Justice," 37.
122 Richard Rorty, "Kant vs. Dewey. The current situation of moral philosophy," in *Philosophy as Cultural Politics. Philosophical Papers*, vol. 4 (Cambridge: CUP, 2007), 201.

reflective equilibrium requires readiness to sacrifice – in the name of justice – one's theoretical convictions, and, hence, even part of one's self, and, second, it is assumed that justice is not finite (although concrete decisions are) and cannot be contained once and for all in any set of dogmatic convictions. *Love or charity, when it comes to judgment in situation, literally disrupts any dogma, any absolutism.*

Now, coming back to Santayana, his association of justice and love is not limited to the context of charity. Charity involves the recognition of human misery and unhappiness, as well as mercy for and solidarity with this "living dust." Charity, as Santayana describes it, may be considered in the context of Schopenhauerian ethics of compassion and may be associated with Santayana's acquaintance with Buddhist philosophy, not to mention the obvious associations with Christianity. Whatever are its sources, and they seem to be eclectic, it is important that the idea forms at once a substantive and universalistic foundation for Santayana's general conception of justice. As for the other dimension of love discussed here – the "erotic" one – it is based on idealization, which involves the recognition of the human potential for perfection and inclines Santayana towards the (ancient Greek) idea of justice as harmony, which translates itself into a harmonious organization of diversity, whereby a tacitly assumed right of an autotelic life to strive for fulfillment and well-being may be accommodated. "[T]here is an irresistible sympathy in every sensitive and clear mind for the natural aspirations of all living creatures and for their perfections, each after its kind."[123] It is in this context that Santayana says that *excellence is representative of humans* and proposes that the ideal of natural aristocracy should not be dismissed as a possible form of just government. An attempt to establish – under the *aegis* of justice – a *reflective equilibrium* between charity, which seeks to minimize suffering, and the ideal-seeking pursuit of harmony has been undertaken by Santayana in an insightful and sensitive way, even if never incorporated into a complete and practicable political project.

123 DP, 215.

CHAPTER 8

Santayana on Communism

> Revolutions are ambiguous things. Their success is generally proportionate to their power of adaptation and to the reabsorption within them of what they rebelled against.
>
> LR, 218

∴

An initial inquiry into Santayana's views on communism,[1] as evidenced by his letters and political writings, *Dominations and Powers* in particular, reveals an evolution from a moderate skepticism, not deprived of some rays of hope, to an utter disillusionment. After Santayana severed his professional relations with academia and settled in Europe, he continued exchanging ideas with a number of intellectuals and activists from overseas, some of them of leftist and emancipatory sympathies, among them: Horace Kallen, Kenneth Burke, Sydney Hook, Max Eastman, or W.E. Du Bois. Much as he was an insightful observer, commentator, and interpreter of the events of the day, Santayana's familiarity with Marxist philosophy was probably only second-hand, based on the reading of Marx's Bolshevik interpretations, primarily that of Stalin, and some secondary sources. In 1935 he confesses to his readers, in an almost playful tone: "My knowledge of Marx is so slender … that I should prefer not to speak of him at all."[2] A few years later, in his private correspondence, he mentions becoming acquainted with the writings of the American communists of the day – in particular two books by Max Eastman -"Stalin's Russia and the Crisis in Socialism" (1940) and "Marxism: Is It Science?" (1940).[3] He also follows Sydney Hook's engagement in American left-wing intelligentsia. The letters he

---

1 This chapter is based on my articles: "A story of disillusionment: George Santayana's views on communism and the Russian Revolution," *The Interlocutor. Journal of the Warsaw School of the History of Ideas* 2 (2019): 161–147; and "Santayana on Communism in the Light of his Correspondence," *Overheard in Seville* 37 (2019): 30–41.
2 George Santayana, "Why I am not a Marxist."
3 Letter to Max Eastman, 31 Dec. 1940, LGS6: 430, and letter to Nancy S. Toy, 21 Dec. 1940, LGS6: 425.

exchanged with Eastman are evidence of his interest in and appreciation of his colleague's work, even though he straightforwardly distances himself from Eastman's political sympathies.[4]

Interestingly, Santayana notices a number of assumptions common to pragmatism, especially that of John Dewey, and communism, which at once marked differences between these schools and his own philosophy.[5] Regardless of the fact that he finally rejected Soviet Russia's totalitarian ambition and method, he presented his own materialism as incompatible with the so-called dialectical materialism, just as his naturalism differed from the Deweyan, evolutionary type of naturalism.[6] These two cases of incongruence are not unrelated. To put it in a nutshell, Santayana was critical of both philosophies on account of what he called their "ingenuity." The materialism/naturalism declared by these doctrines was, in his view, a cover-up for a specific, instrumental kind

---

[4] When reading Santayana's correspondence, one should keep in mind that, unlike, for example, in the essays of the collection *Soliloquies in England*, where his use of the notion "liberalism" is rather orthodox and refers to the classical liberal theory and the liberal rule, in his private letters, especially to his American colleagues, Santayana uses the term "liberals" loosely, as an umbrella term for representatives of different progressivist worldviews and movements, and "liberalism" stands for the bulk of moderate emancipatory tendencies in modern socio-political thought. He thus labels the representatives of mainstream pragmatism, like John Dewey, "liberals," whereas the left-wing, often pro-communist intellectuals and activists in the United States are referred to by him as "radical liberals." This use reflects the political nomenclature of the era in the United States. For more information on this issue see for example: Guenter Lewy, *The Cause that Failed: Communism in American Political Life* (New York, London: Oxford University Press, 1990).

[5] For some examples of the early discussion of similarities between the philosophies of John Dewey and Karl Marx see: Jim Cork, "Dewey, Karl Marx, and Democratic Socialism," *The Antioch Review* 9, no. 4 (winter 1949): 435–452; and: Sydney Hook, "Experimental Naturalism," (1935) in: *Pragmatism, Democracy, Freedom*, ed. Robert B. Talisse and Robert Tempio (Amherst, NY: Prometheus Books, 2002): 29–45. The first text, in contrast to Santayana's criticism, reveals somewhat naively uncritical acceptance of the Marxist version of materialism.

[6] In short, Dewey's naturalism, referred to as evolutionary, transactional, situational, contextual etc., assumed that experience and perception are continuous with nature, which is ever changing. Moreover, human mind and experience are viewed in terms of an integral, social process, expressive of the principle of growth. This kind of naturalism seems secondary in relation to Dewey's main premises being radical empiricism. Santayana's naturalism, in contrast, postulated ontological primacy of the realm of matter, not only independent of and prior to any human experience but also partially recondite from the perspective of human cognitive capacities. A detailed discussion of the difference in question goes beyond the scope of this book. Let me only add that it requires a reference to the dualisms – such as matter-essence or body-spirit – present in Santayana's philosophy (even if one recognizes them as modern, non-orthodox interpretations of traditional dualisms) and rejected by Dewey. For more on Dewey's naturalism see for example: Thomas M. Alexander, *John Dewey's Theory of Art, Experience and Nature* (New York: SUNY Press, 1987).

of idealistic philosophy, which – by reducing reality to the field of action – endowed humans (collectively) with a prodigious creative power and control over the world, a divine *fiat* of sorts. Thus, both doctrines underestimated the limitations to which human agency is subject, and represented what Santayana called the "dominance of the foreground" – a biased perspective (in one case the perspective of the proletariat engaged in a class war, in the other that of social experience), which they proclaimed to be absolute so that it might better serve certain interests. For Santayana these must have been examples of philosophizing with a hammer, or, phrasing it otherwise, turning theory into a power tool. Dewey's anthropocentrism, or rather action-centrism, overshadowed the recognition of the autonomous realm of nature and thus, on Santayana's reading, Dewey abandoned naturalism for an idolatry or a "religion" of collective enterprise and social progress.[7] He might have ascribed to Marx what he ascribed to Dewey, namely – "the quasi-Hegelian tendency to dissolve the individual into his social functions" and to subject "individual initiative … to overwhelming democratic control."[8] At the same time, both philosophies, from Santayana's perspective, underestimated the limitations imposed on human cognition and action by factors other than merely external and contingent, or, in other words, controllable factors.

Santayana decisively denied Marxism the status of being "scientific." He thought it was a crypto-metaphysical, or a crypto-religious doctrine, where humanity and history were united within a teleological, finalistic, if not eschatological dimension. In one of his letters he wrote: "I entirely accept historical materialism, which is only an application of materialism to history. But the phrase carries now an association with the Hegelian or Marxian dialectic, which if meant to be more than the doctrine of universal flux, is a denial of materialism."[9] In another letter, addressed to Max Eastman, he wrote: "[t]hat Marxism is not a science, for me is a truism. It is a last revision of Hebrew prophecy, as Hegel's system is also."[10] Rather than being a genuine materialism or a science, Marxism seemed to be "an idealism that prefers material images. … in formulating its dream … [A]n idealist who uses mechanical or economic or pragmatic terms remains a dreaming idealist."[11] He thus expressed views

---

7   George Santayana, "Dewey's Naturalistic Metaphysics," in *Obiter Scripta. Lectures, Essays, Reviews*, ed. Justus Buchler and Benjamin Schwartz (New York and London: Charles Scribner's Sons, 1936), 213–240.
8   Santayana, "Dewey's Naturalistic Metaphysics," 217.
9   Letter to Harry Slochower, 18 Sept. 1937, LGS6: 75–76.
10   Letter to Max Eastman, 31 Dec. 1940, LGS6: 430.
11   Letter to Max Eastman, 31 Dec. 1940, LGS6: 430.

shared later by some critics of Marxism. "Neither Marx nor Engels are materialists in the exact or historical meaning of the word," writes Leszek Kołakowski in his canonical study.[12] Marx's "faith in the 'end of history'," according to the same author, is "not a scientist's theory but the exhortation of a prophet."[13] The "dream," of which Santayana writes, ceases to be harmless as soon as it usurps the right to a forceful transformation of the human reality, with no or little respect to its costs.

As for the foundations of Santayana's advocacy of humility in philosophy, which makes him so different from Marx, they already have been discussed in this book at length. Suffice it to say that Santayana views reality as material, contingent, and devoid of any essential "meaning," regardless of the fact that it is reflected objectively in an abstract realm of truth. Humans, trapped in-between recondite matter and unreachable truth, far from being masters of it, dependent on their animal faith and finite hermeneutic capacity, map fragmentary patterns of reality, in a way biased in accordance to their finding themselves in the world.[14]

One should not lose sight of the fact that Santayana enjoyed the belief that no single political option was universally the best for mankind. His relativism in this respect may have been limited by his ideas about human condition and nature, but, other than that, it was on a broadly understood context that the assessment of this or that system depended. Thus, on some occasions Santayana did express hopes that the revolutionary changes in Russia,[15] inspired by Marxist ideals, might indeed bring some desirable changes to humans entrapped in the vicissitudes of the decaying liberal order, or, rather – chaos. There are a number of examples in his writings.

He had no principal "hostility" to socialism and communism, according to his letter of 1921 to Horace Kallen, even though he decisively dismissed the idea that they ever might or should become universal and lasting. He seems to have thought that at certain places and in specific historical moments communism

---

12   Leszek Kołakowski, *Main Currents of Marxism*, trans. Paul S. Falla (New York: W W Norton, 2005), 332.
13   Kołakowski, *Main Currents of Marxism*, 307.
14   For a concise discussion of Santayana's idea of material contingency, his insistence on epistemic humility, and his conception of truth in a comparative context of Richard Rorty's thought see: Angus Kerrr-Lawson, "Rorty has no Physics," *Overheard in Seville: Bulletin of the Santayana Society* 13 (1995): 12–15.
15   Two revolutions took place in Russia in 1917. During the February Revolution the tsarist autocracy was overturned and a new democratic government was installed. The October Revolution overthrew the new Provisional Government and the Bolsheviks introduced the Soviet dictatorship, starting a bloody civil war, which lasted until 1923.

might be justified as a sort of cathartic medium. While it should be accepted only as a last resort and "only when inevitable,"[16] there was a possibility, he admitted, that the early twentieth century was just the right moment for a communist revolution in a crisis-ridden Europe. In 1935 he wrote in a letter: "My sympathies are anti-English now: gradually, since the war, all my Anglomania has faded away … I prefer the Bolshies; and perhaps everywhere, through one approach or another, it is to State socialism that we are bound."[17]

What hopes did he possibly attach to communism? He seems to have hoped that it might cater for the most pressing needs of the many, doing away with the most burdensome vices of capitalism, without encroaching on many fundamental liberties cherished by civil societies, such as freedom of speech, opinion, association, religion, travel, etc. In another letter, written a decade later, one reads:

> I am more drawn by the Zeitgeist … towards communism than I was towards liberalism in the old days. Communism would turn the world, physically and spiritually, into one vast monastery, giving the individual sure support and definite limited duties while leaving him free and solitary in the spirit. That doesn't seem to me a bad ideal, even if certain selective forms of society might have to dive under while the universal brotherhood prevailed. It would not, in any case, prevail equally, or forever.[18]

The origins of these wishful speculations probably rest in his critical assessment and pessimistic premonitions concerning the fate of the liberal ideals in the democratic and capitalist world. As discussed in chapter six, his diagnosis uncovers moral nihilism, intellectual chaos and social alienation in the upper social strata, the crisis of self-rule in mass and faction-ridden democracies, the hypocrisy of governments and the conformity of professional politicians, forming a sort of parasitic organism within society, and, finally, lamentable living standards of the poor.[19] "Conviction has deserted the civilized mind," one reads in his final book, "and a good conscience exists only at the extreme left, in that crudely deluded mass of plethoric humanity which perhaps forms the

---

16 Letter to Horace Kallen, 21 Nov. 1921, LGS3: 39–40.
17 Letter to Robert Shaw Barlow, 19 Oct. 1935, LGS5: 248–249. Meanwhile, the same year, publicly and on a theoretical plane, he distances himself from Marxism as evidenced by his article of 1935, "Why I am not a Marxist."
18 Letter to Max Eastman, 26 Dec. 1945, LGS7: 202–203.
19 See: DP, 379–380.

substance of another material tide destined to sweep away the remnants of our old vanities, and to breed new vanities of its own."[20]

Ironically, he notices, the "banners of humanitarianism and equality" previously put forth by liberals, have been taken over "by a return wave of communism and dogmatic unanimity."[21] Some of Santayana's comments seem to confirm the Marxist conviction about the class nature of liberalism and the associated cultural deprivation of the poor. Liberalism, we read, "secured vital liberty [only] for the rich and for the geniuses, ... for the liberty fostered by prosperity is intellectual as well as personal." The marriage of culture and education with prosperity, and, consequently, class, deepened the degradation of many by making it difficult for them to access what, in Santayana's eyes, was the only democratic gateway to the participation in a voluntary human "aristocracy" – a unique plane of a potential human "equality" called culture, and liberal arts in particular. The revolutionary ideals, however, which arose in response to various faces of injustice, were born in the womb of the formal liberties guaranteed by the liberal order. It was "on the varied fruits of this moral and intellectual liberty that the spirit of unanimous mankind might feed at first."[22]

The most upright and surprising expression of Santayana's flirt with the idea of universal communism is found in a response he gives to the question: "Through whom might wisdom rule the world?"[23] One reads:

> Perhaps the Soviets ... they are a real power, with an autonomous army. ... Secondly, the Soviets are theoretically international ... Thirdly, they represent the Dictatorship of the proletariat, that is, of the nondescript masses of human beings without country, religion, property, or skill. *We are all born proletarians, and remain such all our lives long in our physical being and in respect to those radical animal wants which are alone coercive. The dictatorship is therefore not artificial here, but simply a recognition of the fundamental conditions of our existence.* At that level, and in those respects, we live under the control of universal material forces; it would be childish not to recognize them and irrational not to confront them with foresight and method. Lastly, such foresight and method are foreshadowed in the Soviet doctrine of Historical Materialism. ... if

---

20   DP, 254.
21   DP, 310.
22   All the quotations in this paragraph: DP, 310.
23   DP, 453.

the management [of economy] were competent, a universal communism, backed by irresistible armed force, would be a wonderful boon to mankind.[24]

Leaving aside the fact that Santayana was just about to acknowledge that he had been misled attaching such grand hopes to the Soviets, these words testify to his effort to reconcile elements of his materialism with the communist doctrine, which required, at least, circumventing the whole factionist dimension of communism. This could happen only on the verbal and imaginative plane, and in the quotation above has been achieved by the price of switching from the literal to a metaphorical use of the term "proletariat." Having recognized the rudimentary material slavery, the homage humans pay for staying alive, and the inevitable situation of bowing to necessity, Santayana speculates on the possibility that a communist regime – under the condition of a genuine economic competence – might free people from the toll of daily struggle for survival and the shackles of narrow-minded consumerism, thus liberating them to a cultural and spiritual life. The idea of establishing a political order meant to enable individuals to develop the arts and virtues that their "souls" are naturally inclined to, including forms of spirituality broadly understood, reappears in Santayana's writings and seems to constitute a modest, more or less explicit Platonic motivation on his part. This, in my view, is a context helpful in understanding the hopes he attached to communism.

To emphasize, Santayana uses the term "proletariat" figuratively, just as he does with some other terms, such as "barbarism," saying that all people are innately proletarians inasmuch as they are incarnate, finite beings, who suffer and have certain fundamental needs. This constitutes the only basis for the idea of universal equality. "Proletarians thus tend to become equal in the only thing in which equality is possible – in their misery. And this is a great bond" and the source of the idea that "all men are equal by nature."[25] This is to say that the human condition is the equalizing agent. *The great bond of misery* – an image very much in the spirit of Schopenhauer indeed – may be the ground for the feeling and attitude of fraternity and solidarity. This attitude contains an element of charity or an emotionally charged *understanding* of the "equal vital franchise of all creatures ... [that] must all be impartially pitied. For how precarious is the special life stirring in each of them, how buffeted at every turn, how diseased and how tormented" will be envisaged by a *dramatic*

---

24   DP, 455. My emphasis.
25   DP, 369.

imagination enabling one to "reproduce the dramas actually enacted in the world."[26] Equality of this type, however, is a "mystical equality," accessible only through a spirit transcending its own egoism. It starts with understanding that all creatures are "capable of living only in incompatible ways"[27] and "the most ungrudging recognition of inequality and even mutual hostility" among incarnated beings.[28] The mystical equality, sought by some religions and philosophies, is rare and not easily practicable in real life and on a large scale, yet elements of it, such as solidarity with others in misery, which may require personal sacrifice, may be conveyed through culture and only then be adopted by politics.

To provide opportunity for the realization of the natural variety of individual needs and talents, the Soviet state, Santayana says, would have to guarantee freedom of expression, religious affiliation, travel and migration, and "renounce all control of education, ... manners, and arts."[29] In other words, it would have to protect pluralism, which is conducive to vital liberty and spiritual freedom, both of which constitute, from Santayana's perspective, the primary justification of the whole endeavor. This is where a tension between pluralism, being a response to the fact of the natural diversity of humans (both as individuals and as collectivities) and the expected equality and unanimity of all appears. A metaphorical framing of the idea of equality of all people allows to reconcile it with the empirical diversity and pluralism. It is important that, except for the "proletarian" equality, people potentially share in yet another dimension of it:

> We are proletarians and unwitting communists only *in the absence of these things* [the liberties listed above]; *in their presence, we all instantly become aristocrats*. Everything except the mechanical skeleton of society, all culture ... must be left to free associations, to inspiration founding traditions and traditions guiding inspiration. ... [A] just universal government would not disturb them.[30]

Elsewhere we find the idea slightly rephrased: "The real equality between men is ... [either] an equality in misery ... [or] an equality in spiritual autonomy and pride."[31] In the former case we all are "proletarians," in the latter – "aristocrats."

---

26   DP, 368.
27   DP, 367.
28   DP, 370.
29   DP, 455–456.
30   DP, 455–456. My emphasis.
31   DP, 368.

The said aristocracy should be understood with reference to the dignity anchored in *an inalienable autonomy and authority of each human judge* – an autotelic, conscious human being, discovering not only the shape of their uniqueness among other unique human beings but also the possibility of a spiritual unity with others. Exclusively in an environment respectful of natural variety would "the principle of spiritual wealth in spiritual liberty ... be vindicated."[32] This idea is reflected in the already discussed, Santayana's imaginary commonwealth, where diverse forms of life coexist and, possibly, communicate in a peaceful way. An ultimate gain such a society seems to offer is the possibility of choice and of spiritual development, in the broadest sense of this term, to all those who desire it. In any case, if the "aristocratic" type of equality is to prevail, the burdens of the "proletarian" equality, which tends to produce, paradoxically, unceasing power struggles and huge inequalities, should be mitigated by the state.

Keeping in mind that for Santayana diversity is not only a fact about life and human society, modern society in particular, but also a good to be protected, pluralism as organization of differences, as well as virtues needed to sustain the pluralistic equilibrium, are inescapable conclusions of Santayana's political thinking. The said "organization" is – unlike in communism – not to be achieved solely or predominantly by means of central, rational planning. It is always partly local, traditional and inherited, so the margin of rational intervention is to be negotiated with the existing reality. Depending on circumstances, a society may not be a classless society, yet the existing social differences should be mitigated so as not to debilitate people's potential by turning them into slaves of material necessity and victims of the unlimited appetites of others. History teaches that this aim is hardly achievable solely by legal and economic means. It is crucial that in such a society exists a plurality of ways of gaining recognition. In other words, culture is crucial. It was also clear for Santayana that democracy is not the only possible form of political organization where these conditions could be met.

Ultimately, communist practice failed when measured against the basic criteria set by Santayana, such as moral representation or rational authority. It failed also against the criteria of its former advocates and adherents,

---

32 DP, 368. Santayana speaks here of the only real equality, which is "entirely spiritual ... Essentially and inwardly, each man is autonomous, the only seat and absolute final judge of all judgments; and this transcendental centrality of spirit is the same in every man, and its authority, in each case, equal and inalienable. And this every man acknowledges when he speaks to any other creature and posits that other mind." DP, 368.

leaving many of them – inasmuch as they survived – disillusioned. Unable to thrive in the situation of liberty and assert its popular legitimacy, the communist regime resorted to mass manipulation and large scale violence, showing its totalitarian character. Santayana came to a conclusion similar to that of Andrzej Walicki, who argued that there is a genetic relation between the fact of the totalitarian enslavement of people and the attempt to materialize the Marxist idea of freedom. The said idea of freedom entailed the possibility and the necessity of a full and rational control over socio-economic forces, a "collective mastery over people's own fate."[33] Moreover, the said freedom seemed to concern not the concrete individuals of here-and-now, but an abstract, future community of humans who have reached identity with their ideal essence, contradicting Marx's own insistence on considering only the "real" man. Santayana had a clear intuition of the inhuman cost of implementing similar utopias. Leaving aside the fact of ineradicable diversity of humans, which limits both the scope of unanimity among them and the effectiveness of external control, he believed that doing away with an element of unreason in the human world was an impossibility and "could only come at the price of eradicating the bodies which are the material basis for unreason to flourish."[34] These intuitions found their grim confirmation in the development of the Soviet communism into a paradigmatic totalitarian system, characterized by a brutality of unprecedented scale in modern times. This is what Santayana wrote about the Soviet Union under Stalin's leadership:

> it is (...) really the ambition of the self-appointed inner circle of the Communist party that not only rule absolutely but intend to keep the whole world unanimous by "liquidating" all dissentients. And half by the wonderful power of propaganda and mass-suggestion and half by systematic extermination of all other ways of thinking, this artificial unanimity has actually seemed to cover vast regions of Europe and Asia like a blanket of Siberian snow. The depth of it is unknown, but the silence is impressive.[35]

---

33   Andrzej Walicki, *Marksizm i skok do królestwa wolności* [Marxism and the Leap to the Kingdom of Freedom] (Warszawa: PWN, 1996), 19.
34   Till Kinzel, "Santayana, Self-Knowledge and the Limits of Politics," in Padron and Skowroński, *The Life of Reason in an Age of Terrorism*, 98.
35   DP, 457.

Life itself proved the ultimate critic of communism and there is no superior critic than life, noted Alexander Izgojew, a Russian émigré intellectual.[36] Similarly, Santayana sees communism as failing from the viewpoint of the authority of facts. As a materialization of Marxist doctrine, it rendered itself illegitimate in many ways: by betraying its own emancipatory spirit (reliance on mass terror and forced labour), by failing against the standard of moral representation, by disavowing the myth of the scientific authority of Marxism and proving incompetent in practice. The origins of the failure have been sought both in the perversities of the practical application of Marxism and its erroneous theoretical assumptions. Among the Marxist "myths" that Santayana rejected were those listed in Kołakowski's analysis, namely – that "there can be a perfect identity between collective and individual interests," that it is possible to remove all the sources of antagonism among individuals by enabling them to merge within the social "whole," and that there is a possibility of a full emancipation of man, or, in other words, the attainment of his ideal nature.[37] The utopian idea of a full emancipation of man would entail bridging the gap between necessity and freedom, which means not simply alleviating the burden of the human condition, but doing away with the human condition whatsoever. This is where Santayana is most clearly at odds with Marxism, at least in its classical, orthodox version. Even though he believed necessity may and should be understood to some extent, respect for human finitude, humility, and the awareness of an irremovable human dependence and existential contingency were part of his philosophical credo. Marx, in turn, notes Kołakowski, "did not believe in the essential finitude and the limitation of man ... Evil and suffering, in his eyes, ... were purely social facts."[38] These differences between Santayana and Marx are unbridgeable differences between an essentially non-utopian, pluralistic worldview and a utopian project. The said negligence of finitude finds expression also in the totalitarian aspiration to establish justice on earth, which means achieving a perfect convergence of legality and justice. This, as pointed out by Hannah Arendt, has hitherto been recognized as unachievable due to the discrepancy between the generality of positive law and the uniqueness of each human case, "with its unrepeatable set of circumstances." Finally, totalitarian government abolishes legality and

---

36 Aleksander S. Izgoev, "Socialism, Culture and Bolshevism," in *Out of the Depths (De Profundis). Articles on the Russian Revolution*, trans. and ed. William F. Woehrlin (Irvine, California: Charles Slack JR Publisher, 1986), 126.
37 Kołakowski, *Main Currents of Marxism*, 108.
38 Kołakowski, *Main Currents of Marxism*, 338.

applies "the law" (of History or Nature) "directly to mankind without bothering with the behaviour of men."[39]

Looking back at the early correspondence with Horace Kallen, Santayana thinks communism should "be accepted only when inevitable, and confined to the community to which ... [it is] fitted, and by no means to be set up by the philosopher as ideals compulsory at all times and places over all men." These limitations pertain to all grand socio-political designs, the fallibility of which is grounded in human ignorance and ... madness. As long as we think "in aesthetic or moral terms which correspond to no lines of cleavage or motion in nature,"[40] these designs are based on arbitrary theoretical constructs, such as the doctrine of class struggle, which – regardless of its critical value – became a "dubious schema utilized by demagogues."[41]

When the application of an ideal turns out a disaster, Santayana comments, "we are consumed with astonishment and indignation at what we think the folly and wickedness of mankind, whose actions and sentiments are so strangely oblivious of the units we wished to preserve."[42] Similarly, a Russian thinker, Semen Frank, objected to the tendency to blame the masses for the miscarriage of political projects, noting that "[t]he people are ... [only] tools in the hands of a governing minority."[43] And not unlike Santayana, who spoke of the strategy of blaming immaturity of the people for the failures of the Soviet state, Frank asks, ironically, "[w]hat sort of politicians rely in their programme and agenda on an abstract ideal of the people instead of assuming the real, concrete people?"[44]

The fundamental question of "the people" and "the proletariat" on behalf of whose authority the Bolsheviks reached for power seems to Santayana as problematic as the future consequences of the whole undertaking for the people:

> [D]oes the proletariat exercise any power at all? Or do the vested interests at work regard the special interests of the proletariat or of their own prestige or chosen ambition? Here is a revolution entangled in the complexities of its own success and carried by its organized instruments into

---

39 Arendt, *The Origins of Totalitarianism*, 462.
40 Both quotations come from: letter to Horace Kallen, 21 Dec. 1921, LGS3: 39.
41 Petr Berngardovich Struwe, "The Historical Meaning of the Russian Revolution and National Tasks," in Woehrlin, *Out of the Depths*, 212.
42 Letter to Horace Kallen, 21 Dec. 1921, LGS3: 39.
43 Semyon Lyudvigovich Frank, "De Profundis," in Woehrlin, *Out of the Depths*, 221–222.
44 Frank, "De Profundis," 221.

> enterprises of which it cannot plan the course or see the end. Meantime, what may we expect the spiritual condition of the people and the character of the liberal arts to become in this future realm of equality and unanimity?⁴⁵

Santayana's answer to the question about who exercises power is: a sect, a party of conspirators, who, notwithstanding their sense of mission, "remained essentially politicians, counting not so much on the loose lost orphans of society as on the organized working class, that could be indoctrinated, trained and mobilized into a political army."⁴⁶ In 1952, in a letter to a friend, Santayana, utterly disillusioned, ascribes a deep cynicism to the Soviet elites: "It is already notorious that in Russia the governing clique lives luxuriously and plans 'dominations' like so many madmen. ... There would be no 'communists' among factory hands if they knew their true friends."⁴⁷

The Soviet government failed also from the viewpoint of the criterion of reason. In *Dominations and Powers* Santayana comments on the irrationality and crypto-religious features of this totalitarian system:

> In such a conspiracy there is the same intrepid consistency or internal rationality as in any theocracy ... Both reform and reason would thus be banished from the scene, and eclipsed by faith and by prescribed action ... the undertaking is not only horrible in its methods but vain in its promise.⁴⁸

The eclipse of reason within the system was yet another factor corrupting the moral and spiritual condition of the society that was being established on the ruins of the Russian past, after traditional institutions and values were destroyed and all the inherited sources of unity and harmony dissolved. Not unlike Russian émigré authors mentioned here, Santayana enjoyed a conviction that morality precedes law and extends beyond it, providing relatively stable reference points for rational (self-)government. When moral unity in a society is seriously undermined or collapses, as it occurred under the pressure of the mass terror practiced by the Soviet regime, "the government cannot be rational; it can never be an art; for the country supplies no guiding purpose to its rulers".⁴⁹

---

45 DP, 349.
46 DP, 347.
47 Letter to John W. Yolton, 2 May 1952, LGS8: 443.
48 DP, 321.
49 DP, 380.

In *Dominations and Powers*, Santayana sees that an important obstacle in the realization of the promised social paradise was lack of economic competence in the new Soviet system and the inefficiency of an economy deprived of a free market.[50] The central planning of the state-controlled economy, one of the key features of Soviet totalitarianism, resulted in "an economic chaos contained in a political state of nature,"[51] in John Gray's words. As such, it contributed to the moral degradation of its participants, who became unwilling perpetrators in this self-reproducing system. The described by Gray disastrous moral and economic effects of communist social experiments were part of the degeneration of civil society and its transformation into two layers: an impoverished mass fighting for basic goods and a narrow, wealthy elite. The fate of Soviet communism confirms Santayana's skepticism as to the aspirations of social engineering and the idea of rational control over all spheres of life. Since diversity and relative inequality are, according to Santayana, natural – they stem from what he calls the generative order of society – radical attempts at erasing the forms thus engendered may be expected to bring about unwelcome results, including a "return to nature" – or, in other words, the coming into light of the suppressed generative order – but in an unexpected, violent form of "barbarism."

Rational leadership, then, in Santayana's view, would prefer selective continuity and reform rather than destruction of what has been established in the past. He envisages it as disinterested and knowledgeable, "steady and traditional, yet open to continual readjustment," aware of the its own inability to

> define or codify human nature: that is the error of militant sects and factions. But it can exercise a modicum of control over local and temporal impulses and keep at least an ideal of spiritual liberty and social justice before the public eye.[52]

Soviet communism, as summarized by some of the Russian intellectuals of that era, was characterized by an intended discontinuity occurring through the negation of history, tradition and reality itself, and their replacement by

---

50   Santayana writes: "But how, if all profit on land and equipment is abolished is the state to continue paying always higher wages for shorter hours of work, and supplying a more complete system of free social services? Evidently when a government has assumed possession of all means of production and controls all business, it cannot distribute ... more than industry, so organized, will produce; and it will probably ... produce rather less than was at first produced by rival capitalists and private enterprise." DP, 381–382.
51   PLIB, 163.
52   DP, 382.

an abstract ideological construct, the omni-presence of a single ideology being another key trait of totalitarianism.[53] This, by the way, is nothing other than an extreme, nightmarish *politicization of life*. Correspondingly, Santayana ascribes to the revolutionaries "hatred of any view that recognized realities."[54] In particular it was the past that "was the great enemy, the dreadful past." A new kind of man emerged, one who could afford no other past and – implicitly – no other destiny than that prepared for him by the state and propagated in its ideology of the new world order. The undifferentiated mass "would glorify undifferentiated existence. Such may be the ultimate voice of revolutionary democracy."[55]

The unanimity sought by communists disregards the fact that human needs, demands and the ways humans realize their vital liberty "are centrifugal and divergent, so that the goods they pursue are incompatible existentially."[56] In a striking semblance to what René Girard puts forth in his theory about the relation between undifferentiation and violence, Santayana notes that "[t]he more equal and similar all nations and all individuals become, the more vehemently will each of them stick up for his atomic individuality … But when all are uniform the individuality of each unit is numerical only."[57] Enforced equality, rather than leading to brotherhood, may result in atomization and, eventually, mutual hostility.

> Uniformity between classes or between nations is not favorable to peace, except as it destroys units capable of action. There must be organic units at some level or there would be no potential moral agents or combatants; but similarity in these units, if they live in the same habitat, renders them rivals and therefore, in spite of their brotherly likeness to one another, involves them in war. … Similarity is therefore a danger to peace, and peace can be secured only by organization. But the collateral completeness of similar units excludes organization; and then war becomes inevitable at the first shock of competition, unless some higher power, itself organized, stifles the conflict.[58]

What is likely to happen with a society of atoms, or "ciphers," under the conditions of terror and material misery, has been presented persuasively by Gray.

---

53   Valeryan Nikolaevich Muravev, "The Roar of the Tribe," in Woehrlin, *Out of the Depths*, 166.
54   DP, 350.
55   DP, 350.
56   DP, 310.
57   DP, 180.
58   DP, 364–366.

In the absence of both social hierarchy and civil society institutions, people were reduced to the Hobbesian state of nature, where (equal) agents became rivals and were preying upon one another when competing for goods, which were in permanent scarcity.[59] Thus, access to material resources and a constant civil war became tools of political control, illuminating Santayana's crude contention that government stands for latent war. Besides, when social diversity is done away with, "the qualitative riches of the community will be terribly diminished and reduced to the lowest common denominator; the principle being that no one shall enjoy anything that everybody may not enjoy with him."[60]

The following passage seems to me to be a mature, synthetic expression of the late Santayana's views on the totalitarian fruits of the Bolshevik Revolution. Let me quote it in its entirety.

> The moral inspiration of communism is brotherly, pacifistic, ascetic, and saintly. Christianity was originally communistic, and all the religious orders continue to be so in their internal economy and discipline. It is built on tenderness, on indifference to fortune and to the world, on readiness for sacrifice, on life in the spirit. It cannot be militant. But what is now called communism is more than militant, more than a doctrine and a party bent on universal domination; ... It is ferociously egotistical, and claims absolute authority for the primal Will of a particular class, or rather a group of conspirators professing to be the leaders of that class. This class, far from embracing all mankind, does not include all the poor, nor the fundamental rural population that traditionally till the soil and live on its products, but enlists only the uprooted and disinherited proletariat ... Thus the authority of the "Communist Party" usurped without previous delegation, like the authority of conquerors and bandits, proclaims itself to be absolute and to extend prophetically over all mankind. And whose interests meantime does it serve? At bottom only the imaginary interests of a future society, unanimous and (like the Prussians of Hegel) perfectly free because perfectly disciplined to will nothing but what the State wills for them. Meantime, in order to clear the ground for that ideal plenty in peace, war must devour millions of the faithful communists themselves, as well as millions of their surprised and unconverted fellow creatures; there must be slaughter of enemies, forced migrations of whole peoples,

---

59 PLIB, 185–186.
60 DP, 444.

disappearance of institutions, civic and religious, destruction of all traditions ...⁶¹

To conclude, whatever Santayana's initial hopes related to communism were, they were motivated predominantly by the ideas of spiritual gains, greater personal liberty and the establishment of peaceful coexistence among culturally diverse peoples, possible due to a more competent economic management and more just allocation of the costs of necessity. Did Santayana's disillusionment with the Soviet embodiment of communism make him abandon altogether his ideal of a universal commonwealth? It seems not, even though one should keep in mind that it was but a tiny, futurist and quasi-utopian fraction of his political thinking.

In a letter to a friend, written a few months before his death, he mentions his "playful speculations" about a model of what a rational government might be.⁶² His ideas seem to be only to a small degree influenced by the Marxist doctrine, otherwise colored by Platonic inspirations, Schopenhauerian idea of the bond of misery transcending all boundaries among people, and an idealized vision of *Pax Romana*. Governmental control, explains Santayana, would by no means extend beyond security issues and a few strictly economic spheres of common life, leaving all the remaining ones free. Ideologically, the state would be as neutral as possible and represent "no arbitrary moral tradition, no gospel of its own."⁶³ A model of leadership Santayana occasionally returns to is that of so-called Roman Peace, under which ethnic and religious groups are free to cooperate in some areas and in some others remain idiosyncratic and orthodox, their safety ensured by the imperial power. The unattached, idiosyncratic or recalcitrant individuals might migrate freely, physically and intellectually. According to my reading, Santayana tries to divorce the (centralized) management of the military and certain economic matters from self-government in all other areas. Thus, by applying distinct principles and approaches to different spheres of life, the empire would realize a specific formula of the of separation of powers and competences. One may also say it would fulfill the liberal postulate of separating the public from the private.

The very idea of an empire emerged in response to a question about the possibility of peace, both internal and external, in the conditions of economic globalization, when "the world is positively crying for a universal government, and almost creating it against all national wills."⁶⁴ Santayana found no warrant of

---

61   DP, 320.
62   Letter to John W. Yolton, 2 May 1952, LGS8: 443.
63   DP, 454.
64   DP, 453.

peace in the existing alliances of sovereign nation-states. His imagined empire represents a way of avoiding the dangers of an unprincipled growth of global market economy on the one hand, and of militant, religious or ideological, rival states/empires, on the other. He arrives at an idea of a semi-authoritarian state, whose authority is based, on the one hand, and to the largest degree possible, on the "authority of things," as revealed by science and experience, and, on the other, on a powerful military, acting as a deterrent to war and internal conflicts among diverse, to use Santayana's language, "moral units."[65]

Looking at historical examples of imperial powers, Santayana evokes, among others, the Empire of the Caliphs and the British Empire as ones that ran a pragmatic politics and might have seemed, from the perspective of their subjects, as ideologically more neutral and non-interfering in comparison with some other empires. They nevertheless failed because they possessed a "sense of superiority, a great indifference, if not contempt, for what is not theirs."[66] Perhaps, speculates Santayana, the United Sates might play the role of "the secular arm of Reason in checking the unreason of the world."[67] He associates the presidency of Franklin D. Roosevelt with a great governmental autonomy, organization, and efficiency, able to overcome some weaknesses typical of democracy, such as inconstancy and shortsightedness. Such competences, when combined with virtues such as honesty, expertise, and readiness to cooperate, ascribed by Santayana to the American people, might make a possible American hegemony worth considering. However, what makes America

---

65 Here one may say that Santayana either contradicts his own anti-militarism or indicates that a powerful army might be put to a good use in a different geo-political situation. By way of digression, it might be of interest to compare and contrast Santayana's futuristic speculations with some other visions of this kind attempted by his contemporary intellectuals. A proper context for such a discussion has been provided, for example, by George Orwell in his essay entitled "James Burnham and the Managerial Revolution." In it Orwell scrutinizes critically Burnham's diagnosis concerning the factual crisis of democracy and capitalism, the rise of oligarchies, as well as his predictions of the future domination of a new, hierarchical, "managerial" kind of society. Orwell admits that Burnham's diagnosis is correct in many respects but his political predictions have proved largely wrong due to, among other things, psychological and cultural factors, such as Burnham's fascination with power, his American background, and his strong Machiavellian assumptions about politics. See: George Orwell "James Burnham and the Managerial Revolution." Orwell is referring here to the works of James Burnham, most notably: *The Managerial Revolution* (New York: The John Day Co., 1941).

66 DP, 454.

67 DP, 457. Krzysztof P. Skowroński thinks Santayana's attitude towards the vision of America's global hegemony was moderately sympathetic. "His attitude toward American culture was reserved; towards the United States generally favorable; and toward Americans cordial." Krzysztof P. Skowroński, *Santayana and America*, 164.

a debatable ally of universal humanity are its militant ambitions, orientation towards rapid economic progress, aggressive industrial and political expansiveness. These reflections end with a serious question mark as to whether American hegemony would be capable of self-reflection and self-restriction required to establish a more balanced and human-friendly environment.

Unfortunately, Santayana neglects or underestimates the function that private property and enterprise realistically perform in warranting individual liberty and self-government. Whereas he admits that the failure of the Soviet regime consisted, in a substantial degree, in the economic failure (state-owned means of production, state-controlled and centrally-planned economy), he nevertheless does not specify the nature and scope of the governmental control of economic matters in the imagined empire, as one would expect him to do. One may also point to the following aporia. In his criticism of liberalism, he is sensitive to the impact of economic and legal regulations on the scope and effectiveness of individual autonomy and cultural liberty. He enumerates ways in which the hegemony of enterprise and free market renders freedom illusory or empty. Yet, he fails to ask about a similar risk related to a form of state-controlled economy vaguely proposed by him. Obviously, he must have assumed this risk to be smaller, but the question remains unasked.

To an extent Santayana clarifies his intentions in a letter to a friend, written after he had been acquainted with some reviews of his final book. In it he tries both to "soften" the individualistic aspect of it and to dispel the impression that he advocates a sort of state-controlled economy that might threaten basic property rights. The empire he had imagined would consist of "moral societies," each having freedom to decide in all matters of culture, local government, social institutions *and* private property on its territory. The control of the state ("Scientific Universal Economy") would extend over some strictly economic matters, most probably those concerning all the peoples ("moral societies") involved.[68] This level of managing necessity would allow government to control major issues that require for their solutions the same or similar measures. One may think of matters such as climate, health, the military, certain heavy industries, part of transportation system, etc., the list being adjusted in accordance to circumstances. As one may infer from a number of dispersed remarks in the letters of Santayana, governmental control might also extend over issues such as monopolies, control of capital accumulation and virtual capital, introducing some measures of capital diffusion, for example by controlling the distribution of profits from major industrial enterprises.

---

68   Letter to John W. Yolton, 27 Apr. 1952, LGS8: 440–441.

CHAPTER 9

Conclusions and Further Reflections on Why Culture Matters

Santayana's political hermeneutics, as it has emerged from this study, is characterized, on the one hand, by syncretism and an intimidating breadth of thematic scope and, on the other, an integrity, which it owes to the naturalistic commitment as well as the humanistic and individualistic orientation of the author, expressed both in the initial assumption that "each man is by nature an end to himself"[1] and the idea of vital liberty serving as an ultimate moral horizon for human government. While vital liberty is an individual attainment, it never occurs in a void, but in a society, in a medium of culture, and in specific political circumstances. The question posed by Santayana is this: under what conditions society and government are more of a benefit for its members than a burden. The relation of socio-political arrangements, then, to the attainability of vital liberty becomes both a target of criticism and the measure of judgment.

The life of reason, *modus operandi* of a good *politeia*, is, in fact, a naturalistic and pragmatic ideal of a pluralistic environment in which diverse individuals and groups may achieve completion and satisfaction, with regard to broadly understood circumstances, and while coexisting in a possibly peaceful manner with one another. As I have stressed repeatedly, human diversity, insofar as it reflects the natural variety of endowments and ideals possible, and plays a culture-forming function, being thus conducive to vital liberty, is assumed to be not only an ultimate social fact but also a good to be sought and protected. Now, in the light of the ideal of the life of reason, it is assumed that "[a]rt, which is action guided by knowledge, is the principle of benefit."[2] The basic principle and virtue proper to the art of government and self-government is rationality, a higher-order human prerogative aiming at, first, reasonable satisfaction of needs and desires, and, second, reconciling or harmonizing often irrational and conflicted diversity. Wisdom, which except for rationality involves experience, far-sightedness, and the understanding of the conditions of human well-being, allows for setting major goals guiding action. By

---

1 DP, 73.
2 DL, 95.

associating the art of government with the life of reason, Santayana makes politics – without denaturalizing it at any means – transcend a merely instrumental strategy of controlling animal impulses engaged in an eternal struggle. We are thus – to refer to Santayana's categories – at the level of politics in its "nobler" sense, one ascribed to it both by Plato and Aristotle. It requires of those engaged in governing to represent, except for professional competence, some politically significant virtue. Santayana, in general, is reticent towards the possibility of a beneficent and lasting government relying exclusively on procedural arrangements.

I have stressed throughout the book that the individualistic *spiritus movens* behind Santayana's political hermeneutics is the pursuit to increase the chances of individuals to live good lives in ways relatively compatible with their natural potential, non-interfering with analogous attempts of others, and, whenever possible, entering in a harmonious relation with them. In correspondence to these aims, my conclusion is that a set of *principles of human benefit* relevant for human communities may be elicited from Santayana's philosophy. These include the principle of: 1) perfection, which involves respect for finite forms, virtues, arts, and a sustained, selective continuity; 2) rationality; 3) limited benefit from material progress (or: the principle of spiritual vindication); 4) *nemesis*, by which I mean epistemic humility and the recognition of unintended consequences of human action, and 5) preserving disinterestedness, which embraces the comprehension of *autotelia* and an attitude of a sympathetic and supportive distance. These principles may also be seen as a response to what Santayana criticized as dehumanizing tendencies that characterize modern culture and the cynicism permeating politics.

While Santayana is convinced that there is more than one model of a socio-political organization conducive to human well-being, one may still point to what is obviously *excluded* from the array of acceptable options, namely – a totalitarian system as a radical negation of diversity and vital liberty, or, in Cassirer's words, a system based on "the principle of *Gleichschaltung*."[3] Totalitarianism, *de facto*, makes culture as such redundant. To this I would also add any modern system that either by way of neglect or through unnecessary oppression, leads, through material and moral degradation of human life, to the exclusion of large groups of people from a proper participation in culture, thwarting their pursuit of vital liberty.[4] One may think of oppressive

---

3   Cassirer, *The Myth of the State*, 285.
4   Santayana seems to accept past and traditional oppression, for example in the form of feudalism, as part of the generative order. He is much less willing to accept new, "artificial" and militant forms of oppression, such as, for example, extreme social injustice in sharing the

autocracies, dictatorships in particular, oligarchies, and societies based on uncompromising, rigid, and exclusive hierarchies, based on dogmatic, superstitious or purely egoistic principles, privileging some individuals on the basis of, for example, wealth, heredity, or race.

This being said, one may have an impression that Santayana devoted not enough attention to the issue of justice and did not venture to develop an explicit and complete theory of it. Nevertheless, focusing on what he did say on justice, I have attempted my own interpretation with the support of two hermeneutic keys, namely- the notions of harmony and charity. What emerges from this reading is an eclectic, modern, and reflective approach, which seeks to explain justice in terms of three of its possible motivations – the pursuit of harmony by a disinterested reason, the admiration and recognition of multiform human excellence, and a universal incentive, reflected in different religious and philosophical traditions worldwide, to minimize suffering. While all of them are meant to express some shade of impartiality, the first one is a principle of the life of reason, the second and the third may be described as different facets of love – love as idealization or a premonition of perfection in the other, and love as a sense of sympathy with the suffering other, accompanied by a desire to relief them. The first of the two types of love reappears in Santayana's writing in different guises – for example in the form of the idea that eminence is universally representative, discussed in the section on the aristocratic ideal. The following passage is an articulate expression of the idea:

> To worship mankind as it is would be to deprive it of what alone makes it akin to the divine – its aspiration. For this human dust lives; this misery and crime are dark in contrast to an imagined excellence; they are lighted up by a prospect of good. Man is not adorable, but he adores, and the object of his adoration may be discovered within him and elicited from his own soul. In this sense the religion of humanity is the only religion, all others being sparks and abstracts of the same.[5]

---

costs and benefits related to the development of industry. This approach is perfectly rational when considered in the framework of Santayana's categories. One should expect a new order, introduced intentionally, under the banner of progress and democratization, to be less cruel and more just than the traditional one. The problem according to Santayana was that while certain beauties of the traditional order had been irretrievably lost, the social promises of the new one were not being fulfilled. Masses of people were forced to pay the costs of modernization, while very few enjoyed its benefits beyond measure.

5   LR, 262. In order to articulate Santayana's humanism I decided to quote a passage that may seem problematic in conjunction with Santayana's decisive rejection of anthropocentrism.

One also reads that in order to approach "the Life of Reason nothing is needed but an analytic spirit and a judicious love of man, a love quick to distinguish success from failure in his great and confused experiment of living."[6] The context of Paul Ricoeur's ruminations on love and justice helped me illuminate the fact that Santayana in his reflections on justice chooses metaphors from beyond the circle of retribution and vengeance, and from beyond the dominant utilitarian model. Other, practical aspects of just politics, such as equality of opportunity and elements of welfare state have also been given attention in this book.

All these dimensions of justice may be associated with the two levels of governance that according to my interpretation may be found in Santayana's thought – that of managing necessity (the level of necessity) and that of harmonizing diversity (the level of liberty). The two represent, as I have suggested, a specific formula of the separation of powers and competences. The art of harmonizing diversity must be founded in the art of managing necessity. As a naturalist, a materialist, and a critical philosopher, Santayana is careful to distinguish between human needs, interests, demands and preferences. Basic needs, as objective and common, part of the dimension of necessity, render themselves to an impartial, non-ideological interpretation in terms of interests and their "scientific" management. Yet, precisely this dimension of governing life or managing necessity forms a sphere of potential abuse, which I have discussed in this book with reference to what I call Santayana's negative anthropology. The thinker has no illusions about the pre-political principle according to which some lives thrive at the price of the belittlement of some other lives. In the absence of virtue, politics is reduced to its "meaner" sense, where government is an instrument of withholding war and distributing necessity and power. Dealing with a plurality of often conflicting units, it may well seek, cynically, to organize their existence according to a principle of enforced domination. Santayana's humanism and individualism stand behind his incisive criticism of the ways politics and society dominate rather than empower individuals.

I have emphasized in the book that, like Plato, who was a critic of the democracy of his own era, Santayana is sensitive to the anthropological placement of contemporary politics. He locates it at the fragile conjunction of material life with language and imagination, and observes that ideologies and fads, spreading like contagions, influence public opinion, and that socio-political

---

I admit that the latter tendency is more typical of Santayana and more frequently expressed. Nevertheless, both threads coexist in his thought without annulling one another.

6   Santayana, introduction to LR1, 5.

phenomena are often co-fabricated by the language of propaganda, which is an equivalent of unprincipled ancient sophistry. During his lifetime, Santayana observed that the "exercise of autocratic power has become almost normal ... for party leaders ... and it is not in themselves or for what they do that they triumph: they triumph as demagogues" and may become "perpetual dictator[s]."[7] Thus, Santayana's critique of the evolution of the existing democracies may be read as a warning against both totalitarian *and* autocratic forms of political organization, now transformed and reinforced by modern technology employed in the service of social control and invigilation. While some of the critical tools delivered by Santayana may still be helpful for understanding and judging reality, at least at a certain level of generality, some of his diagnoses have proved more timely than ever, prodigiously timely indeed.

The art of government, any intentional political reform indeed, is limited by the burden of past conflicts and inherited coercion. "People long coerce one another of their private initiative," writes the thinker, "or follow some tradition before they begin to do so through special military or legal agents. [In the generative order] [g]overnment concentrates domination in its own hands, and regulates it. It neither originates nor abolishes domination."[8] Santayana repeatedly emphasizes that politics can never be emancipated fully from the ancient bond of necessary servitude, which is suffered by humans primarily in relation to nature and fate (or: contingency), and, then, to custom and law. I have tried to show that this servitude, however, which cannot be superseded fully as it is part and parcel of the human condition, is presented by Santayana as potentially complementary to the highest human good called vital liberty. It is through art (as a form of activity) and virtue that humans may aspire to an equilibrium between powers and dominations, and a harmony between liberty and necessity. The associated role of the government would be, in short, to mitigate the influence of natural necessity and introduce peace where there is conflict.

As John Lachs remarked, we still lack answers to some fundamental questions concerning the relation of individuals to communities. Perhaps no definitive answers exist, in which case, however, we are not exempted from asking the questions. Santayana offers his readers a broad, critical-hermeneutic reflection, which, while establishing a reflective distance from its subject, aims at enhancing self-understanding, illuminating human errors and limitations, revealing paradoxes involved in the practical application of theoretical

---

7   DP, 117–118.
8   DP, 82.

constructs. As I have tried to show, his philosophy does provide some moral guidance, though without an underpinning of a naïve optimism. It conveys sensitivity to certain – usually overlooked or considered as "dated" – attitudes like criticism, patience, moderation, humility, disinterestedness, understanding of and sympathy with otherness. Meanwhile, the thinker is deliberate in *not giving priority to any specific form of government or political doctrine*. He sees a philosopher's task in terms of enlightening human will so that it "sees in the first instance how to attain its purpose without making or inflicting unnecessary sacrifices" and is able to "revise or rescind itself."[9] These higher-order skills may be crucial given how demanding and fragile liberal and democratic ideals are. Embodying and preserving at least some of them to the common benefit would require a sustained effort and exercise in (self-) education and (self-) criticism.

Despite the fact that his primary definition of politics and government might suggest otherwise, Santayana explicitly opposes the Hobbesian idea that self-preservation and power accumulation is the highest aim of man and the source of his morality. It is not that these instincts are not real. Yet, there are other, equally real facts "competing" with the grim reality of strife, which is not to say that they ever annul the more "primordial" and violent dimension of human existence. One of them is the indissoluble bond between humans and the medium of culture in which they live. Culture may cultivate other impulses or channel the same impulses differently and assume unexpected forms. Culture may well idealize self-sacrifice rather than self-preservation. It is in the womb of culture that a *political culture* emerges. Among the sources of human morality culture happens to be one of the most prominent. It does not alleviate the relativity of morals as an essentialist conception of human rights or a universal and fixed human nature might do, but raises it beyond pure subjectivism, to a supra-individual level and makes it more resistant to momentary caprices and fashions.

Searching for the sources of morality and ideals beyond the individual and his direct circumstances is visible already in *The Life of Reason*. In it Santayana complains about an unfortunate separation of moral reflection from anthropological and existential one in contemporary philosophy. Rather than starting with asking: What is? Or: What ought to be? one asks an abstract question: "What ought I do?" as if there existed a separate sphere of morals, a self-standing

---

9   DP, 120–121. Meanwhile, it is not my intention to suggest that Santayana considers philosophy, as Plato did, as the noblest possible human vocation, an art (*techne*) that raises one far above others. Rather, his relation to philosophy oscillated in-between love and ironic distance.

"compartment." Some unfortunate conceptions of human morality, then, seem to Santayana to stem from abstractness, lack of deeper anthropological insight as well as "artificial views about the conditions of welfare; the basis is laid in authority rather than in human nature, and the goal in salvation rather than in happiness."[10] Other than that, too often are morals derived primarily and directly from religion, which "unhappily long ago ceased to be wisdom expressed in fancy in order to become superstition overlaid with reasoning."[11] Now, binding morality to the agent and their circumstances on the one hand may confirm relativism, on the other, however, may restrict it as long as this and other agents share a nature, belong to a specific type of natural beings, etc.

I have pointed to the fact that the thinker does not use the traditional notions of natural rights or laws; he preserves the notion of human nature, at least in a weak version, the human condition, and an idea of human constitution - one of a concrete, mortal, psycho-spiritual being, endowed with potentialities, desires, and aspirations, and a propensity to find fulfillment in pursuing them. The said fulfillment does not ask for any additional justification, it is for its own sake and constitutes a sort of a borderline moral idea. This idea, which is one where constitution (or nature) is a source of ideal commitments, is central for Santayana's political thought and makes it at once naturalistic *and* idealistic, or, in other words, one where the ideal is inspired by nature, but, as I have stressed, not by facticity. What is more, this idea may help free Santayana's political ideas from an individualistic seclusion and the ghost of a radical kind of moral relativism which condemns any moral judgment to sheer arbitrariness as soon as it concerns anything beyond the narrow context of the speaker.

Throughout the book I discuss the way Santayana's moralism and humanism are, in a sense, grappling with his relativism. This is particularly the case in the context of social and political reflection, where certain technical subtleties of Santayana's metaethics, as contained, for example, in *Realms of Being*, for pragmatic reasons give way to more commonsensical assumptions concerning human agency, rationality, and the ability to form a trustworthy moral judgment concerning others, without which the ideas of moral representation, rational authority, responsibility, and justice would seem dangerously elusive and void. So, for example, an experienced and competent politician, when forming a moral judgment, has at his disposal and takes into account not only his personal, idiosyncratic, psychic impulses and personal preferences but

---

10   Santayana, introduction to LR1, 18.
11   LR1, 18.

also a rich experience, an insight into the objective needs of the people he represents and the goods that correspond to them, as well as a certain knowledge of the world and the realm of human affairs at large. Additionally, if he happens to be virtuous, his virtue gives him access to the understanding of the aforementioned principles of human benefit, the status of which is natural and aspires to some universality. Some of this knowledge may be conveyed through inherited traditional institutions, but politics, as a sphere of rationality and far-sightedness, cannot rely blindly on inheritance. Now, this heterogeneity of the sources of moral judgment, seems to suggest, tentatively, that there exist limits to Santayana's moral relativism, or, in other words, that his moral relativism tends to restrict itself, especially when regarded in a socio-political context. Such limits, if they exist, will be revealed in the process of examining human nature and the conditions of human well-being. Santayana appreciated the ancient thinkers for, among other things, their continuous effort to do so. More importantly, they will be revealed in and through moral imagination and virtue, which radically expand individual psychic resources turning them into a more reliable basis for moral judgment and authority, at least in a socio-political context.[12] Now, to what extent these limits are universal and fixed for humans, and to what extent they are mutable and culture-specific, remains an open question.

The criticism of the individualism endorsed by Santayana as sterile from a perspective of community may contain a grain of truth but seems to overlook, first, the historical context, second, the significance of individual virtue and attainment to any human community, and, third, the naturalistic and humanistic paradigm to which it belongs. One should keep in mind that Santayana witnessed the rise of mass societies, accompanied by a propaganda of a thorough "socialization" of man, which in the context of the totalitarianisms of his time was, to say the least, ambiguous. George Orwell and Aldous Huxley were warning against anti-individualism. Questions arose about intellectual autonomy and morality when one is incapable of resisting the pull of the crowd or the impersonal mechanisms of the system. It seems important, then, to clarify the type of individualism endorsed by Santayana, a task which I have taken up in this book. I read it as connected to a prominent trait of humanism in his thought, which, next to his naturalism and the idea of spiritual life, constituted one of very few ideal allegiances of the philosopher. While I do not

---

12 This will be the case regardless of the fact that, strictly and technically speaking, moral judgments express a natural bias of a single organism rather than truths about material reality.

intend to label Santayana "a humanist" in any doctrinaire sense – as a naturalist he enjoyed a belief that humanity is but a form of animal life – I think that it is correct to say that the main context (and rationale) for his well-known critiques of egotism, fanaticism, barbarism, militarism, and, even, capitalism, is humanistic. Actually, one may hardly find a better frame for the idea of wisdom in his thought than a humanistic (and a humane) one. This is illustrated by a beautiful passage from *Dialogues in Limbo*, where Socrates speaks of the human good: "Are all fashions equally good? Are all transitions equally happy? (…) Have you learned how to live? Do you know how to die? If you neglected these questions your self-government would not be an art, but a blind experiment."[13]

These words encapsulate the meaning of the interconnected ideas of *ars vivendi* and wisdom. Both are part and parcel of Santayana's humanism and so is his individualism, remaining, as I have argued in this study, at a far remove from a Spencerian-type of egoistic individualism of power. Rather, in its eclecticism, it may be associated with Socratic self-knowledge, an Aristotelian, autotelic understanding of life, a humanistic articulation of individuality by the Stoics, the Spinozist ideal of intellectual autonomy and even, to some extent and despite Santayana's quarrel with romanticism, a post-romantic individualism of authenticity.[14] Furthermore, when Santayana opposes what he calls the "brute humanity" and associates the coming of the brute humanity with the idea that "[c]ivilization is perhaps approaching one of those long winters that overtake it from time to time,"[15] he seems to be speaking on behalf and in defense of the virtues of a "polite humanity." Let me stress again, then, that the *Apollonian* individualism Santayana endorses, is very much unlike both the predatory, modern individualism associated with egoism and the social

---

13 DL, 95.
14 Santayana's philosophy, including his political and cultural reflection, exhibits – debatably, and, given his criticism of romanticism, paradoxically – certain modest affinities with romantic philosophy. I would mention here, tentatively, as worth consideration, his idea of vital liberty, the inalienable freedom of an autonomous human judge, at least partial historical and cultural relativization of politics, interest in psychological motivations and mythological underpinning of certain phenomena, distrust in reason as a truly effective *power*, or the idea of universalistic patriotism. Of course, he rejected romantic, essentialist nationalism, collective individualism, promethean and messianic ideas applied to history and politics, or, in other words, idealization of history. Nevertheless, this seems to be an interesting issue still to be explored.
15 George Santayana, preface to *Character and Opinion in the United States* (New York: W.W. Norton & Company, 1967), viii-ix.

atomism, which involves depersonalization and in which individualism, especially in large societies, sometimes tends to result.[16]

To connect a few points made by me so far in this chapter, let me evoke once again the issue of the limits of Santayana's moral relativism and say that if they exist, as I am inclined to believe, they originate in the implications of his naturalistic, pluralistic, and individualistic humanism. They reveal themselves, for example, when Santayana discerns within culture certain threads and tendencies that he calls emphatically "inhumane" and describes as "sins against humanity." Even though the thinker does not consider these judgments as "absolute" in any metaphysical sense, he thinks them true and valid from a humanistic (and a humane) perspective and in the light of the fact of human diversity, and hopes, perhaps even believes, that his readers share his moral intuitions, whereby they form a community of certain humane orientation. By calling something "inhuman" he does not mean that it is, in any sense, unnatural or metaphysically evil, but rather, that while being natural, it still conspires against the vital interests of a specific kind of natural being – a human being. Recall that for Santayana the dignity and specificity of a human being rests primarily in understanding, creation and appreciation of beautiful forms, and sympathy with otherness. When Santayana complains about certain aspects of modern culture, such as loss of chivalry, fear of discomfort, and subservience and conformity to majority option, calling them "a shocking degradation modern society has condemned the spirit,"[17] he speaks not on behalf of this or that ancient habit or a way of being but rather of human imagination that has been instrumentalized and enslaved by motivations, aspirations, and interests antagonistic towards human dignity thus understood.

To give a few more examples, in one of his texts, Santayana says "[n]othing will repay a man for becoming inhuman."[18] The inhumanity here consists

---

16   There is an insightful chapter "Depersonalization and the Importance of the Liberal Arts" in Krzysztof P. Skowroński's book on Santayana and America. In it the author enumerates the ways in which Santayana's approach towards the individual is meant to prevent the dangerous phenomenon of depersonalization and its personal and social consequences. Skowroński lists, among other things, anti-dogmatism, avoidance of unreflective mimesis, prudence and responsibility for one's choices, perfection or self-realization instead of sheer hedonism, participation in culture, and, more specifically, the liberal arts. One needs to be aware, however, that Skowroński uses the term "atomism" in an affirmative way and a very different one than I do – namely, he understands it as tantamount to a sort of personality "nomadism" or, in any case, referring to an integral personal identity. Leaving these verbal differences aside, I wholeheartedly agree with Skowroński's argument here. See: Skowroński, *Santayana and America*, 45–49.

17   DP, 207.

18   George Santayana, "Logic of Fanaticism," *The New Republic*, 28 November, 1914.

in egotism and xenophobia expressed in a "hatred of the rest of the world." Elsewhere one reads about "crime against humanity," being a kind of *hubris* that leads to sacrificing the human good in the name of egoistic and megalomaniac schemes. Faust – a reappearing figure in Santayana's writings and an archetype of these inhuman tendencies – stands for a bearer of an infinite desire that he is keen on realizing without regard to the cost. Thus, he is bound to "grow feeble, vicious, and sad, like other sinners."[19] In politics and society, an inflexibility, an excessive, militant integrity not founded in wisdom, a scary, "absolute singleness of will ... works havoc."[20] Egotism, conceit, and unprincipled craving for power, being flows of character in a private person, turn into a fatal "sin" in a politician, a faction, or a government.

Now, given that "government [in the second, "meaner" sense] is essentially an army carrying on a perpetual campaign in its own territory,"[21] Santayana has good reasons for seeing the politicization of life, starting with the politicization of language, as a danger for culture. What sort of danger? The danger of becoming illiberal, inauthentic, and servile, which means losing the emancipatory, formative and dignifying potential that culture, and liberal arts in particular, represent to a human being. For similar reasons Santayana thinks personal virtues are needed for governing oneself and others. *Virtues (integrated by individuals but conveyed by culture), as trans-political "powers," may be the only chance to withstand the otherwise irresistible thrust of different forms of competition, conflict, manipulation, and struggle for domination. An inherent idea in Santayana's political thinking, then, is not overestimating politics.* To put it in other words, into the relation between an autotelic human life striving for some form of fulfillment, and government, an intermediary or a third party, namely – culture, is introduced. Santayana's intention is to make this third party an ally of individuals. That is why, as I claim, *his political thought is inseparable from his reflection on and criticism of culture.* To divorce the two or simply ignore the latter is to deprive the former of some of its most precious insights.

What is more, the individualism and the humanism – both mildly rebellious given their critical potential – endorsed by Santayana are relevant for politics in that they constitute a safe guard against totalitarian tendencies. The quality of human environment is not insignificant for the emergence and success of a totalitarian regime, as authors such as Hannah Arendt or Ernst Cassirer pointed out. It seems that the threat of totalitarianism, the essence of

---

19 DP, 231.
20 DP, 229–30.
21 DP, 79.

which is anti-individualism, uniformity, and a total politicization of the common world, can hardly be countered without recourse to human individuality. It is an individual who is the bearer of virtues, the primary seat of suffering, judgment, and, when necessary, the source of the spark of multifaceted resistance. Though a single individual, when isolated, may be powerless, a number of similar individuals may constitute a community, a minority of like-minded persons who perhaps may start a movement. But this actual community needs to be founded in and nourished by a virtual human "community," not limited by time and space – in other words, human culture. Humans may and should be able to benefit from the fact that broadly understood culture has deeper roots and longer influence than politics. It remains in their best interest, then, to preserve at least partial autonomy of culture as well as individual, intellectual, and moral independence from the ever-expanding power of politics in its "meaner" sense. In other words, humans may seek in culture protection against the evils of politics.

Now, to counter my own conclusions, I admit that *a contrary situation is perfectly possible too!* People may and often do seek protection against prejudice or irrational and cruel customs sanctioned by their specific, traditional cultures in the legal and political sphere. This, however, I would reply, is an expression of their longing for justice and a socio-political order which is, at least, an approximation of the life of reason. Thus, we are at the level of politics in its "nobler" sense, where both politics and culture work towards the empowerment of people rather than their enslavement.

Santayana was too well aware of the role of culture as a supra-individual and trans-political medium in forming individuals and communities, to overestimate politics, especially politics of the day. Besides, aware of the significance of unintended consequences of human action, he attaches more hopes to the long-term effects of the development of philosophy and liberal arts for the condition of society, culture, or civilization than about the immediate consequences of current politics. Politics is but one dimension of the world of human affairs, and it sadly happens to be one of the least disinterested ones. Reading Santayana in-between the lines, one may conclude that culture tends to be wiser than politics and less contaminated by the actually competing forces and their interests. However, while culture penetrates social and political life, a reverse process seems to be more potent in the contemporary world. The appearance and global spread of internet made culture more fragile, more forgetful and more sensitive to diffused and unpredictable influences than it has ever been before. This fact prompts one to reconsider both the issue of the autonomy of culture and that of the sources of individual autonomy as even more pressing.

Without intending to cloth Santayana as an idiosyncratic liberal, I have pointed to the fact that, in some respects, such as his endorsement of individualism, tolerance, and pluralism, Santayana is close to the original liberal perspective. In some others, such as his focus on the share of tradition, continuity, and virtue, or, in fact, a set of specific virtues preferred by him, he draws on the heritage of the ancients. I also tried to show that Santayana's criticism of modernity does not make him necessarily an anti-modern thinker. Despite the presence of some conservative traits in his thought and what may seem as a nostalgic sympathy for older, organic forms of socio-political organization, Santayana's anti-dogmatism, his futurist speculations, the hermeneutic-critical form of his reflections, as well as the ambiguity and provocativeness it is permeated by, reveal a modern, if not post-modern dimension of it. Santayana's thinking is always ready to recognize and trespass its own prejudice, even though his very materialism and his views on truth make him an unlikely candidate for a post-modern thinker. As beautifully phrased by Morris Grossman, a "remarkable duplicity" and "controlled ambiguity" are "at the heart of the smiling sadness of the entire Santayanian corpus."[22] As for the ambiguity on Santayana's part, besides being intriguing in itself, it may be considered as a dialogic expression of authentic dilemmas in front of some problems of the human world that – in their intricacy – resist an exhaustive rational analysis and a definitive solution.

Let me conclude by evoking Wilfred M. McClay's humorous remark that "[i]t may seem mildly self-subverting to invoke such a spirit of *Gelassenheit* [as represented by Santayana] as a form of cultural improvement; and to be sure, one does not want perversely, to turn Santayana into the new guru of moral uplift and self-help."[23] Santayana's astonishingly rich legacy nevertheless remains and one does well to appreciate it "for what it is and what it could mean to us ... and appropriate it on whatever terms make sense to us." My modest aim when writing this book has been to breath into Santayana's political *hermeneia* some of the vitality it deserves, a philosophical kind of vitality, which arises from and through dialogue and interpretation. Far from hoping to exhaust the interpretive possibilities of his political reflection – which, I am convinced, opens before an inquisitive reader an enormous variety of paths as well as many opportunities for criticism – I seek to provoke further questions and research.

22 Grossman, *Art and Morality*, 235. Another scholar who notices a post-modern quality in Santayana's thought is Thomas M. Alexander. See: Alexander, *The Human Eros*, 228.
23 Both quotations in this paragraph: McClay, "The Unclaimed Legacy," in GTACOUS, 144.

Bibliography

Adorno, Theodor and Max Horkheimer. *Dialectic of Enlightenment*. Translated by John Cumming. New York: Continuum, 1989.

Aksiuto, Kamil. *Szczęście i wolność: utylitarystyczny liberalizm Johna Stuarta Milla*. Warszawa: Wydawnictwo Studiów Politycznych PAN, 2016.

Alexander, Thomas M. *John Dewey's Theory of Art, Experience and Nature. The Horizons of Feeling.* New York: State University of New York Press, 1987.

Alexander, Thomas M. *The Human Eros. Eco-Ontology and the Aesthetics of Existence.* New York: Fordham University Press, 2013.

Amir, Lydia. "The Democritean Tradition in Santayana, Nietzsche, and Montaigne." *Overheard in Seville* 38 (2020): 74–92.

Arendt, Hannah. *The Origins of Totalitarianism*. New York: Harcourt Brace Jovanovich, 1973.

Aristotle. *The Nicomachean Ethics*, translated by Benjamin Jowett, introduction by H.W.C. Davis. Oxford: Clarendon Press, 1908.

Aristotle. *Politics*, translated and introduction by Martin Ostwald. Upper Saddle River, New Jersey: Prentice Hall, 1999.

Bell, Daniel. *The Cultural Contradictions of Capitalism.* New York: Basic Books, 1976.

Bell, Daniel. *The End of Ideology*. Illinois: The Free Press of Glencoe, 1960.

Benjamin, Walter. "The Work of Art in the Age of Mechanical Reproduction" (1935). In *Illuminations,* translated by Harry Zohn, edited and introduction by Hannah Arendt, 217–252. New York: Schocken Books, 1969.

Bergson, Henri. *Two Sources of Morality and Religion*. Translated by R. Ashley Audra and Claudesley Berenton. New York: Henry Holt and Company, 1935.

Berlin, Isaiah. "Two Concepts of Liberty." In *Contemporary Political Theory. An Anthology*, edited by Robert E. Goodin and Philip Pettit, 391–418. Oxford and Maiden, Mass.: Blackwell Publishers, 1997.

Brodrick, Michael. *The Ethics of Detachment in Santayana's Philosophy*. New York: Palgrave Macmillan, 2015.

Burke Edmund. *Reflections on the Revolution in France*. Edited by William B. Todd. New York: Rinehart & Co., 1959.

Burke, Kenneth. *A Grammar of Motives*. Berkeley: University of California Press, 1945/1969.

Burnham, James. *The Managerial Revolution*. New York: The John Day Co., 1941.

Cassirer, Ernst. *The Myth of the State*. New Haven and London: Yale University Press, 1946.

Clausewitz, Carl von. *On War*. Edited and translated by Michael Howard and Peter Paret. Princeton: Princeton University Press, 1984.

Geertz, Clifford. *Interpretation of Cultures*. New York: Basic Book, 1973.

Grossman, Morris. *Art and Morality. Essays in the Spirit of George Santayana*. Edited by Martin Coleman. New York: Fordham University Press, 2014.

Constant, Benjamin. *The Liberty of Ancients Compared with that of Moderns*. 1819.

Cork, Jim. "Dewey, Karl Marx, and Democratic Socialism." *The Antioch Review* 9, no. 4 (Winter 1949): 435–452.

Dougherty, Jude P. "We are modern and want to be modern." *Studia Gilsoniana* 4:3 (July-September 2015): 241–249.

Eastman, Max. *Marxism: Is It a Science?*. New York: W.W. Norton and Company, 1940.

Flamm, Matthew Caleb. "Liberalism and the Vertigo of Spirit: Santayana's Political Theodicy." In *The Life of Reason in an Age of Terrorism*, edited by Charles Padrón and Krzysztof P. Skowroński, 115–133. Leiden: Brill, 2018.

Flamm, Matthew Caleb, Giuseppe Patella and Jennifer A. Rea, eds. *George Santayana at 150*. Lanham: Lexington Books, 2014.

Flamm, Matthew Caleb and Krzysztof Piotr Skowroński, eds. *Under Any Sky: Contemporary Readings of George Santayana*. Newcastle, UK: Cambridge Scholars Publishing, 2007.

Frankfurt, Harry G. "Freedom of the Will and the Concept of a Person." *The Journal of Philosophy*, 68, no. 1 (1971): 5–20.

García, César. "Santayana on Public Opinion." *Overheard in Seville: Bulletin of the Santayana Society*, 23 (2005): 23–27.

Geuss, Raymond. *The Idea of Critical Theory. Habermas and the Frankfurt School*. Cambridge: Cambridge University Press, 1981.

Girard, René. *Battling to the End: Conversations with Benoit Chantre*. Translated by Mary Baker. East Lansing, MI: Michigan State University, 2009.

Gray, John. *Enlightenment's Wake*. London and New York: Routledge, 1995/2007.

Gray, John. *Liberalism*. Minneapolis: University of Minnesota Press, 1986.

Gray, John. *Post-Liberalism. Studies in Social Thought*. New York and London: Routledge, 1993.

Gray, John. *Seven Types of Atheism*. Penguin Books, 2018.

Gold, Milton. "An Historian's View of Art." *Criticism*, 3, no. 4 (Fall 1961): 267–280.

Hayek, Friedrich A. *Individualism and Economic Order*. Chicago and London: University of Chicago Press, 1980.

Hessen, Sergey. *Państwo prawa i socjalizm*. Translated and introduction by Sławomir Mazurek. Warszawa: IFiS PAN, 2003.

Heney, Diana. "Metaethics for Mavericks: Santayana and Nietzsche on False Idols and True Poetry." *Overheard in Seville: Bulletin of the Santayana Society* 35 (2017): 78–92.

Heney, Diana. "Santayana on Value: Expressivism, Self-knowledge and Happiness." *Overheard in Seville: Bulletin of the Santayana Society* 30 (2012): 4–13.

Hobbes, Thomas. *Leviathan*. Edited and introduction by J. C. A. Gaskin. Oxford and New York: Oxford University Press, 1996.

Hook, Sydney. "Experimental Naturalism" (1935). In *Pragmatism, Democracy, Freedom*, edited by Robert B. Talisse and Robert Tempio, 29–45. Amherst, NY: Prometheus Books, 2002.

Huxley Aldous. *Brave New World Revisited*. New York: Harper & Brothers, 1958.

Kerr-Kawson, Angus. "Freedom and Free Will in Spinoza and Santayana." *The Journal of Speculative Philosophy, New Series* 14, no. 4 (2001): 243–267.

Kerr-Lawson, Angus. "Rorty Has no Physics." *Overheard in Seville: Bulletin of the Santayana Society* 13 (1995): 12–15.

Kinzel, Till. "Santayana, Self-knowledge and the Limits of Politics." In *The Life of Reason in an Age of Terrorism*, edited by Charles Padrón and Krzysztof P. Skowroński, 93–102. Leiden: Brill, 2018.

Kirk, Russell. *The Conservative Mind: From Burke to Santayana*. Chicago: Henry Regenery Co., 1953.

Kisner, Matthew J. *Spinoza on Human Freedom: Reason, Autonomy and the Good Life*. Cambridge, Ma: Cambridge University Press, 2013.

Kołakowski Leszek. *Main Currents of Marxism*. Translated by Paul S. Falla. New York: W. W. Norton & Company, 2005.

Kremplewska, Katarzyna. "Further Reflections on Culture, Humanism, and Individualism in the Context of Santayana's Political Thought." *Overheard in Seville: Bulletin of The George Santayana Society* 38 (2020): 66–73.

Kremplewska, Katarzyna. *Life as Insinuation. George Santayana's Hermeneutics of Finite Life and Human Self*. New York, Albany: SUNY Press, 2019.

Kremplewska, Katarzyna. "Managing Necessity: Santayana on Forms of Power and the Human Condition." In *The Life of Reason in an Age of Terrorism*, edited by Charles Padrón and Krzysztof P. Skowroński, 28–42. Leiden: Brill, 2018.

Kremplewska, Katarzyna. "Santayana on Communism in the Light of his Correspondence." *Overheard in Seville: Bulletin of The George Santayana Society* 37 (2019): 30–41.

Kremplewska, Katarzyna. "A story of disillusionment: George Santayana's views on communism and the Russian Revolution." *The Interlocutor. Journal of the Warsaw School of the History of Ideas* 2 (2019), 161–147.

Lachs, John, ed. *Animal Faith and Spiritual Life. Previously Unpublished and Uncollected Writings of George Santayana with Critical Essays on His Thought*. New York: Appleton-Century-Krofts, 1967.

Lachs, John. *Freedom and Limits*. Edited by Patrick Shade. New York: Fordham University Press, 2014.

Lewy, Guenter. *The Cause that Failed: Communism in American Political Life*. New York, London: Oxford University Press, 1990.

Lippman, Walter. *Public Opinion*. New York: Harcourt, Brace and Company, 1922.

Lukes, Steven, ed. *Power*. New York: New York University Press, 1986.

Mazurek, Sławomir. "Wydajność i wolność (kryzys kultury industrialnej w diagnozie Borysa Wyszesławcewa)." In *Filantrop czyli Nieprzyjaciel i inne szkice o rosyjskim renesansie religijno-filozoficznym*, 24–41. Warszawa: IFiS PAN, 2004.

Mill, John Stuart. *Autobiography*. Oxford: Oxford University Press, 2018.

Mill, John Stuart. "On Liberty." In *On Liberty, Utilitarianism and Other Essays*, edited with introduction and notes by Mark Philip and Frederick Rosen, 5–114. Oxford, UK: Oxford University Press, 2015.

McClay, Wilfred M. "The Unclaimed Legacy of George Santayana." In George Santayana, *The Genteel Tradition in American Philosophy and Character and Opinion in the United Sates*, edited by James Seaton, 123–147. New Haven and London: Yale University Press, 2009.

McCormick, John. *George Santayana: a biography*. New York: Alfred A. Knopf, 1987.

Moreno, Daniel. *Santayana the Philosopher. Philosophy as a Form of Life*. Translated by Charles Padrón. Lewisburg: Bucknell University Press, 2015.

Oakeshott, Michael. "Philosophical Imagination." Review of *Dominations and Powers. Reflections on Liberty, Society and Government* by George Santayana. *The Spectator*, November 2, 1951.

Ortega y Gasset, José. *Dehumanizacja sztuki i inne eseje*. Translated by Piotr Niklewicz. Edited and introduction by Stanisław Cichowicz. Warszawa: Czytelnik, 1980.

Ortega y Gasset, José. *Dehumanization of Art and Other Essays on Art, Culture, and Literature*. Princeton, NJ: Princeton University Press, 1968.

Orwell, George. "James Burnham and the Managerial Revolution." In *The Collected Essays, Journalism and Letters*. Vol. 4, *In Front of Your Nose 1945–1950*, edited by Sonia Orwell and Ian Angus, 160–181. Harmondsworth: Penguin, 1970.

Orwell, George. "The Prevention of Literature." In *The Collected Essays, Journalism and Letters*. Vol. 4, *In Front of Your Nose 1945–1950*, edited by Sonia Orwell and Ian Angus, 81–95. Harmondsworth: Penguin, 1970.

Padrón, Charles, and Krzysztof P. Skowroński, eds. *The Life of Reason in an Age of Terrorism*. Leiden and Boston: Brill, 2018.

Pinkas, Daniel. "Santayana, Judaism, and the Jews." *Overheard in Seville* 36 (2018): 69–78.

Pinkas, Daniel. "Egotism, Violence and the Devil: On Santayana's Use of the Concept of Egotism." In *The Life of Reason in an Age of Terrorism*, edited by Charles Padrón and Krzysztof P. Skowroński, 181–195. Leiden and Boston: Brill, 2018.

Plato. *The Laws*.

Plato. *The Republic of Plato*. 2nd edition. Translated by Allan Bloom. Toronto: Basic Books, 2003.

Przybyszewski, Stanisław. *Zur Psychologie des Individuums*. Berlin: Fontane & Co, 1892.

Rawls, John. *A Theory of Justice*. Cambridge, Mass., London, England: Harvard University Press, 1971/2005.

Ricoeur, Paul. "Love and Justice." In *Paul Ricoeur: The Hermeneutics of Action*, edited by Richard Kearney, 23–39. London, Thousand Oaks, New Delhi: Sage Publications, 1996.

Rodrik, Dani. *The Globalization Paradox*. New York and London: W.W. Norton & Company, 2011.

Rorty, Richard. "Justice as larger loyalty." In *Philosophy as Cultural Politics. Philosophical Papers*. Vol. 4, 42-55. Cambridge: CUP, 2007..

Rorty, Richard. "Kant vs. Dewey. The current situation of moral philosophy." In *Philosophy as Cultural Politics. Philosophical Papers*. Vol. 4, 184–202. Cambridge: CUP, 2007..

Russell, Bertrand. "The Forms of Power." In *Power*, edited by Steven Lukes, 19–27. New York: New York University Press, 1986.

Saatkamp Herman J., Jr. "Santayana: Cosmopolitanism and the Spiritual Life." In *George Santayana at 150*, edited by Matthew Caleb Flamm, Giuseppe Patella and Jennifer A. Rea, 93–110. Lanham: Lexington Books, 2014.

Santayana, George. *The Birth of Reason And Other Essays*. New York: Columbia University Press, 1968.

Santayana, George. *Character and Opinion in the United States*. New York: W.W. Norton & Company, 1967.

Santayana, George. *Dialogues in Limbo*. Ann Arbor: University of Michigan Press, 1957.

Santayana, George. *Dominations and Powers. Reflections on Liberty, Society and Government*. New York: Charles Scribner's Sons, 1951.

Santayana, George. *Dominations and Powers Reflections on Liberty, Society and Government*. With a new introduction by John McCormick. London and New York: Routledge, 2017.

Santayana, George. *The Genteel Tradition in American Philosophy and Character and Opinion in the United States*. Edited and with introduction by James Seaton. New Haven and London: Yale University Press, 2009.

Santayana, George. *The Genteel Tradition. Nine Essays by George Santayana*. Edited and introduction by Douglas L. Wilson. Lincoln and London: University of Nebraska Press, 1998.

Santayana, George. *The German Mind: A Philosophical Diagnosis*. New York: Apollo Editions, 1968.

Santayana, George. *The Letters of George Santayana, Books One-Eight*. Edited by William G. Holzberger. Cambridge MA: MIT Press, 2002–2008.

Santayana, George. *The Life of Reason or the Phases of Human Progress*. One-volume edition. New York: Charles Scribner's Son, 1954.

Santayana, George. *The Life of Reason. Reason in Society*. Critical Edition. Vol. 7. Edited by Marrianne S. Wokeck and Martin A. Coleman. Cambridge MA: MIT Press, 2013.

Santayana, George. "The Logic of Fanaticism." *The New Republic*, November 28, 1914.

Santayana, George. *Obiter Scripta. Lectures, Essays, Reviews*. Edited by Justus Buchler and Benjamin Schwartz. New York and London: Charles Scribner's Sons, 1936.

Santayana, George. *Soliloquies in England and Later Soliloquies*. New York: Charles Scribner's Sons, 1922.

Santayana, George. *Some Turns of Thought in Modern Philosophy. Five Essays*. Cambridge: Cambridge University Press, 1933.

Santayana, George. "Spanish Opinion on the War." *The New Republic*, April 10, 1915.

Santayana, George. "Why I am not a Marxist." *Modern Monthly* 9, no. 2 (April 1953): 77–79.

Santayana, George. *Winds of Doctrine. Studies in Contemporary Opinion*. London: J. M. Dent & Sons Ltd., 1913.

Schilpp, Paul Arthur, ed. *The Philosophy of George Santayana*. Evanston, Illinois: Northwestern University Press, 1940.

Schopenhauer, Arthur. *On the Basis of Morality*.

Seaton, James. "Santayana as a Cultural Critic." In *Under any Sky: Contemporary Readings of George Santayana*, edited by Matthew Caleb Flamm and Krzysztof Piotr Skowroński, 111–120. Newcastle (UK): Cambridge Scholars Publishing, 2007.

Seaton, James. "Irving Babbitt and Cultural Renewal." *The Imaginative Conservative*, September 18, 2016. Accessed on November 18 2020. https://theimaginativeconservative.org/2016/09/irving-babbitt-cultural-renewal-seaton-timeless.html.

Seaton, James. "Santayana on Fascism and English Liberty." *Limbo*, no. 29 (2009): 81–100.

Simmel, Georg. *The Philosophy of Money*. Translated by Tom Bottomore and David Frisby. Edited by David Frisby. London and New York: Routledge, 1978/2004.

Singer, Beth J. *The Rational Society. A Critical Study of Santayana's Social Thought*. Cleveland/London: The Press of Case Western Reserve University, 1970.

Skowroński, Krzysztof Piotr. *Santayana and America. Values, liberties, Responsibility*. New Castle (UK): Cambridge Scholars Publishing, 2007.

Strauss, Leo and Joseph Cropsey, eds. *History of Political Philosophy*. Third edition. Chicago and London: Chicago University Press, 1987.

Talisse, Robert B. and Robert Tempio, eds. *Pragmatism, Democracy, Freedom*. Amherst, NY: Prometheus Books, 2002.

Talmon, Jacob. L. *The Origins of Totalitarian Democracy*. London: Secker & Warburg, 1952.

Taylor, Charles. *A Secular Age*. Cambridge, Massachusetts, and London, England: The Belknap Press of Harvard University Press, 2007.

Taylor, Charles. "What is wrong with negative liberty." In *Philosophy and the Human Sciences. Philosophical Papers*, vol. 2, 211–229. Cambridge: Cambridge University Press, 1985.

Tocqueville, Alexis. *Democracy in America*. Vol. 2. Translated by Arthur Goldhammer. New York: The Library of America, Literary Classics of the United States, 2004.

Toynbee, Arnold J. *A Study of History*. One-volume edition. New York and London: Oxford University Press, 1947.

Toynbee, Arnold J. *War and Civilization*. A selection from *A Study of History*. Selected by Albert V. Fowler. New York: Oxford University Press, 1950.

Vega, Lope de. *The New Art of Writing Plays*. Translated by William T. Brewster. Introduction by Brander Matthews. New York: Dramatic Museum of Columbia University, 1914.

Walicki Andrzej. *Marksizm i skok do królestwa wolności*. Warszawa: PWN, 1996.

Wallach, John R. *The Platonic Political Art. A Study of Critical Reason and Democracy*. University Park, PA: The Pennsylvania State University, 2001.

Weber, Max. *Politics as a Vocation*. Translated and introduction by H.H. Gerth and C. Wright Mills. New York: Oxford University Press, 1946.

Weber, Max. *The Protestant Work Ethic and The Spirit of Capitalism*. Translated by Talcott Parsons. Introduction by Anthony Giddens. London, New York: Routledge, 1930/2005.

Wolf, Ursula. "How Schopenhauer's ethics of compassion can contribute to today's ethical debate." *Enrahonarn. Quaderns de Filosofia* 55 (2015): 41–49.

Woehrlin, William F., trans. and ed. *Out of the Depths (De Profundis). Articles on the Russian Revolution*. Irvine, California: Charles Slack JR Publisher, 1986.

Znaniecki, Florian. *Upadek cywilizacji zachodniej* (1921). Warszawa: Wydawnictwa Uniwersytetu Warszawskiego, 2013.

Index

Adorno, Theodor   13, 125, 134
action   33, 54, 59, 104, 123
   as art   23, 122, 180
   authorship of   63
   field of   27, 29
   free   63
   rational   31, 181
   unintended consequences of   34, 38, 236
Aksiuto, Kamil   155
Alexander, Thomas M.   217n.6, 247n.22
alienation
   of arts   137–138
   of humanity   124
   of man from work   20, 139–140
ambiguity
   in politics   98–99
   as a feature of Santayana's writings   10, 16, 24n.3, 107, 130, 247
   of technological progress   130
Amir, Lydia   116n.113
anarchy   70–74
anthropology
   negative   37, 40–42, 75, 238
Arendt, Hannah   174, 226, 245
aristocracy   100, 198, 196–201
   meritocratic   186
   natural   205–206, 215
   of spirit   142, 221, 224
   spiritual versus parasitic   193n.54
Aristotle   23, 30n.14, 40, 58, 104, 122n.3, 197, 206
art
   dehumanization of   141–142
arts   76, 88, 122–147, 201
   liberal   138–144, 204, 205, 244n.16
artist   138–144
authoritarian
   tendencies in politics   107, 157, 159, 161, 186, 193, 208
authoritarianism   193

Babbitt, Irving   13–15
barbarism   18, 49, 108, 114, 117, 130
Bell, Daniel   100, 103n.59, 174
Benjamin, Walter   180n.130

Bergson, Henri   63, 211
Berlin, Isaiah   72
Bible, The   213n.120
   See also The New Testament
biology
   politics and   113
Bois, W.E.B. Du   216
Bolsheviks, the   219, 227
Bolshevik Revolution, the   96, 164, 231
Brodrick, Michael   210n.109
bourgeoisie   135, 139
Burke, Edmund   96, 97n.42
Burke, Kenneth   28, 216
business   131–137, 166

capitalism   14n.42, 125–127, 133–134, 136, 144–145, 160–161, 174, 203
   state   194
Cassirer, Ernst   5n.11, 81, 106, 115, 245
Catholicism   14n.43
catholic culture   15, 90
Cervantes, Miguel de   87
charity
   in relation to justice   202–216
chivalry   107, 109, 111
civilization   41, 198
   decline of   117, 169–171
   industrial   160–161
   war and   108n.81, 109
communism   53, 161, 193, 194, 216–234
conformity   85, 196, 244
conservatism
   of Santayana   13–17, 80, 131, 182, 247
Constant, Benjamin   46, 84
consumerism   137
Cory, Daniel   2n.2
cosmopolitanism   18
crime   118
   militancy in politics as   108, 117–118
crowd   84, 111, 165, 199, 242
culture   21, 21n.68, 24, 36, 88, 111, 112, 125–126, 131–137, 201, 223
   importance of   235–236, 240, 244–246
   liberalism and   169–177
   political   48, 50, 80

INDEX

customs 80–81, 90, 246
cynicism
  in politics and culture 111, 114–115

Darwinism 79
democracy 54, 60, 67, 178–202
  in America 49–51, 100
  globalization and 82
  mass 162, 193
  natural versus artificial 186–187
  politicians in 104, 189–190
  propaganda and 105
  social versus aristocratic 197–201
  threats to 98–99, 101, 126, 162, 164
  totalitarian 52, 52n.34
depoliticization 21
Dewey, John 5, 94n.36, 217–218, 217n.6
disenchantment 146
  See also secularization
diversity
  in America 201
    cultural and human 18, 42, 145, 151, 154, 158, 166, 238
    justice and 203, 206, 209, 215, 223–225
dominations and powers 33–36
Dominations and Powers 2
  reception of 6–8
  structure of 11, 23–27, 33

Eastman, Max 216–217
economy 77, 81, 127, 128, 161, 194, 195
  state-controlled 229, 234
egalitarianism 146, 157, 171, 183, 187
egotism 18n.64, 67n.91, 245
elites 128
  as creative minority 117, 123, 205
  social function of 175, 192, 200, 199
  See also aristocracy
eminence
  crisis of 199
  as representative of humans 186, 197
empire 83
  Santayana's speculations on 15, 24, 26, 118n.118, 119, 166, 195n.61, 232–234
English liberty 44–54
enterprise 126, 132, 136–137, 142–143, 146, 166, 234
equality 49, 77, 100, 157–158, 165–166, 187, 200–201, 204, 221–224, 230

essences 28–29, 40
excellence 80, 122n.3, 191, 197

fatalism 64, 94–96
finitude 64, 99, 115, 203, 212
  and humility 226
  and liberty 57, 63
Flamm, Matthew Caleb 17
Frankfurt, Harry 65
Frankfurt School 13, 21, 62n.34, 90, 102n.59, 125, 130
freedom 44–74, 84–85, 153–155, 179–185
  negative 157–158, 163, 167, 175
  spiritual 62, 66, 76, 223
  individual 51, 71, 164, 173, 185
  vacant 45, 57, 63–64, 66, 69–70

García, César 101, 112n.99
Gasset, José Ortega y 140–142
Geertz, Clifford 21n.68
generative order 30–32, 42–43, 54, 90, 91, 96, 97, 112, 138, 203, 229
genteel tradition in America 15, 44–46
Geuss, Raymond 102n.50
Girard, René 80, 108, 166, 230
globalization 82, 135, 209, 232
government 91–94, 99, 112, 114–115, 159–161, 178–196, 204–205, 228, 232, 234–236, 239–240
  autocratic 111, 239
  just 197, 204, 205, 215
  representative 182, 186–187, 189–192, 197
  war and 92, 93, 110, 238
  See also self-government
Gray, John 12, 17, 22, 37, 46–47, 149, 156, 162, 175–176, 229

harmonizing diversity 11, 19, 42, 209, 238
harmony
  justice and 202–215
  principle of 54, 65
Hayek, Friedrich 160, 175, 203
Heraclitus 87, 110
Hessen, Sergey 160–161
hierarchy
  social 100, 193, 206, 231
history 12–13
  Marxist vision of 218–219
  politics and 104–105
  Soviet communism and 229–230

Hitler, Adolf   165
Hobbes, Thomas   57, 78, 157
Horkheimer, Max   125, 134, 137
Hook, Sydney   6, 90, 216
humanism
　of Santayana   15, 17, 21, 44, 79, 97, 147, 237n.5, 238
human condition   34, 37–38, 41, 57, 70, 183, 222
human nature   13, 32, 37, 97, 116, 150, 156
humility   39, 50, 67, 209, 219, 236
Huxley, Aldous   14, 242

ideology   102n.59, 60–61, 86, 99, 102–103
idolatry   102n.59, 146
imagination
　directive   89
　function of   29, 40, 71
　militancy and   98–100
　moral   79, 118, 209
individualism   16, 17, 18, 21, 45, 49, 51, 54, 67n.91, 79, 81, 91, 112n.99, 149, 157, 160, 187, 238, 242–245
　Apollonian   17, 243
　Collective   4
　predatory   21, 243
industrialism
　criticism of   127–128
　See also technology
inequality   69, 203, 206, 229
　social inequalities   77, 88, 143, 171, 175, 202, 204, 224
interventionism
　state   161, 175–176

James, William   45
judge
　each person as an autonomous   154, 224, 224n.32
　man as a poor   61, 183
judgment
　private   101–102, 103, 134, 155, 214–215, 241–242
justice   202–215, 194–195, 226, 237–238

Kallen, Horace   216
Kant, Immanuel,   153
Kerr-Lawson, Angus   94n.35, 155
Kimball, Roger   46

Kirk, Russell   8, 13
Kołakowski, Leszek   219, 226

labour   76, 123, 127–128, 193
　forced   226
　unions   192, 194
　worship of   145
　See also work
Lachs, John   17, 54
laissez-faire   160–161
League of Nations, The   108, 132
Lenin, Vladimir Ilych   96, 165
liberalism   17, 51, 53, 144, 205, 217n.4, 221
　criticism of   148–177
　culture and   169–177
liberty   44–74, 84–85, 124–125, 187, 188, 203–204, 208, 239
　English type of   48–54
　in liberalism   150, 151, 154–160, 165, 167–168, 173, 174–175
　spiritual   194, 224, 229
　vital   44, 55–57, 62–63, 64–65, 68–69, 99, 221, 223, 235–236
Lippman, Walter   101n.53
Locke, John   78, 153
love
　as foundation for justice   202, 213–215, 237–238

Machiavelli, Niccolò   93, 113–116
madness   28, 227
managing necessity   11, 19, 42, 119, 192, 208, 234, 238
Marcuse, Herbert   52n.34
Marx, Karl   40n.48, 216, 218–219, 226
materialism   55, 59, 64, 94–95n.36, 96
　Santayana's versus dialectical   217–218
　historical   221–222
matter   27–29, 131, 217n.6
Mazurek, Sławomir   160–161n.48
McClay, Wilfred M.   19, 51
McCormick, John   3, 6, 8
militancy   87–121
militant order   30–31, 42–43, 86, 87, 97
militarism   108, 109, 130–131, 143
Mill, John Stuart   155, 156, 170
mimetism   130
　as a feature of human nature   37
minority

INDEX

creative   123, 200, 205
  governing   117, 227
  tyranny of   164, 186
money   132–133
Montesquieu, Charles de   19, 201
Moreno, Daniel   9, 14, 14n.42, 35–36, 95–96
Mussolini, Benito   93n.33, 165, 207n.95
myth
  idolatry and   102n.59
  -making   45, 80
  presence of in culture   89–90
  of the state   81

nationalism   4, 66, 164
naturalism   13, 18, 24, 32, 95, 97, 112, 198
  Santayana's and Dewey's
    compared   217–218
nature   33, 44, 56, 57–58, 96, 181, 184, 217n.6
  government and   205, 208, 229
  and ideal   241
  state of   41, 78, 157, 231
necessity   38–42
nemesis   38, 236
New Testament, The   35
  See also The Bible
Nietzsche, Friedrich   116–117
nihilism   107, 118, 220

Oakeshott, Michael   7
oligarchy   77, 99, 126, 162, 186, 188, 207, 233n.65, 237
Orwell, George   104, 233n.65, 242

party
  political in democracy   178–179, 188–191
particularism   167
patriotism   81–84
  rational   82
perfection
  moral   210, 210n.109
  principle of   179–184, 215, 236
Plato   2, 5n.12, 18, 26, 31, 38, 41, 60, 78–79, 84, 84n.32, 92n.27, 113, 167, 189, 211, 238
pluralism   42, 212, 223–224
  value   25
politicization
  of culture and life   85, 120n.130, 166, 169, 230, 245, 246

politics
  ambiguity in   98–99
  compromise in   196
  crisis of   180–181
  culture and   240, 245–246
  cynicism in   113–115
  as governing life   35
  disengagement from   65
  militancy in   92, 92n.26, 92n.27
  naturalistic view of   32–33
  necessity and   78, 239
  professionalization of   187–188
  psychology of   5, 11
  rational   31, 57, 151, 157, 242
  religion and   135, 212
  understanding   23–28, 34–35
  virtue in   236–238
poor, the   128, 143, 192, 220–221
poverty   100
pragmatism   45, 217, 217n.4
progress   77, 124, 127–129, 130–131, 151–152
propaganda   105–107, 130, 132, 167, 239, 242
property
  private   73, 166–167, 175, 234
proletariat
  communist   221, 227, 131
  figurative use of the notion   222
  Toynbee's conception of   117
propaganda   105–107, 130, 161, 164, 166–167
Protestant work ethic   145, 174
Przybyszewski, Stanisław   139
psyche   29, 34
  as agent in politics   57–61, 106–107
  polis and   124
public opinion   99, 101, 103–105, 112n.99
Puritan   145

rational order   31–33, 42–43, 112
Rawls, John   202–205, 207
realms of being   27–32
Realpolitik   41, 92, 113, 115
relativism   10, 18, 25
  politics and   113–121
  the limits of Santayana's   241–242, 244–245
representation
  moral, in politics   182–185, 189, 191–192

revolution   52, 70, 96–97, 219–220, 231
   The French   52, 70, 96–97
   The Russian   132, 160
Ricoeur, Paul   213–214
Roosevelt, Franklin D.   233
Rorty, Richard   210, 214, 219n.14
Russell, Bertrand,   60

Saatkamp, Herman J., Jr   18, 165
sanity   29, 103
Schopenhauer, Arthur   209–210, 209n.104
Seaton, James   7, 13, 15n.50, 50, 52n.34, 203
secularization   144–147
self-government   61, 73, 127, 163, 167, 178–201, 187, 236, 243
separation of powers   191, 232, 238
Simmel, Georg   133
Singer, Beth J.   8n.25, 94–95n.36
Skowroński, Krzysztof Piotr   1, 8, 14n.42, 233n.67, 244n.16
slavery   75–77, 206
socialism   194, 219, 220, 161
society
   capitalism and   127, 136
   crime in   118
   civil   167–169
   diversity in   224
   degeneration of under communist rule   228–231
   generative stage of   38–39, 90
   the individual and   36, 38, 49, 58, 69, 112–113, 148–149, 163, 173
   mass   84–85, 130, 131, 135
   naturalist view of   198–201, 204
   secular   145–146, 168
   structured   198, 200, 204
   subjection to   73, 75–77, 79–81, 83, 86
   privileged groups in   175
   See also artist, elites, the poor, working class
solidarity   222–223
Solidarity, Polish trade union   95
Soviet Bloc, the   132
Soviet regime   228–229, 234
Soviet Union, the   193, 225, 227
Spain   4
Spinoza, Baruch   154–155
spirit   25, 27, 28, 56, 64, 64n.81, 66, 121
Stalin   225

state   92n.26, 149, 161, 166–168, 201, 202, 207
   interventionist   161–162, 175
   nation-state   4, 82, 110
   servitude to   78–79, 81
   welfare   194, 199, 161
Stoics, the   131

Talmon, Jacob L.   52n.34
Taylor, Charles   145–146, 174
technology
   relation of man to   76–78
   military   130
Tocqueville, Alexis de   49, 54, 100, 167
tolerance   71, 149, 150, 165, 209, 247
totalitarian   105–107, 155, 165
   regime   225–228, 236, 239
totalitarianism   161, 174, 193, 229, 230, 236, 245
Toynbee, Arnold J.
   on the decline of civilizations   117, 124, 143
   on elites   129
   on empires   119
   on *lingua franca*   91n.24
   on war and militarism   108–109, 130–131
tribalism   186, 188
tyranny   93–94, 96
   of majority   164, 167, 183

unanimity   53, 196–197
   communism and   225, 228, 230
   contemporary democracies and   188–189
   liberalism and   152, 165
United States of America, The   3–4, 44, 191, 217n.4
   hegemony of   233–234
   liberty in   48–50, 54
   pluralism in   201
   See also the genteel tradition
universalism   15, 151, 203
utilitarianism   155–156
utopia   31n.18, 155, 226, 232

Vega, Lope de   87
virtues   11, 42, 124, 245
   democratic   52, 182, 233
   meaning of   35–36, 122n.3
   military   109
Vysheslavtsev, Boris   160–161

Walicki, Andrzej   225
Wallach, John   92*n*.27, 199–200*n*.78
war
   manifestations of   87–120
   existential origins of   87–88
   transformation of   111
Weber, Max   92*n*.26, 144–145
welfare   82, 155, 161, 194
wisdom   65, 103, 124, 235–236, 243
   political   190
   practical   32, 36, 39, 123*n*.3

work
   alienation of   125–126, 128, 139–140
   compulsion of   51–52
   dehumanization of   136–137, 144, 145
   forced   76, 126
   See also labour
working class   144, 192, 193, 228
World War I   4, 162, 164, 172
World War II   5, 128, 132

Znaniecki, Florian   193*n*.54

Printed in the United States
by Baker & Taylor Publisher Services